May We Rant and Roar No More:

A
sea kayak journey
around
Newfoundland

Michael Paul

Pottersfield Press, Lawrencetown Beach, Nova Scotia, Canada

National Library of Canada Cataloguing in Publication Data

Paul, Michael

May we rant and roar no more: a sea kayak journey around Newfoundland

 ISBN 1-895900-43-3

1. Paul, Michael—Journeys—Newfoundland.   2.Sea Kayaking – Newfoundland.
3. Newfoundland—Description and travel.   I. Title.

GV776.15.N48P39 2001   917.1804'4   C2001-902028-7

Cover design: Dal Graphics

Pottersfield Press gratefully acknowledges the ongoing support of the Nova Scotia Department of Tourism and Culture, Cultural Affairs Division, as well as The Canada Council for the Arts. We acknowledge the financial support of the Government of Canada through the Book Publishing Industry Development Program for our publishing activities.

Pottersfield Press
83 Leslie Road
East Lawrencetown
Nova Scotia, Canada, B2Z 1P6
To order, telephone: 1-800-NIMBUS9 (1-800-646-2879) toll free
Website: www.pottersfieldpress.com

THE CANADA COUNCIL | LE CONSEIL DES ARTS
FOR THE ARTS | DU CANADA
SINCE 1957 | DEPUIS 1957

NOVA SCOTIA
Tourism and Culture

Canada

for the children of "The Rock"
and my mothers

Until they become conscious they will never rebel,
and until after they have rebelled they cannot become conscious.
— George Orwell

An honest book's the nobelest work of man.
— Henry David Thoreau

Foreword

All of my school friends had moved on to seemingly greener pastures like Halifax, Fort McMurray and Vancouver. The cod moratorium was into its sixth season and the nets, traps and boats were in a continued state of decay on the shore. Unbeknownst to me at the time, the Newfoundland government was gearing up for the largest observance of an historical event that the island had ever encountered; the belief that John Cabot had landed on its shores exactly five hundred years earlier, in his ship *The Matthew*, was a potential goldmine from the tourism industry's perspective.

Such was the climate of my return. The environment was in a shambles.

If I should celebrate anything with the printing of this, my first and perhaps only major piece, it's my rejuvenated discovery that free speech does, in fact, exist. And while I'm sure some, perhaps quite a few, of my observances and views expressed within these pages are not accepted by others, I'm grateful that there were folks out there who saw validity in allowing one more voice of a young person to be heard.

It was written in a two month isolated hiatus from civilization in a one-room cabin, whose front piers were constantly soaked with the salt of the cold North Atlantic. And, please note, never with the slightest intention of it arriving to this stage of "digestion." I'd simply arrived at a point where my head was so full, I required no more stimulus and as an act of survival, an outpouring of this monumental event in my life had to be literally disposed of on paper. If I'd known the energies it would sponge out of me, perhaps I would have burned each sheet in the woodstove next to my bed as they were produced.

The journey really began when I found myself on the Indian subcontinent less than a year before — battling ancestral demons and cursing the greed of the modern world. Two years of dedicated wandering found me repulsed, sickened and scared. I made substantial strides toward understanding, sympathizing and integrating myself with people — people simply alive and focused on essentials. An existence not long ago similar to that of the pre-Confederation Newfoundlander. I was on the other side of the planet, striving to learn of another culture and wanting desperately to be active in preserving some diversity . . . when I realized I'd never given nearly as much effort to the culture from which I came. I had to go thousands of miles away from my homeland before I realized the most important thing I could do was to, in fact, go home.

Michael Paul
May 14, 2001
Notre Dame Bay
Newfoundland

I

5.20.97 I think if we'd been entertained with more stories and yarns of times in our own coves and bays, we'd have more sense of an identity, fondness and yearning, a pride, to remain and create integral and honest lives for ourselves, to stay and fight for the lifestyle which is rightfully ours.

Yet here we remain. Disjointed, families torn, bitter and overwhelmed with neglect and regrets. Instead of maintaining a culture, we've sold it, like so many unappreciated heirlooms, for television, the Sears catalogue and potato chips.

In each bay of this island there were heroes, and those who rightfully should have influenced us kids. Instead we were given Spiderman and Barbie as inferior substitutes. Equally as important, if we'd been honestly told stories of the life which had evolved off this island, we could've had more of an immediate appreciation and respect of the circumstances to which we were raised.

We never realize how substantial life here is until we leave — and then for most of us, it's too late.

Tomorrow my journey begins.

The winter had slowly begun to beat its retreat. It had been a season not without its challenges, for I'd returned to a life, I had to realize, that was not solely my own. I'd found myself once again living in the home of my parents. The house I'd been raised in. But I'd been away for so long, had established my own code of ethics, and was soaked in the contentment of my independence that often times it created friction, for which I was considerably responsible. Yet, with the time permitted in readjusting ourselves to the fact that we'd all developed (even to my surprise those who had stayed behind in the same environment), we'd all grown. A simple respect was established.

I'd embarked on a strict training regimen during the preceding couple of months. There was snow to utilize and enjoy. Incredibly it had been four years since I'd been substantially exposed to it. Most days I skied hard and reached a physical level that I felt was satisfactory for my proposed kayak journey around the island of Newfoundland.

This period also contained a slow retreat back into the ingestion of seafood as well. The decision did not come easily, yet I felt it would be beneficial when faced with circumstances of outport families offering their hospitalities This being inevitable of course, and it would aid in soothing the potential uneasiness sure to be created by my "strange" vegetarian diet.

The gear necessary had all been accumulated, to rest in meticulously organized piles throughout the house. Even the boat had mysteriously found her way into the living room one day, her stern unashamedly extending into the dining room. It was there that enthusiastic packing sessions, testing of gear and longing meditations from the cockpit occurred. As preparations reached a frenzied pitch, all family members extended help as gear bags were made and reflective tape was sewn on equipment and clothing.

We'd an uncharacteristically extended winter, with ice remaining well into May. Even Pop was incredulous as to spring's late arrival stating, "B'y, as long as I been in dis bay — well over seventy year now," looking reminiscently into space, "never been a year the ice haven't been gone by now! Boy, you can sure pick 'em."

At that stage, it seemed they'd all resigned themselves to my dedication to the journey. They knew the dangers as well as I, yet by that time had grown accustomed to my peculiar adventures, my relentless pursuits. It didn't make the parting any easier.

My brother had secured me a ride with a friend's father, who'd be driving his transport to the south coast. If we could get the boat somehow secured among his load I was welcome to come along.

"Ya gonna do what?" he'd questioned astonished. "This boat, whadya call 'er?"

"A kayak."

"Oh, yeah. Seen one o' dem on TV, goin' down a river. And you're gonna row one o' dem on d' sout'coast?! B'y, I s'pose I can be party t' sum'n like dis. Ya folks realizes o' course, dey ain't ne'r gonna see ya again."

I thanked him for restricting those comments solely to our telephone conversation, and hung up. A long pause.

"Woohoo!" I'd screamed, dancing through the house. The family hadn't seen that much exuberance from me, well . . . ever. The long nights of cutting up charts, studying navigation, and doing endless situps was finished. The following day, that slim, yellow boat and I would be rolling to the south coast.

An eerie quiet overcame the other members of my family — as if they were attending a wake. Was it sheer selfishness to put them through it? But it was uncontrollable; some genetic implant that they didn't have — a longing itch that could only be relieved by unknowns and adventure that they simply could not comprehend.

The next morning all gear was packed into the car. It had been religiously fondled over, repeatedly, to ensure I'd not forgotten some essential piece or that nothing was going which was of little use. Everyone clambered aboard, and with the girl on the roof we travelled in near silence the entire fifteen-minute drive to the truck.

The flatbed was loaded with massive industrial pipes and steel tubes, an intimidating load of metal. My heart sank a little as the thought of being left behind entered my mind. How were we going to get my 17-foot boat safely secured amongst that? It towered menacingly above our heads as we waited forlornly for Jim's arrival. Minutes later he emerged from his car and scratching his head below his worn, grease-stained ballcap, commented, "Well . . . never figured 'er t' be so long."

He quickly began studying the load for any possible resting sights and added, "She's a queer lookin' t'ing, ain't she."

Miraculously, there was a large pipe wedged up on the very top of the pile. We wrestled the partially loaded boat up and gingerly eased her into the space. Minutes later she was invisible even from below and securely nestled for the long road haul.

Quickly all my supplies were hoisted up into the cab of the truck by brother, sister, mother, and father. The only family I'd known since they'd taken me in as an infant. Only our parting remained. For them to stand there that day in the cold, unwelcoming hours of a spring morning that had yet to declare itself and watch their brother, their son, leaving wide-eyed and anxious into a future of grave uncertainty was a true testament to their support and unquestioning love. Would I be prepared to watch my own son leave on *his* journey toward manhood and truth, as my father did that day, well knowing that he may never return?

As we pulled out of the parking lot that day, I watched as my family slowly retreated into the welcoming warmth of the car and wondered seriously if I'd ever see them again. Lost in those thoughts, it was a long time before I was even aware of where I was, of where I was going, and even of the presence of the man bouncing along in the seat beside me.

He broke the silence with, "So how ya figurin' on gettin' all that stuff in that lil' boat o' yours?" motioning to the great pile of food bags, pots, sleeping bag, life jacket, tent, spray skirt, stove, fly rod, and various other items that had found their way in a hasty shambles onto his sleeping quarters.

"Oh, there's a proper place for all of it. No room to spare though," I'd joked, sounding more convincing than I felt at the time.

Was I ready for it? The ice had only retreated a week earlier, allowing me one daytrip. I'd spent a morning rolling the boat (with limited success) and only the previous day had I even paddled a fully loaded kayak for about ten minutes to see if she sat evenly in the water, to determine if any of the gear would need to be readjusted. In total, I'd sat in a kayak no more than a dozen times. Was an inaugural trip of well over 4,500 miles a bit too adventurous?

Jim sent a questioning look of wariness in my direction.

I returned the sentiment.

I'd surmised that my best route would be along the south coast, starting in Port aux Basques and to begin heading eastward. Due to the ice-free conditions, it would allow for the earliest departure date. When I made it around to the northeast bay of my home, I could rest up, reassess and decide then if I would attempt the next leg. If so, then I'd return by land to Port aux Basques and proceed down the west coast (to utilize the prevailing westerlies) and round the northern peninsula for the return paddle back to my hometown in Notre Dame Bay. All this, hopefully, before the stiff winds and cold temperatures arrival in the fall announcing winter's imminent descent.

We'd discussions also that day of Jim's work and the tribulations of being away from his family for such extended periods of time. When he'd first started, there were very few occasions when he wasn't home following only a couple of nights on the road.

"Now, b'y. I'll look up and find m'self in Texas somewhere and wonder how d' Jesus did it get t' dis?" he ranted and shook his head dumbfounded.

I'd sat silently then and remarked later of the long processions of trucks that joined us in our convoy to the south coast. How much of the stuff they were shipping was needed? How much of it was just plain garbage? And why had we sold ourselves out of the bays for this road? Because the rest of the glorious country had it, we deserved one as well? Purely so some crazed bureaucrat could pamper his hernias, is all I could figure.

We've got supposedly sympathetic government officials now desperately seeking ways of bringing the almighty tourists to our island. Seems to me they keep destroying all the things which would hold us unique to begin with — like the coastal boats that once steamed along the shore, bonding communities to the sea and to each other, or even the railline which singularly connected the island's inhabitants by land.

My thoughts developed unpleasantly for such an auspicious occasion, so I brought up the weather. Nearing our destination, it had grown considerably worse and my concerns were justified when Jim remarked, "Ya won't be gettin' out o' here t'day, my friend. She's blowin' sou'east."

As we rounded a corner and he gently geared down for the considerable forthcoming grade, Jim reminded me how uninviting the weather could be down on the southwest coast. "Der's times I've come down dis here slope, and you sees dat pond dere. She'd be blowin' sou'east like she is now — an d' wind, by God, she'd be blowin' d' water up d' hill!"

Comforting. His words were altogether entirely . . . comforting.

Jim of course had been correct in his predictions. The weather was "unfit": a cold, damp drizzle of sleet, fog and blowing gales. My trip to the put-in complete — I was grounded. Our mid-afternoon arrival, coupled with the uninviting weather, would allow for a relaxed, quiet evening in which to mentally prepare.

In a mad downpour, we got my boat out from her resting place where she'd weathered the journey unscathed. And with a ceremonious nod of his head, Jim wished me a curt farewell and quickly retreated into the warm, dry comforts of his truck. Left to the imposing elements, I shambled quickly to secure all the gear within the boat.

There she lay on a small pitch of withered, dead grass and resting up against a guardrail. I'd retreat myself, shortly thereafter, to the dry shelter of the ferry terminal, leaving her to battle her own demons in the elements to which she'd eventually grow accustomed.

By evening the storm had begun to move on and I was able to get out, retrieve some things needed, and see that she was secure for the night. I was greeted by two guys only a few years younger than me. They were to leave on the ferry the following morning — headed for Alberta to find work, excitement, the city, and girls.

Seeing those two, as they stood on the eve of their own grand adventure, I was reminded of the day I first left on my own. Those same feelings of newfound independence, mystery and, well . . . yeah, lust too; of leaving the shallowness and mundane ways of the bay where everyone knew "what you were at" before you'd even the chance to be at it! And I realized that for some of us, regardless of the circumstances, we'd have to leave, to see for ourselves and experience some of the outside world. I only hoped they'd experience enough, that it would make them want to come back.

My options for instrumental accompaniment were of course limited. My faithful companion of previous adventures, Pop's mouth organ had staked its claim to the breast pocket of my vest. In addition, I'd found in my possession, a small, metal, finely twisted mouth gadget which would undoubtedly provide hours of pleasure — a jaw harp. This instrument entranced me when I first encountered it in India. Not indigenous to the culture there, it does have an East Indian aura to it and did not sound strangely misplaced among sitars or tablas. It was the proven catalyst for my next friendly encounter.

The following morning found the weather still unsettled. Yet, confident that I'd at least get underway at some point during the morning, I greeted my travel companion with words of encouragement. All preparatory tasks completed, I sat cross-legged and had begun to play while studying the sea conditions for subtle telltales of improvement.

"Hi. Whaya got der?" A young boy of eleven stood before me and continued, "I 'eard ya from d' car. We're goin' t' Saskatoon. Y'ever been dere, sir? . . . I hear's dere ain't no sho' dere."

His questions didn't seem to require any answers.

"Me ma an sister is already dere . . . I lives in Carbonear, least I did. We's all movin' cause Dad ain't got no work . . . Nan and Pop's stayin' 'ere d'ough." His eyes dropped to his feet before looking out to the horizon, as if it would reveal all the questions that he had no answers for.

He was leaving the island of his birth, his grandparents, his friends, his universe to go to a land with no shore, as foreign to this bright, conversive friend of mine as the craters of the moon. Few places remain on this continent where a young child can still feel comfortable enough to approach a stranger and begin a conversation. Fewer places still where parents will allow their children the freedom to do so on their own. Children of course have little of the stereotypical fears that haunt adults.

"Ya goin' on d' boat too?" he asked, tightening the collar around his neck to counter the stiff wind which had breezed up.

"No. I'm leaving on a boat, though, a little smaller than yours. Right there behind you. You missed it sure, when you came over." I pointed in the direction of my boat, still lashed onto the guardrail from the previous night's storm.

"Wha's dat?"

"It's called a kayak. I'm gonna leave pretty soon and paddle down the shore."

His eyes became two round saucers. "In dat t'ing dere?!" He was incredulous. To my delight he asked to sit in her. As he was air-paddling a few strokes (canoe style) he asked simply, "Wha's 'er name?"

I paused. Good Lord. I was about to embark on this wild journey without a name for my boat! Sacrilege. Without further thought on the matter I stated, "*Destiny.*" A fitting title and the spontaneity in which it was proclaimed seemed appropriate. *Destiny* it was.

Before we parted ways, he asked if I could play some more of "dat weird chummy" and I happily obliged. A fog bank was beginning to form, and with it the wind was sure to die out.

I'd changed, undaunted by the conditions or exposed vantage point, into my fleece pants and layered clothing. A quick look around and I was ready. I was trembling with excitement. Before me lay a day of intense unknowns, drama-filled and challenging. My spider senses were tingling.

The large ferry beside me, destined for Cape Breton and the "other world," had begun to warm up her engines. An omen. I began to mentally stage out my approach to the water. Dead low tide. It might prove more difficult than I'd originally foreseen.

Between *Destiny* and the water lay an unnatural, sloping mess of boulders used as landfill. Once that obstacle was overcome, I still had to find a launch site that would allow me to pack the boat before climbing aboard. Regardless of tide, it was still a couple of fathoms deep. Before attempting the task, I reassured myself that it was probably the worst launch site I'd encounter the entire trip. Once in, I'd have pebble and sand beaches and slipways to bid me farewell.

Once I'd figured on the easiest route and set about it, things went smoothly and soon afterwards I had *Destiny* floating.

The fog had arrived and a light drizzle had begun to fall.

The final approach ensued . . .

But I was denied my moment by the unwelcome arrival of a large, overzealous dog, who quickly planted his muzzle deep into the confines of my crotch, and was soon accompanied by his faithful owner, a kid of my own age straight out of college.

"Ah, sorry bud. Like, I just let him off to get a run in and do his business before we got on the boat . . . hey, nice kayak." The guy had taken notice of my boat. The dog, forgotten, was left to rudely explore my privates.

"I'm a warden over in the park," the guy proudly exclaimed. "I do quite a bit of this myself. Looks like you're just about to leave. Like, whereabouts you headin'?"

I explained my scenario quickly and then inquired of his destination, fully assuming he had grown up in one of the nearby towns. "The season's about to begin — I thought you'd be home gettin' ready to start by now," I winced for I'd still his dog's muzzle up my ass.

"Oh no, like, I'm from PEI. I'm just going home for a few days vacation."

My heart sank. I'd little patience to speak with him after that about my trip, boat or his work. It was cold. I'd have liked to've discussed with him his knowledge of the area and inquired how many men he'd seen there who'd lived their entire lives in the ecosystem, who were out of work and heading to Saskatoon, uprooting their families, like my earlier friend's father.

It was not the time to dampen my spirits. The ocean beckoned.

Paddling out of the safe harbour that morning, there was no elaborate send-off of fireworks or shouts of encouragement. There was simply myself and *Destiny*.

There was some residual swell remaining from the past day's storm, and as my body became aware and made adjustments I looked back. The ferry to the mainland was just emerging from the channel. As it headed westward toward the land of wealth and technological advancement, I looked down and confirmed my course setting from a compass, an ancient relic of bygone days.

And so I began my journey east, into the land of interdependence and pride.

I thought also, not of my last acquaintance, but of my young friend from earlier that morning. I wished him well, and without thought slowly dipped my finger into the frigid north Atlantic and, ever so slightly, touched the salt tear to my forehead. *"Hare Krisna, Hare Krisna, Krisna Krisna, Hare Hare Hare Rama, Hare Rama Rama Rama, Hare Hare."*

With half a mile of visibility to contend with, I was quickly put to the test. There was no one left to consult with or bail me out. It is the greatest incentive to learn. When you have no other choice but to grasp ideas and details in order to survive, the mind is capable of unquestionable resourcefulness and clarity.

Points on the chart had to be recalled; heads of land distinguished; compass bearings remembered; places to theoretically come ashore with the given swell direction, if and when the direction of the wind changed; the next possible landing site; the distance and time to it; the tide rising or falling; how long I'd been out; the speed I'd been travelling . . . These are only a few of the essential elements that one has to recall to safely navigate through the waters off the coast of Newfoundland.

My first day's paddle consisted entirely of these details. And self-questioning. Was I prepared to devote that much energy and time into ensuring my own safety? If I wasn't it was up to me to pull ashore in a community that night, and to have the balls to call home for a truck to come get me. I wasn't crazy, and unless I devoted myself entirely, mentally and physically, then the ocean was going to swallow me up.

It was a mammoth decision. It was irrelevant how much money or time or preparation had gone into it. It wasn't until this point in the journey that the decision could be made.

That day, on the leeward side of Isle aux Morts, I'd step onto land a different person than when I'd left it, only a couple of hours before.

In question was the distanced, fiercely independent coldness of my character. There would be times on the journey when I'd need someone's help. Period. The ocean was too powerful to take on alone. Would I have the maturity to ask for help? This was something I was not good at, something quite foreign to me.

Leaving the "Island of the Dead" following lunch, I still didn't know the answer.

"I sees you ashore buddy, I'm takin' your temp'ture!"

That was it! It was in crossing God Bay that my answer came.

The only spoken words that I'd encounter the entire day came from a fisherman out in his boat, checking his nets. Upon approaching I could see the astonished look on his face. A bewildered questioning of whether or not what he saw was actually there. From out of the fog had appeared a bright yellow craft of some sort — only to be seen occasionally, when both boats were in sync on the rolling swell.

As I passed, he'd drawn back his ballcap and was scratching his head. The net lay drifting out of his boat again as he just stood there. While I was still in earshot he gave a jovial holler, "I sees you ashore buddy, I'm takin' your temp'ture!"

I *had* heard correctly.

It was the secret of the universe and I was the happiest man in it.

There was no question as to what I'd find myself doing the next day.

2

5.22.97 It's a beautiful day to be alive. Here I lay —
very content, full, warm, blissful and still energetic on this,
the full moon. I've estimated to have covered only 13-14
nautical miles, yet I must take care to ease myself into the
long paddles. This was in just under 6 hours. Relatively big
seas and fog all day. A lot of boats out, seeing them continu-
ously. I had to climb the hill up above my tent to reconfirm
my position. This fog is wild. I'll sleep well — if I can shut my
brain down.

Upon entering, the blast of heat hit you like a solid wall. Then slowly,
it enveloped you — as if re-entering the womb. You were overcome
with the sense of protection and safety. It provided many more services
than mere goods. A haven for numbed little fingers to warm their hands
over the stove; a centre for news and conversation; an occasional escape
from the daily routine of life at home. The outport store.

Essentially it wasn't what was there which made it so substantial. It
was the items which were not. Simplicity. All the imported goods which

were required to provide a comfortable life for the people in the cove could be found on the well-tended shelves of that one room, this one room being merely an extension to the family's home.

I entered thankfully and was greeted with the warm smile of a girl my age. I'd only begun the journey of course, and being two days into it had little need of anything. Regardless, I'd found myself drawn to the store. I'd entered through a portal in time — the early days of my grandparents spread before me.

Amazed, I discovered even the old twenty-ton cash register remained, which required the brute finger of a gorilla to depress the keys. The clean, brown paper on the big roll for wrapping, and the well-worn countertop which had borne witness to many an exchange of currency . . . and even more proclamations of credit and invitations to barter. That old system of trust and requirement which had once dominated the coves before the roads came.

This *was* the end of the road literally. For beyond this point there was over one hundred nautical miles where the influence from the outside barely existed. One of the most uninhabited sections of coastline left on the planet.

The girl was then joined by her mother, who'd entered from the house. We spoke at length of the store's history and the number of generations that it had been in the family. Yet, this would be the last. People drove to Port aux Basques now, so it was hard to keep up. The girl saw little future in it and was taking nursing in Town — she'd returned only for the summer to help out.

I'd called my own family to reassure them and in bidding farewell, looked around the warmly lit room — at the bundles of wool, the sections of stove pipe, and the two friendly faces and prayed that my children would get the chance to warm their hands in a room like this following a fine morning of sledding back o' the hill.

Up to that stage, I'd seen very little of the actual coastline and surrounding scenery. The fog had continued throughout the second day. Giving a moist, dream-like quality to my experience, it was like being enclosed in a giant pillow. With this damp blanket of air little wind seemed to be generated, and within its protective embrace I began to feel comforted. Occasionally it would thin a little and I'd get a faint glimpse of the stark grey cliffs, then just as quickly it would thicken again and the imposing shoreline, no further than a quarter of a mile, would be lost as if it ceased to exist.

A lot of efforts were made in refining my stroke and becoming completely comfortable with the handling of the boat on that second day.

My shoulders and hands had become a little sore, yet it was to be expected as my body grew accustomed to the extended periods of exertion. The temperatures were cold, but remaining comfortable was little trouble while paddling, only becoming a factor once I'd come ashore and began to cool down. Priority quickly focused then on getting into a full set of dry clothing. This usually meant a morning ritual just prior to departure, of fitting myself out in the clothes of the previous day, still damp and frigid. The evening's occasions of reaching into the bag for the dry set was divine — such sweet comforts for a day well spent.

I'd only been ashore for a short time, having completed the chores of bringing *Destiny* up above the tide line, building a fire and setting up camp, when I heard the familiar drone of an outboard engine approaching. Three men from a nearby community had been out to their cabin for supper. They'd seen the smoke and came in to say hello. Upon coming ashore they were immediately drawn to my boat. They'd never seen anything like her.

"You come from Port aux Basques in she . . . in the past couple o' day? My Lord Jesus, you got some nerve."

"And you says you're from here," inquired another from all fours, as he eyed the line of *Destiny's* keel. "Ya sure don't sound Newf t' me."

"Oh, I guess I've been away for too long," I replied.

Only after they were satisfied — at least partially convinced — of the boat's seaworthiness, did we return to the fire.

Their complete lack of awareness concerning the outside world was fascinating. They'd little or no interest in anything that didn't pertain directly to them. The boats were their lives, the sea their only means of travel. There was a reassurance felt in being on that dangerously rugged shore with them. They were as comfortable sitting around a driftwood beachfire as they would've been in the shelter of their own houses back in the community. They already were, quite simply, at home. They were some of the most contented faces I'd ever seen. I felt privileged to be in their company that evening.

> 5.23.97 It doesn't get any better than this. Here I am
> — I've got my own little sheltered bay to myself for the night.
> I've paddled in some wild conditions — crossed over to
> Petites in total fog for an hour and hit it dead on. Limitless
> exploration on and off land. I'm feeling good and strong and
> never so alive in my life! Incredible how much work there is
> to do even after the paddling is complete. That's in some
> ways the easiest part of the day. Tomorrow I'll pass the
> halfway mark to Burgeo, 40 miles from here.

The next morning I was pleased to discover that I'd awoken with a smile on my face. My feet were cold. I'd had to wear my tuque throughout the night. There was a fine layer of frost over my whole sleeping bag and the inner walls of the tent. I'd spent the previous two days in less than favourable conditions. But there I was . . . smiling. In fact, I hadn't felt so content in my entire life.

The wind had switched to nor'west, leaving a calm, tranquil sea. The barometer was slowly rising and I'd premonitions I'd see the sun's unveiling that day. Anxious to return to the water, I leaped happily from the relative warmth of the tent as a hazed, angelic sun rose above the naked hills. The days were getting longer — summer loomed. Pushing off that morning, I looked heavenward and gave praise for all I'd been blessed with. I was in my element. Even if, for some unforeseen reason, the trip ended abruptly I thought it would've all been worth it. All the preparations were rewarded in waking in that desolate little cove that morning . . . with a smile on my face.

Because I was content to simply appreciate the movement, the paddling developed into a passive meditation. An entire morning would transpire and I'd be delighted to note that the rhythm of my stroke had yet to be broken. Once I attained that level of consciousness, my mind was free to focus entirely on breathing, or the occasional visit from a seabird, or on pleasant nothingness.

If all went as planned, my entire summer would be composed of blissful mornings such as this.

This would be the day of my first visit to a coastal village accessible only by water. I'd paddled for nearly five hours and with only a brief shore stop for lunch, I was all the more delighted when I rounded the last point and paddled solemnly into the peaceful cove. I was amazed with the beauty and harmony it instilled. The entire community was built along the sloping hills of a granite coliseum. Its focal point was a grandiose, cascading waterfall.

The sound was delicious. The steep surrounding cliffs seemed to radiate and amplify it further. From the comfort of every bed in the cove the townsfolk could gauge in the mornings how much water had fallen the previous night. Such were my thoughts upon entering.

Immediately following these thoughts, before I'd even come ashore, I considered how beneficial it would be if I simply remained in such a community for the season. I thought of the friendships that could develop and the knowledge and appreciation I could gain from such an experience. But such profoundly deep and substantial relationships with people would nearly be impossible, I surmised. The constantly transient nature of the journey would never allow the time essential for such bonds to be nurtured. There would be a season for all things. At that time, I needed a physical and mental challenge, as well as a newfound respect for the island and its people.

It's essential that we not overburden ourselves with too many goals and aspirations at once. This is the sole, underlying mistake of Western civilization. We seem to believe we can be more efficient by conducting numerous tasks at once, while in the end we're left to discover that because none of them were given full care and attention, they all peak at a level inferior to our initial intentions. As a result, the populace as a whole is left with feelings of guilt, inadequacy and defeat. With these thoughts concerning the human condition, it was obvious that I was once again approaching the vicinity of fellow *homo sapiens*.

As I approached the small beach to the right of the cove, I saw a man standing up above on the cliff. The sun had finally burned off the remaining fog and he was out at his garden. The fact that people were even capable of tending gardens in this environment was a true sign of their durability. It was from his garden that I'd get my first uninhibited view of the coastline I'd been paddling along.

Rugged. At first glance it seemed completely void of all life. Treeless barrens, scoured by eons of exposure to salt and vicious weather. Stunning.

By that time, I'd disembarked and removed my paddling garb and ventured up for a chat.

"Can you believe it?" he said. "The end of May and I can't get at the ground yet." He was busy with his prong, moving about the kelp he'd put atop the soil in the fall. Underneath was still solid, frozen ground. "She been a late year. You findin' it cold out in her?"

"No. A little chilly in the mornings is all."

"Yeah, I 'llow she is," he grinned knowingly. "Where you come from?"

I explained and noticing that he'd not been overly surprised by my arrival inquired, "Have you seen many paddlers down this way before?"

"Oh yeah, not this early now mind you, but every couple o' years a group o' two or t'ree'll row in t' d' cove."

He spoke with the calm reassurance of quiet, contented retirement. He said his name was John and like most of the inhabitants, he'd a jolly rotundness to him, testament to many a fine meal. He was adequately dressed and seemed to enjoy the idea of merely being outside, following the stretch of bad weather and the long, drawn-out winter.

Resting his arms up against the fence, he continued, "They usually come like you did and paddles to Burgeo. Had a couple camp up back o' d' hill for a time one year. Nice t' see b'y — a few new faces aroun', right."

I asked him many questions about the community and his family. He stated simply with an air of indifference that all his kids had moved away. Next he spoke of a mine which had recently closed nearby and of the three families who'd left within the past year. I looked around at the houses surrounding the cove. A number of them were boarded up. Three families. That was about 15 percent of the town. John quietly surmised that there was little chance of the town's survival into the next generation, if everyone didn't have to pull out before then.

"How about the school here — how many children?"

"Two, b'y. She only goes up t' d' ninth level, then the kids haves t' go and live wit' folks down Burgeo or Port aux Basques."

Youngsters were taken out of their homes at fifteen. I'd sobered up from my long, unburdened paddle with the arrival of that last bomb.

"Well . . . I think I'll take a walk around the cove before I head out again, John." I needed a little time. "I'll talk t' you again before I leave."

"Right y' are. I'll be here, watchin' me ground taw'n out," he replied with a hearty laugh.

Quaint little paths ran between the houses. At the top of the falls was a bridge leading over to the other side of the cove.

Many people had seen me paddle in and came out to say hello. Others were out hanging clothes, to take advantage of the precious few rays of sun we were being graced with. It wasn't difficult to see how fast news travelled in a small community such as that. Some of the older folks were at their windows to have a look and quick nods of acknowledgment soon followed. It always brightened my spirits whenever the courtesy was administered. Apart from the few young children, there was no one left in the community below the age of thirty-five.

Returning from my stroll, I marveled again at the peacefulness instilled in the small cove. Why was it?

The lack of noise I figured was a main reason. Like the general store, the things not heard brought about an awareness of the more natural sounds that were. The sound of falling water took precedence over the noise of automobiles. The swell outside . . . and the still silence of John's prong resting idle against the fence, waiting for the thaw.

"You know of a good spot to camp a little ways along the shore, John?"

"Oh, yes . . . whadaya, gonna head out? You're welcome t' come into the house, b'y."

"No thanks. She'll be a nice one t' camp out, and it'll be good to get a little more paddling in today."

"As you like. Well, you come out o' the cove and head straight t'ru dem islands der," pointing with his nose. "'Undred an' ten degree she is, when you get's outside. See d' point a couple o' mile beyond it? Just beyond dat is a lovely spot for ya."

"Grand. I can't thank you enough," I said, shaking his hand.

"B'y, I can't figure I did too much fer ya but you're welcome."

"You've got a lovely spot, sir. Perhaps I'll get to visit again."

I made my way down below to the beach during our final chat and prepared to push off again. John gave me a final wave and I headed out of the cove. The time had passed quickly and the sun was beginning its descent. It would be an extremely full day by the time I got ashore and settled that night I thought. I wondered would I ever see the friendly cove again.

It was only a three mile paddle to the point John had spoken of. The wind had, surprisingly for that time of the day, picked up a bit. Yet it had remained nor'west so it would help speed me along. Coming around to 110 degrees, the islands lay directly ahead. I settled into a comfortable rhythm and took notice of an extra soreness in my wrists. I'd probably gone a little too far that day, this early into the trip. Tomorrow, I decided, I would take it easier.

Upon reaching the islands, the weather had taken a bizarre turn. It had swung over northerly and I was now getting direct wind onto my port side. There was only half a mile between the shore and myself, yet a considerable lop had developed. I picked up the pace. It was changing too fast. I felt a sense of urgency overcome me. In another ten minutes it had stiffened further. I was forced to paddle with twice the amount of effort with my right arm.

It didn't make sense. I was surrounded by whitecaps, yet the shore was so close, it was so late in the day . . .

There was considerable strain on my right forearm now.

Why was the boat so hard to keep straight?

I was making slow progress, yet I kept the boat headed directly towards the point. I glanced back and realized I might have been maintaining my course with the point in front of me but I was being blown offshore!

I discovered not long afterwards that by raising the adjustable skeg there was less drag; she tended to head up into the wind easier. This put less strain on my right arm as well. I quickly decided also that heading directly for the point was a mistake. If conditions remained I would eventually get there, but if the winds were to increase, I'd risk the chance of getting blown offshore completely. Heading towards the inner shore of the bay, I'd be taking the winds more directly in front of me, and the closer I got the less there'd be, due to the high cliffs.

Once I'd made those few adjustments, the feelings of doubt subsided and I merely had a strenuous workout ahead. My arms were hurting. There was no other choice but to continue.

I eventually reached the point and wild spasms of relief overcame me. Shortly thereafter, I came ashore on the little beach and collapsed. My first legitimate test from the ocean. I lay there, amazed at how quickly it had gotten ugly.

Slowly, a faint glimmer of a smirk developed around my mouth, to be replaced soon after by the broadest, most enthusiastic smile imaginable! Shit, it felt good!

I'd found something to challenge me . . . somethin' to keep me "fresh."

The condition of my arms had little bearing on my decision to remain ashore the following day. It was simply a beautiful chance to explore the barrens. My first incentive to do this came in the form of a visitor, for looking outside of my tent that morning I was happy to see a young caribou. He'd come down during the early hours and was busily eating away at the moss. He looked up initially when I'd opened the tent, then satisfied that I was of little threat went back to his breakfast.

Secondly, that morning I looked around and was overcome with the foreignness of my surroundings. Was this the same island I'd grown up on? I'd spent my life on the leeward side of the island, a land of low-lying wooded hills and rocky coastline. Now, I was camped above a long, crescent-shaped sandy beach and surrounded by steep, exposed cliffs with a vast expanse of tundra stretching inland. I'd a caribou for a breakfast companion, an animal I'd never even seen on my side of the coast. I'd been to the other side of the planet, yet I had never explored the other side of my own island.

And so the day was spent. But not before a second visitor arrived. I'd packed a small lunch and was preparing to set out along the shore for a hike when John came along in his boat.

"Some mornin', ain't it? Thought I'd get out an' come over t' d' bay for a run. So, how'd ya make out yes'day eve'nin'? Got a bit rough, wa?"

He'd been pretty smooth with the approach, but it was obvious that he'd come over to see if I was alright. I was touched.

"Yeah, she gave me a workout alright. Learned a lot. Why don't you come ashore for tea?"

"No, no. Gotta get back. D' missus gets home from church pretty soon."

We stood there then, both searching for an adequate farewell.

"Well, you take care o' y'self now, hear?" he said finally.

"You too . . . and John," I sputtered, "thanks."

"Don't mention it," was his solemn reply.

I left shortly afterward and hiked the remainder of the morning.

There was a nesting pair of eagles up in the trees further inside the shelter of the bay. They were to have their young soon, if they'd not had them already. I watched in awe as one would soar out over the bay in search of food, then I was amazed when it would rush down and snatch an unsuspecting fish from the surface. Taking his cue, I fished as well that morning with my fly rod, spending some time practicing in the many little pools that dotted the landscape.

In returning late that afternoon I came overland along the barrens. I'd made my way up through a small outcrop of rock, focusing only on the area directly in front of my feet, when I looked up and startled a very large caribou not five metres away. We'd spooked each other and merely stood there for a few seconds before he took off.

I dropped my rod and small pack and dashed over the plain after him. For well over a mile I kept pace with the majestic creature. The energy release felt great. The landscape was endless.

Having played with me long enough, the last I saw of him was a bold silhouette, slowing again to a relaxed trot as he scaled the next hill and was gone. I crouched then on all fours, exhausted and elated from my run and drank from a pool ceaselessly, until my head ached with the numbness of the stark water . . . and during that brief yet memorable collection of events, I *was* a caribou and this *was* my land.

> 5.25.97 I've had a young caribou guarding my camp all day. A fine scoff of fish and brewis tonight went down well. It's incredible how fast it is to prepare. So filling and oh so Newfie!
>
> Every 10 minutes I'm discovering a new technique or idea that improves the whole camping experience and makes things easier. My wrist was terribly sore after yesterday's marathon, yet a day of rest (fly fishing?) seems to have improved it greatly. Also wrapped it in a bandage to minimize movement all day.
>
> These barrens have me spellbound — so beautiful and intricate. The flies have yet to emerge in any numbers which is a blessing, can't say the same for the army ants. A beautifully exhausting day — I'll sleep well.

5.26.97 — 0900 hr — The barometer's fallen 10 points in the past 8 hours! There are 40 knot winds outside and it's precipitating in the form of hail. It's a challenge to go out and shit, yet I've never felt so alive. Winds are still from the east. Forecast is for it to diminish this evening, snow, and then switch around to SW tomorrow. Yet that's what they said last night. The tent's holding up as beautifully as ever and all gear is secure and safe. I'm as warm as can be expected, dry and content for now to be huddled up here in my little cave. This will give the wrist some extra rest which is an added plus; it's doing quite fine now — we'll see following a few hours of paddling. Paddling the coast of Newfoundland, this is to be expected and there's certainly no point in growing anxious or getting upset. Must be patient.

1630 hr — weather update. Barometer is at 989 mb. It's dropped 10 more points in the last 4 hours! Registering +50 knot winds at Burgeo. Most of the rain and hail has let up.

2000 hr — It's stopped precipitating for the first time today and my friend the eagle has been out flying. Perhaps just restless like myself. I've been napping on and off all day, so I hope sleep will still come easily. Been reading also and a pot of cabbage soup has just been finished, so, God willing, conditions will improve over the night and I'll be able to proceed. Burgeo and beyond for tomorrow?

5.27.97 — 1000 hr — I'm all packed and ready. The sun is shining yet it's blowing a gale. *Big* swell from the west and gusting winds from the north a cold one at that! The waiting game continues . . .

2000 hr — It did finally die down, about an hour ago just after I'd made the call to set up camp again. So for the third night I'll spend it here in just a little bit of paradise.

There is great concern though. I'd indications that my wrist was well on the way to recovery — apart from a little tenderness all but extreme movement was fine. So in the afternoon I removed the pressure bandage and now it's quite painful. Even carrying gear, chopping wood, etc. causes great pain. I'm in a state of confusion, disappointment, and great loss. All the joy and wonderment of this week and the prospects of a fantastic summer are in question. I've worked so hard and long for this adventure — and it's going so incredibly well — to perhaps end like this, and so soon would be devastating.

Tomorrow morning's paddle will decide. Yet I pray it'll go smoothly for I'm not sure how much it can take. To continue into complete isolation for many days is quite unrealistic at this time, not to mention stupid.

What am I going to do? I can't imagine giving this up and returning home in failure. I can pray for a miracle recovery — that's all I've left . . . How long before it heals well enough to resume the trip? All the happiness I've received has just been drained out of me in a few hours. Because I'm not indestructible. My arms, hands, everything I felt would be quite sore and maybe a problem are excellent. Yet I'm a bloody disabled. Seeing my shadow tonight as I prepared a meal over the fire was terrible; arm limp to the side and useless. This just can't be the way it's going to end.

3

I had feelings of devastation in the hours preceding the decision but in the end I simply accepted my fate. Yet loading my boat the next morning, I'd still held a faint glimmer of hope that once I touched my blade to the water's surface, all pain would magically fade and I'd proceed down the coast as desired. It was not to be.

I'd awoken thankfully to a fine morning, following my storm-extended stay. The young caribou who'd greeted me the first morning was no longer to be seen. He'd remained with me throughout the entire ordeal, as if a guardian angel had been sent to reassure and boost my spirits. Now that I'd accepted my fate of having to turn back, his services were no longer required.

There was little doubt in my mind whether or not I'd return. How much damage I'd sustained due to my carelessness and anxiousness was unclear. It was obvious I'd made some judgment errors and had not paced myself correctly in the first days of paddling. How long would it be before I'd the chance to redeem my mistakes?

The paddle back to the welcoming little cove that morning was sheer agony. There was a faint swell and no wind, yet I felt little enjoyment from these normally ideal conditions. I'd had to replace the tight bandage around my forearm; the dull throb even without movement was considerable. Moving my wrist or opening my hand created the sound of a rusty, unused door hinge creaking open for the first time in untold seasons.

Finally, after a number of hours I entered the cove and pulled ashore on the small beach I'd left only days earlier. I'd the hopes of one day returning to see the little town I'd fallen in love with. I'd never have predicted that it would be so soon.

There were a few signs of life among the small cluster of houses. Gentle streams of wood smoke could be seen reaching skyward from a number of homes. Still, it remained breathtakingly silent. I paddled humbly ashore. A man slowly strolled down over the rock-encrusted slope to greet me. "Back agin? Come on up t' d' house b'y and git y'self warmed up. D' name's Tom."

I left everything as it was and followed solemnly. His home was just up over the embankment, and within seconds we were greeted at the door by his wife. They were both in their late forties and immediately manifested the subtle signs of a long, fulfilling marriage. I was led into a room radiating warmth, love and years of contentment. Everything was neatly laid out. The walls were adorned with handcrafted ornaments of welcome and the objects of many a long winter's artistic endeavor.

Following our initial introduction, little else was required until after my first sip of tea. Looking occasionally out to the calm ocean as I did so — for the kitchen table stood against the wall and a large, multipaned window overlooked the sea — I began, "Well, seems I've damaged my arm somewhat. There's no way I can continue my trip. So I had to head back here this morning. Now I'm not sure what's next."

Tom remained quiet and could see the difficulty I was experiencing with the reality of the situation. He allowed me time to continue.

"I guess I'll have to get someone to look at it," I mumbled. "I really can't believe this is happening . . . "

The tea had a difficult time navigating the large obstruction in my throat.

"You just missed d' doctor," he replied quietly. "He only come in once a week. There's d' coastal boat. She's due in about fifteen minutes. Someone'll see ya t'day sure in Port aux Basques."

His wife brought some toast and it gave me time to digest the information.

"All ya gear and boat sure, we can put down in d' store down on d' wharf. Ain't ever locked but no one'd touch 'er. You git y'arm looked aft' an come back when ya can, and she'll be 'ere waitin' for ya."

There was little else to do.

"We'd have to rush," I answered, the logistics of pulling it off, with my fully loaded boat laying down on the beach and ten minutes in which to do it, racing through my head. "You'd be willin' to help me get the boat over? She's heavy."

"Le's go den, b'y," he said, already standing and reaching for his coat.

Getting *Destiny* up over the bank would not be an easy task for the two of us. Wincing from the strain that it exerted on my arm, we slowly carried, shimmied, dragged her along. At one point I heard Tom utter astonishedly, "B'y she's 'eavy for d' size o' 'er, ain't she? I got a bit of a bad back, right."

"Geez, b'y," I replied as I struggled along, "you shoulda told me that before we took this on." I made the call for a rest and as we did so, the loud drone of the boat's fog horn could be heard repeatedly, as she began her approach through the channel.

"Le's go," he demanded. "We'll git ya dere yet."

The tendons in my arm had felt like they were going to snap. Still we continued. I thought to myself, "Forty yards. All downhill now. This bouncing motion is hell. Twenty. There's no way I'm going to make it! I'm going to drop her and crack her in two. Seven . . . (A sudden sweat had broken out on me.) Onto the wharf now — level. . . God, the *pain*! Around the corner."

Someone had seen us coming and had opened the garage door. Strained hellos as we torturously shuffled by.

There! — along the back wall . . . two pallets magically awaiting. Done.

Yet there was little time to bask in our achievement. The boat had docked.

What did I need to take?

I quickly grabbed toiletries, a bit of food, my jacket. Still in my damp paddling clothes and rubber boots . . . there was no time. It would have to do. They held up the boat of course, and turning to Tom I gave him my sincerest thanks and quickly stepped aboard.

"Oh, Tom," I remembered as we pulled away from the wharf. "T'ank the missus for breakfast."

Travelling along the shore that morning a deep sadness overcame me as I recalled my own trip, less than a week before, along the same route.

Yet that morning the fog had stayed away, and in crossing a number of the bays I marveled at the distance, and how I'd crossed them in the fog without really grasping the scope or intimidating nature of the environment. I recognized the cove where I'd camped on the second night and the places I'd stopped for lunches. I remembered the fishermen who had come ashore and stayed for a visit and the blissful occasions of paddling when the rest of the world ceased to exist.

Less than seventeen hours after waking on an isolated crescent beach of the south coast, I found myself back home before dusk — following a wild three-mile paddle, a 23-mile coastal steam, a 17-mile bus ride, and a more than 300-mile hitchhike — on the northeast side of the island.

The land of barrens and quaint coastal communities shrouded in fog again seemed half a world away.

The time spent home provided little stimulation. I'd be surrounded by sympathetic family and friends, yet my thoughts were miles away back on the south coast. I was of little help around the house, and my frustrations were increased when I discovered how many limitations had to be self-imposed if I were to promptly return to the coast. Those were the longest excruciating weeks of my life.

A wonderful diet provided by my mother and complete rest for my arm insured a speedy recovery. The day arrived finally when I felt I could depart again. By then it was well into the second week of June. Bidding farewell, once again, to my wonderfully supportive family I departed with little more than I'd arrived with (for there'd be no room for anything extra once I'd reunited with *Destiny*) and began the long, arduous journey back in time.

Returning to the south and traveling on the coastal boat had me clearly in uncharted waters from another perspective, for I found myself seasick. All those occasions off Vancouver Island working as a deckhand, to raise money to paddle, when I'd tried desperately to sympathize with those sickly looking faces. The sheer torture of spending a day out on the ocean in hopes of fishing, only to be turned into a pale, grey mass of despair. And I'd silently chuckled as I scrubbed vomit from the deck, thinking they'd *paid* for that misery. That's it boys — over the side with it now. No harm done in feedin' the fish. The rest of us won't laugh at ya, right, fellas? And there's less of it for me to clean up. So I deserved it, I concluded.

I'd spoken with Tom on a couple of occasions by telephone and informed him of my tentative arrival date. It was not a pleasant sea that welcomed me back. The coastal boat dipped and struggled through the high seas. I'd eaten very little since my sparse breakfast and it had taken two days to reach the south coast. Weary and in ill health from the long trip, when the boat finally docked I gladly went ashore.

Tom and a few other men (my friend John included) were on the wharf to greet me. They were all huddled over in the lee of the store seeking shelter from the blasting rain. Tom, fully decked out in rain slicks, had to practically shout when he approached, "Fine bit o' weather t' welcome ya back, eh?"

Not only was he competing with the howling wind to be heard, but there was something else . . . The waterfall. I looked and was amazed. It was barely recognizable from the mental pictures I'd had of it only two weeks earlier. For now, it was a wild torrent of white. The water spilling over the lip was nearly touching the bottom of the bridge. A thick mist, created by the increased amount of water falling, was heavy in the air. Combined with the sheets of rain sweeping about the cove, it created a sobering contrast to the nirvana-like nest it had been on my initial visits.

"Looks like you guys have had a bit o' rain since I left," I smiled and licked the water from my lips. It was salty. Mist created from the swell of the outside ocean was drifting in over the cliffs, into the protected harbour as well.

A quick hello to the others and everyone promptly dispersed to the welcoming confines of their respective homes. It was no day to be paddling, tending gardens or any such thing. It was, as we say, unfit. The warm blanket of a wood fire brightened our spirits and we shut ourselves in from the elements. Like all beings, the sea must be permitted the courtesy to vent her own frustrations. All hands were safely ashore . . . Let 'er go!

That evening was spent in the fine company of new friends. Tom, his wife and I relaxed in the time the storm had provided. Unburdened by schedules or routine engagements, we were content to acquaint ourselves further. We spoke of their original homes as kids in a now defunct community, which was resettled by the Smallwood government, and the many fond memories she'd retained from there. Her father who was a boat builder. The photos of his schooners had me yearning for the days of yesteryear when the coastline was dotted with those majestic displays of craftsmanship. Of a time before outboards, and fish-finders, and draggers.

Their trustworthiness and quick acceptance of me was heartfelt. At one point they both left the house and thought nothing of my remaining there — while he went to help a neighbour who'd lost his electricity and she went over to the store to chat with some of the other ladies.

I'm forever indebted.

6.13.97 Sometimes I feel I may be a little too undeserving of all I've been given. As always, the greatest signs of hospitality and kindness come following very difficult times.

I'm now reassured that no matter what, I'll always be duely rewarded if I persevere and show integrity and courage. I'm exhausted yet feeling so content and inspired once again. They insisted that I stay the night, the weather being most unwelcoming, and we'll see how it is in the morning. I'll sleep tonight for the first time in a feather bed. The entire mattress, about 5 inches thick, is feathers!

By the late evening, the winds had died out and I slept comfortably, to the soft drumming of hail against my window.

Conditions in the morning were workable, apart from the dampness. A considerable southwest swell remained from the storm, yet the winds were negligible. It would be a wet day, but I'd intentions of paddling only a few miles to test out my arm. I'd head over to my old camping spot and then along the shore that I'd hiked. There was a saltwater lagoon on the inner part of the bay where I could try for a fish.

Tom invited me to stay longer of course, but I was adamant that I needed a night out alone, wet or not. *Destiny* was as I'd left her and it wasn't long before we were underway. The swell was a nice challenge and I got some valuable practice with a following sea.

Approaching my old camping spot meant going through a tickle, a narrow channel of water found between an island and the mainland. As I came close enough to check out the conditions I paused for many moments before deciding to head in through. The swell was being funneled in, in such a way that it was rebounding off the mainland and also off the coast of the island just offshore. The result was a small section of water at the approach of the tickle which had a chaotic, nearly random mess of overlapping waves. Apart from one near mishap where the blade of my paddle sliced through the water and I lost my balance, giving me a noted dose of adrenalin, all went well and I was soon paddling along the shore of my past camp.

I stopped there to look around and took great interest in how much more growth had occured since I'd been there. The fresh blades of marsh grass were well along and the purple irises were just about to bloom. My eagle friends were busily fishing still, for undoubtedly they'd hungry mouths to feed by now. Spring had finally arrived on the shores of New-foundland. It was the middle of June, after all.

I'd set up camp and was content to lay in my tent when the rains kept me from exploring. Time to reevaluate. I was given another chance. I didn't want to screw it up a second time. The most important thing was that I was back.

I began visualizing myself from an eagle's perspective of the coastline — my boat and me a mere fleck on the delicate film between two worlds, an insignificant speck of dust in relation to the almighty organism below. From this vantage point, I could better understand the swell's effects upon encountering solid objects such as coastal headlands, islands and shoals. To merely be conscious of the immediate conditions around me without un-derstanding why or looking at it from a much grander scale, would quickly result in my untimely demise. I quickly, out of necessity, began predicting the conditions I'd encounter upon rounding the next point of land.

The coastline offered so little in terms of adequate landing sites that the few that did exist had to be seriously noted. It was foreseeable on an occasion that I'd have to backtrack and paddle ten miles along the coast I'd already travelled to finally come ashore. There were stretches of some-times sixteen miles (a four-hour paddle in fine conditions) where the coast-line was entirely a wall of rock, at times exceeding well over a thousand feet. The backwash of waves created by the swell hitting these uncompro-mising barriers was chaotic — to find myself in it would not be wise. This meant giving the shore a wide berth, quite often as much as a full mile.

I carried with me a small VHF radio but had quickly discovered its uselessness among the imposing cliffs. I was utterly alone if an accident oc-curred. The water temperature here was a balmy five degrees, this being quite warm in relation to the frigid Labrador Current I'd encounter upon rounding the Avalon Peninsula. I soon understood, with exceptional clarity, why the fishermen rarely learned how to swim.

Below me lay deep canyons and spired, steeple-like pinnacles; shoals of uncharacteristically shallow water; sunkers, these commonly found rocks that rarely penetrated the surface, only to make their presence felt with the slow approach of an exceptionally large swell. These things and much more lay beneath *Destiny's* thin shell.

By the time I approached the saltwater ponds, or barasways, of Burgeo days later, the ocean had taught me many things for which no text from a book or detailed diagrams could substitute. Hourly I was becoming increasingly more in tune with my surroundings. I was no longer the child of expendable energies that I'd chastised myself for being only weeks earlier. I'd graduated with an integral, abstract understanding of the principles of ocean paddling. I'd developed a profound respect for the ocean and of my insignificance upon it.

I reflected on these accomplishments when I rounded the point to Barasway Bay. The southwest swell had remained since the storm of my return; it had now evolved into a thick, sluggish surge, following its extensive journey up the eastern seaboard. It was a fine morning to explore the inner shallows of the uniquely developed barasway.

I altered course and began the paddle along the inner shore of the 5-mile-wide bay. Again, a massive amphitheatre loomed in the distance, two miles across with steep sloped encircling walls of sheer rock.

There was a sunker breaking off to port, between me and the shore. Every thirty seconds it could be heard with the approaching swell, a deep, wild suction as the level water surrounding it seemed to be absorbed into the thick, grey mass of sea that would immediately engulf the low lying rocks. I continued along at a comfortable distance, commenting to myself on the incredible force that the ocean displayed.

Suddenly there was something not quite right. Why could I see, with such clarity, the kelp . . . flowing quickly to starboard beneath me?

Oh Christ! I thought to myself.

I looked out to the horizon, just over my right shoulder, and barreling in toward me was a behemoth bulge of sea. Still seventy feet away, the water surrounding the sunker had already made its decision to join the ranks of this imposing conqueror. It dwarfed the preceding "ripples" that

43

had overcome the sunker as I approached. I felt a faint drag as it began to draw me into its deathly advance as well. The swell was too far developed to try and paddle parallel to it in an effort to avoid disaster. If I did so, it would overwhelm me in a great tomb-like cocoon before smashing me onto the rock.

Quickly, for this was my only chance, I paddled backward with all force on my starboard side, then a mad heave forward on the port. This brought me around to face the ever-advancing wall directly. Then with full precision strokes I paddled straight toward it! All my energy, injured arm or not, had to be channeled into reaching the wave before it reached me. My sore arm would be the least of my injuries if I got pummeled onto the rock.

Stroke! Stroke! Stroke! Stroke!

No thoughts, but stroke, stroke . . .

My bow edged its way up over the crest.

Stroke! Stroke! Stroke!

There was a sensation — No, it was happening . . . I *was* being pulled backward with the direct aftermath of the wave.

Stroke! Stroke!

Beneath me barreled the aqua blue of sea-mixed air; a mass of foam yet to be given the chance to reach the surface.

Stroke! Damn it, stroke!

A thunderous crash of sea against rock. A clash of titans.

I still had much to learn.

Arriving in town later that morning, I was greeted with the sight of garbage and sludge of uncertain composition along the shore of the cove. The price to pay for the "gift" of a road, I wondered? All week I'd camped in coves and along beaches that were uncharacteristically clear of humanity's incessant litter.

I'd grown up along shores clogged with man's vile habit. Never could you walk a stretch of shoreline barefoot without the fear of embedding shards of glass into your feet. The lack of people along the south coast was a main factor of course. Yet it would be brought to my attention later that one of the positives to the cod fishery's closing was the lack of garbage being thrown overboard. In the past five years the ocean was permitted to cleanse her shores without the constant daily assault of chip bags, pop bottles and oil cans.

I waded through the "gifts" of the twentieth century and came ashore. There were many people about and several took an inquisitive interest in my arrival. I was still hyped from my encounter with the wave, when I inquired for the nearest store and happily wandered up towards it.

The weather was beautiful and the cove radiated a pleasant warmth. Kids ran along with the exuberance of . . . kids, having been released from the shackles of school for their summer break. The sun bounced off the multicoloured clapboard of the close-set houses. Ladies were hanging clothes and smiling. A number of dogs accompanied me up the well-worn path. I turned and looked out to the horizon, having gained some elevation. The sparkling surface of the ocean glistened among the dotted islands that shielded the community. The long awaited warmth of a summer sun reached my skin. It would be the first summer I'd spend on the island since I was fifteen.

I needed food supplies along with fuel for my stove. Carrots, a few potatoes, a turnip, cabbage, and a sack of onions. Some oranges. Pass on the bananas. Perhaps an extra bag of split peas. That bizarre block of dates, which "may or may not contain sulfites," would have to do. My shopping complete, I headed back down the hill to my awaiting carriage and began looking for some place to store it all.

"Hello . . . Ya hungry b'y?"

Looking up, I saw an older gentleman of about seventy and clinging protectively to his legs was a small girl, undoubtedly his granddaughter. She'd peer out wide-eyed on occasion, one hand tightly gripped a bundle of her pop's pants, the other reassuringly in front of her mouth, thumb notwithstanding.

"I wouldn't want to put you out, sir. I'm fine really."

"No trouble, b'y. I'll get d' missus t' fix y'up som'n. Come on up t' d' 'ouse b'y, luh." He'd turned on his heels and, young girl in hand, was

45

heading up over the hill again. There was little else to do, so I shuffled along to catch up.

It was a very simple lunch, easily prepared for any visitor at any time of the day on the coast. Tea and freshly baked white bread, margarine, pickles and beets, soda crackers and patridgeberry jam. I avoided the sausages by saying that I had in fact eaten a bit of a lunch back along the shore. This worked, so I was indulged with the next course: dessert, consisting of more tea, jamjams and a massive slice of cake.

It was just following noon when I'd arrived, so they'd already had their lunch. They sat listening intently as I told them tales of my coastal journey while I ate. Of course, there were the ever-present inquiries as to friends and acquaintances I might've known over on my side of the island.

Throughout the meal I'd the misfortune of trying to compete with the television that was left on in the adjoining room, a popular midday American soap opera. No one was watching it — it just seemed to be on for background filler. I was the only one who seemed to be affected by its presence or show signs of its distractive curse. Soon thereafter it was responsible for my hasty departure. There was no way I could compete with the lives of those in Genoa City.

A few hours later, following a wonderfully relaxed paddle, I entered a narrow channel I'd been told of and leisurely followed it around to the backside of an island. There was a simple cabin nestled into the back of the hill and I continued on to the next cove, where I proceeded to set up camp.

I'd finished supper and headed over towards the cabin for a walk. Fly season had arrived. Back in the lee of the island where there was little wind, the "nippers" were fierce. I'd ventured out to the point between the two coves, in hopes of catching a draft to provide some relief. I soon discovered that the smoke from my rarely used pipe was a fine deterrent against the little buggers. I was enjoying my plug when the sounds of an approaching outboard became audible.

Three men came cruising around the calm of the inner channel. They were fast approaching when the engine was suddenly cut. Pointing quickly, one of them shouted, "Look. Up agin d' hill. Moose! Do ya see 'im?" I scanned the hill where he'd been pointing and there it was, running excitedly among the rare stand of fir and spruce trees. Soon afterward they came ashore and began switching their lobsters into the holding box just off from their wharf. I walked over to greet them and then wandered away a little to give them time to finish their work.

The eldest gentleman left the younger two to settle things away and joined me. He had big hands, calloused and deeply cut with scars from years of hauling traps and working lines. His face was darkly tanned from the constant exposure to the elements. His chest was thick and his arms well toned. The cool air of evening found me in a tightly fitted long shirt and sweater. He seemed quite comfortable, remaining in his work shirt rolled up above his elbows and half unbuttoned. He'd only moments ago stepped from his boat.

"Nice t'ave ya come . . . James, dat's me son down in d' boat and 'is buddy John up on d' wharf — oh, den dere's me. I'm James too . . . 'e's junior. We comes 'ere and fishes agin d' shore and stays 'ere come suppertime. Where's ya boat at?"

"I'm pulled up over in the next cove. I paddled in from the other side of Burgeo today. No trouble if I spends the night over there, is it?"

"No, b'y," he answered. "Ya welcome t' sleep in d' cabin if ya likes, tons a bunks sure."

The conversation continued like this throughout our entire encounter. The younger men remained respectfully quiet and said little, unless I asked them a question directly. Both were in their mid-twenties. They invited me in for supper and set leftover lobster from lunch on the table before me.

"Y'ave ate lobsta b'fore, ain't ya?" he questioned.

The look in my eyes let him know the answer.

"Well, we'll show ya," he smiled.

"First Newf ever I 'eard tell of," chuckled James Jr. quickly, "who ain't never ate lobsta!" The look in James Sr.'s eye let Junior know something else.

It was a grand experience and we all had a laugh, at my expense in the end. Before dark they walked me back to my camp so they could check out my boat and we parted happily. I had spent a beautiful evening in the company of decent strangers . . . and without a television for miles.

6.16.97 So blissfully content right now. I've been given two meals today — my first lobster included. I've just spent the evening with three fishermen. No politics or world issues, just pure conversation for the sake of human decency. A fabulous day, close calls and altered routes included. Lovely winds and fine people. I simply can't put a price on the spectacular life that I've created for myself.

6.17.97 I've just now awoken and without even looking outside to check the weather, I find myself scrambling to write.

A dream — the most vivid and interesting one I've ever had! I'm travelling by train westward. It's in the early morning hours and mist blankets the plain outside. It must have been out in the southwest somewhere, and the clothing and style of the coach was perhaps 'Thirties era. It all seems rather common and unremarkable when suddenly the train comes to a screeching halt. There's a sense of unease discerned from the faces of the other passengers. An eerie lull falls upon the cabin.

A loud clink and the sliding of a bolt jolts my own attention, and I rise in my seat to get an unencumbered view of the scene unfolding. Men, seasoned-looking men, are quickly entering. One of the last to appear is a remarkably upright and proud gentleman. He walks with purpose and his voice slices unwaveringly through the stale air of the cabin. Mist and refreshing coolness accompany the motley crew. I feel revived and excited.

"Excuse me, ladies and gentlemen. We have no plans of detaining you for long. We've simply halted the train's progress in an effort to reestablish some, shall we say, balance . . . "

Then this charismatic and clearly remarkable leader holds out a sack and begins removing the valuables from the mostly unamused patrons. But not before conducting a simple and ingenious examination. Asking respectfully to see the palms of each person whom he approaches down the aisle, rarely does this act meet his approval and the people are ordered to remove their watches, jewelry and purses thereafter.

I'm clearly intrigued by this strange routine and my intense interest is noticed by the man. Several times there's an exchanged acknowledgment between us as he makes his way down the aisle toward me. There are a couple of encounters that don't warrant the patrons losing their possessions.

Before I have time to understand what it is that is making the difference, he's before me. I offer my hands to him. Incredibly, I can see them clearly in my dream as being *my* actual hands. Calloused, sore and weathered from the many days of coastal paddling, wood chopping and constant exposure. He smiles at me approvingly, for it's clear I have the telltale signs of a life honorably lived.

Returning to the front of the coach, he sincerely thanks all of us present for our time and "donations." Then the fog drifts in around him, as if mystifying his character and preserving the ethical lesson that he represents. Are we the students and he the professor? In bidding farewell he tips his hat and, as if to clarify, states, "I'm merely Black Bart, the Poet."

Could this man have actually existed, or did I conjure up some fabled radical solely in my head?

4

I'd climbed atop a hill. All day I'd paddled into stiff headwinds. The coast had not been welcoming in providing an easy place to land. The extreme tides of the approaching full moon didn't help. For lunch I'd struggled onto a small rock platform only large enough for myself. The water had gone over my boots in getting there. *Destiny* remained in the water, and with every surge of the outside swell she'd hit against the unforgivably brutal rocks. I went through the pains of ringing out my socks and emptying my boots — only to have them get soaked again when I re-entered the water.

It was mid-afternoon. I was damp, cold, and I'd had to paddle to the lee of an island again to find a place to land.

There was a couple in a small cabin up above the beach when I arrived. I felt I'd be imposing if I were to remain, so I climbed the hill to get a view of the conditions and route ahead. A seven-mile crossing would bring me to the entrance of the next community. The extended forecast did not sound promising.

Atop the hill, overlooking the ocean and the continuing coastline to the east, were the remains of a long forgotten graveyard. The effort to get the deceased up to that vantage point for burial must have been considerable. I'd have been eternally grateful to the brothers who did. The view was stunning.

When I die, you can bury me atop that desolate hill. I'll rest with the folks to whom I can relate with the most, from a time long since forgotten. There'll be nothing to obscure my vision. . . of perfection.

After paying my respects and promising to one day return, I sauntered back down to the shore. The conditions seemed to have improved a little with the falling sun. I needed high tide ideally to make the approach to the community a mile upriver. It was in two hours and I felt I should go.

I quickly prepared, anxious to get paddling again to create some warmth, and set off. It wasn't long before I realized the skeg wouldn't lower. I should have turned back and checked out the problem, but I didn't. The result was a much more challenging paddle than it should have been. The rolling sea to port kept pulling me off course (the purpose of the skeg is to adjust for this) and as with my injury-resulting mishap of weeks earlier I had to begin paddling with extra force. Only this time it was reversed.

Struggling and frustrated, and cursing myself for being so stupid, I continued on. Repeatedly I broke rhythm and tried the cable-slide which moved the skeg. Why wouldn't it move?

I gave up on it and concentrated on getting there. I shifted as much weight as possible to my left cheek, causing *Destiny* to heel over slightly. This worked in heading her up into the swell, but I then had to be especially cautious with my centre of balance altered. Already I was detecting an uncomfortable strain in my left elbow. I was over a third of the way there and crossing a deep fiord, a mile inside my position. There was little where else to go but forward.

Suddenly there was a great *foeshh*.

There! — seventy feet off my port bow — a whale! And he was coming towards me. Even my thoughts of injury or capsize were secondary then. My first whale!

There again! Oh shit! thirty feet away then, but it had changed direction and was swimming along with me. My thoughts were all muddled. I only remember, Where is he? Where is he? An eternity passed.

FOOESH . . .

I saw his eye, his fucking eye!

I had to blink a number of times to get the tears out of my own. This time he'd surfaced no more than a boat length away, directly beside me. I barely remembered to breathe, I was so excited — and nervous about where he'd be the next time he came up.

But there was no next time. As mysteriously as he'd arrived, he vanished.

I waited and waited. I scanned the waters. Nothing . . .

I replayed the entire encounter through my mind a dozen times before I realized that I'd reached the cliffs. For 650 feet they towered above me. I felt very small and insignificant.

I'd studied the opening to the river on my chart, but I was still amazed when I reached it. The massive cliffs created an impenetrable wall. Yet there was an opening of no more than six boat lengths across, and just inside it took a gentle curve to the right denying me a view of what lay ahead.

What would happen?

Before me lay the most bizarre, seemingly undesirable location for a town. As I slowly paddled towards it, the cliffs behind appeared all the more imposing — uncompromising. There in that deep crook at the narrow delta of a large river sat a community. Much bigger than I'd imagined, it was positioned at the base of the immense cliffs which enveloped it, on rock scrub left from eons of the slope's gradual erosion. I had to strain my neck to look skyward.

I quickly went ashore on the far right of the town. A number of locals were over at the government wharf to my left. The coastal boat had passed me on my way in and they were still hanging around from *that* excitement — now this. With disbelieving expressions, they seemed unsure of how to approach this strange creature, who'd only moments ago entered their tiny world. Finally, a young man came forward, only a few years older than me. It was obvious, by lack of seniority, that he'd felt it his duty to wander over to investigate. I was chilled and had begun to shiver by this stage.

"Where ya come from? She ain't too civil out dere now, is she?" he began.

"No b'y, guess it's good I got in when I did. My name's Michael," I answered, extending my hand. He seemed uncomfortable with this formality of greeting and quickly shook my hand weakly before returning his to his side.

"Sorry 'bout it being so cold," I added, realizing that it must have been like taking hold of a dead fish. "I'm coming from Port aux Basques, not t'day now mind you, but I've been at her a little while now."

A few of the other men, reassured by then that I wasn't some ill-omened spirit, approached and one of them cut in, "In dat l'il 'ting? Lord Jesus, ya wouldn' catch me goin' cross d' riva in dat."

Everyone laughed before the conversation took on a serious tone again. "Dere's forecast for a storm. Ya won't get outa 'ere in d' mornin'." We all nodded in agreement.

"There's not much level ground around is there," I stated, looking around.

"Only where d' 'ouses be, d'ats 'bout it," the young man answered. "Dere's a bit o' pat' leads agin d' shore. We can go take a look . . . gonna pitch ya tent I s'pose, wa?" The thick accent there was beautiful, yet that first evening I'd everyone flustered in repeating themselves, I'm sure.

The others had slowly retreated back to the wharf and I called out a quick farewell before we headed across the little brook and up along the path. It didn't look promising and I was still in my paddling gear and had wet feet. A light drizzle had begun to fall. Passing the incinerator and helicopter pad, we turned back unsatisfied. A number of young girls passed us then, unperturbed by the damp weather and skipped along the path back to town. They turned often to catch sight of the bedraggled looking visitor and giggled.

"Me buddy Pete got a garden out back of 'is 'ouse. I'll go ask 'e, if ya can put ya gear dere."

Upon returning to my boat, I was amazed. She was lost in a sea of kids, all jostling one another to get a glimpse of the strange yellow boat.

"Git on now and leave d' man be!" my buddy barked.

The children began to slowly recede to let us through. They all remained in clumps, scattered at a close distance to see what would happen.

"What are you guys doin' today? Glad t' be out of school I bet," I acknowledged them. No further invitation was necessary. They closed in and engulfed me. Where'd they all come from?

I had flashbacks of the previous isolated community . . .

"Where's ya from?"

"Wha's ya name?"

"Where's ya engine?"

"Ain't got no computa in dere, 'ave ya?"

"Why ya got a beard?"

The tsunami of questions was remarkable. I got a word in when I could and just kept smiling.

My friend had gone up the path toward the houses. I excused myself and made efforts not to step on anyone as I waded through. I saw an opening and quickened my pace. I looked back and a solid parade of kids was quick on my heels.

Pete was out on his bridge talking with my friend, and it was all settled even before I arrived. The gang returned to my boat and with countless helpers everything was up in the garden in one trip. My buddy had become frustrated with all the children around his feet. I stated that all the extra help was nice for a change, for it usually took me seven trips to do all of it myself. Soon thereafter, he left me to set up.

I'd had thoughts solely of getting into warm clothes and having dry feet when one of the young boys asked, "We's goin' t' play basketball. Ya

54

comin'?" Only a few of his immediate friends remained as it seemed the initial novelty of my arrival had subsided.

I heard myself saying O.K. and we set out for the school yard — magically being joined by others from various homes and paths as we ascended the hill. I recognized many who had greeted me at the shore, but they'd brought reinforcements.

A fine group of misfits gathered. Gender and athleticism were irrelevant. The only prerequisite seemed to be that as yet ill-defined rite of passage between youngster and adult. Was it a skill, this willingness to intermingle between adult activities and the younger people's acts of play? Why, I wondered, did most refuse to step back over this line once it was crossed?

The playing field was a caged-in enclosure, roughly the size of a basketball court. There was a lone hoop, which had lost its mesh a generation ago, nailed to a well-weathered piece of plywood for a backboard. The playing surface was of well-packed dirt, yet it was dotted sporadically with the bold protrusion of jagged rocks and boulders. These undoubtedly had proven themselves too large and substantial to remove. Perhaps they were even part of the bedrock core of the island itself.

Opposite the hoop was the school. A large set of steps led down from the school to the field, providing a great view and simultaneously a spot for battle-wearied youngsters to nurse their respective injuries before rejoining the mayhem.

A mad free-for-all developed. Like a flock of seagulls that had been thrown carrion, they all lunged at that one lone object. The kids ranged in ages from eleven to sixteen. At its beginning stages there were as many as fifteen of us on the field. The hastily divvied-up teams broke down within seconds of the ball's arrival on the court. I watched in shocked horror as a girl's hand got stepped on, or someone else stumbled and skinned their knees, and another got unceremoniously bonked in the nose with a pass. Within minutes the field had cleared of all the half-hearted participants (myself included) and we watched from the steps as "the battle" continued. Definitely a hardy bunch; they've got spirit, I thought. I got to meet a number of them as we sat on the school's steps. We talked mainly of the year's term finishing and what they'd do for the summer.

By that time I simply *had* to get changed. I left them to their game and began heading back to the garden.

"Hey, where's ya goin'?" hollered one of the earlier dropouts from the game, as he came hurrying down the path towards me.

"Gotta get dry, my friend. Been in these wet clothes all day."

As we went through the gate and I began setting up my tent he said, "Sure, Mudder can dry ya close fer ya. I only lives right dere sure." With that he was gone.

Pete, whose garden I found myself setting up camp in, came out then and explained apologetically that he'd have me into his house but that his wife's father had passed on and that he was in the spare room. "We got no fun'ral home o' course, so we 'aves t' keep 'im in d' home."

I thanked him for what he'd done for me already and asked him to give his wife my condolences. He retreated back into his home, and finally I was able to change into dry clothing.

As I was emerging to figure out my next course of action, my young friend returned.

"Yeah. Come on she said, da's no trouble."

It wasn't long after I was inside and sitting at the table that Simon's mother, Mary, decided there was little chance of my staying out in the tent overnight. "What with d' cold an bein' alone, an a storm comin' on . . . We ain't got much, but der's a bed fer ya and we'll find some grub t' fatten ya up on. My die'n ain't you skinny!" she gasped in astonishment.

She was constantly moving. Talking nonstop as she did, she gave me the immediate impression of mildly flustered acceptance, a contentment almost, in the chores and duties that her life demanded. In the adjoining room lay her husband, nearly bed-ridden with the aftermath of two strokes. It was clear that she had her hands full without the burden of a guest to tend to. I insisted that I'd be fine out in my tent. She "wouldn' hear tell of it" — it was her home and I was to stay in it.

Once my sleeping arrangements had been settled, Simon and I went down to the store and shot a few games of pool. Nestled snugly in among a couple of video games and a Coke machine, there was barely walking space around the perimeter of the table. It was great. Even the pool cue was full length, so great skill was required as the thing perched itself wildly up around our ears on every shot.

Like all outport stores, it was the place to hang out and with the inclement weather outside there were no lack of bodies around. I even had a lengthy discussion with a young kid concerning AC/DC's deserved recognition as leading edge artists.

"Yeah," I offered politely. "They may have been one of the most popular acts in the history of rock and roll."

"Were!" he quickly retorted. "Where you been? Dey still playin', b'y."

"Oh," I said, trailing off. "How lucky for us."

Lining the walls surrounding the table were rows of rental videos. I curiously looked at them while Simon took some of his shots. Junk. Pure garbage. Blank, stereotypical, useless Hollywood fluff. Movies. The belittling plots and dialogue had even found its way to those isolated, unsuspecting folks. I emitted a deep sigh of despair.

That night we also agreed to go fishing the next day. He'd be in school for a couple of hours to get his report card in the morning . . . and then we'd be free.

The following morning there was bologna and eggs awaiting me for breakfast. Before I'd even left the confines of Simon's room the sickly smell overcame me. I'd foreseen the occasions when it was going to happen. Up until then I'd avoided the issue. That morning in that little boy's room, a serious decision had to be made.

If I was to be accepted, to seek some kind of understanding of how those people lived in that isolated environment, then I had to commit myself fully. This, of course, meant eating the diet to which they were accustomed to as well. That morning I walked out with a warm smile on my face, greeted everyone and sat before a large plate of bologna (composition entirely unknown) and chicken menstrual cycles. I took a deep breath, sighed heavenward and ate the entire thing.

6.18.97 It's been said that the Buddha died after
accepting the gift of a meal of pork, even though he was
against the consumption of meat.

I spent the morning with Mary and her husband, Joe. The weather was miserable. Big swell from the southeast and torrential rains. She felt that the coastal boat wouldn't make it in that afternoon. She busied herself with baking and tending to Joe's needs, while I marveled at how much she could decipher of his seriously altered speech. Many times he'd ask me a question and I'd understand nothing, then she'd holler from the kitchen, her hands into a batch of cookies, what he said.

As with Pete's situation next door, there were no services available in the small community so they simply did what was required themselves. Joe didn't have access to the medical facilities provided in the bigger centres. Instead, he remained in his own home and maintained his dignity, where surrounded by his family and friends he could die still a man.

There were times when he cried out in pain and despair, and Mary would be in tears trying to make him as comfortable as possible. There were also times when he gave us the grandest smiles, or the following day when he felt strong enough to join us at the table for lunch and it brought everyone such joy to have him there. It didn't matter how much food he spit up. Or if he wetted his pants. He was *there*. And people still loved him enough to put the rest of their lives on hold.

While the rest of society was being conditioned to believe that it's righteous and decent to shut our sick and elderly away, or to use them as mere lab experiments, or to pay someone else to tend to the welfare of our own mothers and fathers because we're too busy, or too repulsed, there was still that isolated community on the south coast of Newfoundland that held folks who still knew that they were alive and that they would die, and that they should laugh but also should cry.

So I helped out in any way that I could.

"Y'any good at fixin' stuff?" she asked me that first morning.

"I can give anything a try I s'pose."

She pulled out her hand mixer and I began taking it apart. The contact on the switch inside had merely worked its way too far. Before Simon returned to go fishing, she was mixing her ingredients for a cake with her newly fixed gadget. She explained as we prepared to head out that the cake was for the bishop's visit. In the excitement of our departure, I'd not comprehended that the bishop was to arrive on his annual visit and young Simon was to be confirmed. Much to the chagrin of Simon.

We dug a few worms over in the remains of an old shed that had fallen and headed out. The small stream I'd crossed only the evening before was now at least eighteen inches higher. It had attained a remarkable crescendo that I had heard from my bed that morning, but which had not been audible upon retiring the night before. Up along the path and along the incinerator, we stopped briefly to say hello to a man stoking the fire — the sides of the metal housing aglow with the intense heat, despite the ravages of the steady downpour. A little further upstream and the trail dissolved.

That was it! The amount of space the locals had from one another was that quarter of a mile trail. Unless you were to scale the steep incline of the surrounding six hundred foot cliffs, that was as far as you got for privacy and seclusion via the land.

We fished for the rest of the morning with no luck. Too early in the year and too much water in the river was the verdict from the locals that evening.

We developed a fine friendship on those small fishing trips, for it wasn't far of course and we returned many times. I realized how much influence I'd had on him when he began singing a song I'd been unconsciously voicing all morning, about a girl who steals cash from all her roommates, only to disappear for two days to get high. Perhaps it wasn't the right influence to portray.

"How 'bout books, Simon. Do ya like t' read?" I inquired.

"Naw, not much. Ain't got none aroun'. Dere's some up t' d' school, but dey ain't no good," he replied sheepishly.

"What ya gotta do is find something that you like, sure. There's books about anything you can imagine."

I picked something, and began telling him about *The Old Man and the Sea*. When I'd finished the story he asked incredulously, "You learned dat dere from a book? Well, das some story." I promised to send it to him, and we slowly walked back into town.

That night there were many visitors and there seemed to be a nervous anticipation of the boat's arrival the next day.

I remained quiet on the subject of the "religious experience'" that was to influence the community. Expressing my opinions at the time wouldn't have helped, and I convinced myself that I should go into it with an objective and hopefully unbiased mindset.

Next morning, the weather remained just as nasty and it was evident that I'd be "hung ashore" for another day. With breakfast survived I was asked would I "have a go" at the VCR. They hadn't been able to use it in many months.

There was no way I could support *that* — not there — not after what I'd seen on the shelves of their store. But I looked at Mary, who'd barely sat down since I'd been there — and at Joe who was laying in bed, staring at the walls all day . . . and asked her where it was.

The VCR got fixed and everyone was joyous.

Simon no longer wanted to go fishing.

I began taking walks.

I hiked up the stream that was by that time bursting its banks from the heavy rains. I was amazed — only two days before, it had been a mere trickling stream and now it was a chaotic torrent of white-water.

I'd needed that respite, for the feast which welcomed me for lunch was sobering still. In the middle of the table lay a massive platter. It was the proud recipient of an entire leg of a caribou. There was an air of exuberance in the house. Joe joined us all at the table and Simon was dressed in his Sunday best. The Bishop had arrived and the VCR had been fixed. I said grace with similar enthusiasm and asked the animal's forgiveness. We dug in.

The church service was scheduled for afterward and I found myself asking if I could attend. I'd even gone and changed into a clean shirt when Mary hollered that we had to go. Joe remained and a neighbor had arrived to spend the couple of hours with him. I leaned down and whispered to him, "Wish me luck." He replied understandingly with a beautifully wide, toothless grin.

Walking the short distance to the church in the rain that afternoon, the vision of lavishly clad clergy being welcomed ashore by gun salutes and long, arched paths of boughs and handmade rugs wouldn't leave my head.

I'd heard many stories of the various faiths' journeys along the coast to preach "the good word" to the people. All it created was fear, misunderstanding and separation amongst the villagers. It brought the outside world one step closer and was directly responsible for the breakdown of the community's togetherness, which was essential for the survival of all the coastal towns.

I'd discover that day that nothing has changed.

I was also well aware that fixing the VCR and renewing their reception of American trash was just as detrimental to that family's well-being — and to that entire community's survival — as the bishop's visit that day.

I felt shame. I doubt that he felt anything.

6.19.97 Two meals of caribou and an Anglican confirmation service and I'm nearly repulsed into silence. Yes, I've rejoined the legions of full-fledged carnivores again. Although it was a tough and long thought out decision, I feel the benefits of understanding and knowledge will be certainly more valuable in the long term. But will my system be able to cope with the drastic changes in diet?

No great problems yet, but a decent bowel movement has not occurred since my arrival two days ago . . . And the sweets in this place! My God, it'll take a month off your life, every day of eating this stuff.

5

Parting meant such sweet solitude. I'd been ashore for two days and now I felt that I had to be out there moving. I was clearly addicted.

I'd hopes that the arrival of the full moon would once again welcome me back to the monastic seduction of the sea. My anxiety reached a feverish pitch and my belly was in turmoil, so the next day's conditions would have to suffice regardless.

I awoke early and was down to the wharves. Within the community, we were completely shut in from the outside state of the ocean. There was little way of knowing the conditions apart from a vague, often incorrect forecast or signs of the clouds moving overhead.

There was a fisherman coming in, so I'd get a first hand report. "Big sea from d' west, b'y, d' fog's pretty t'ick too. Dere'll be no sign o' wind, 'less she burns off afta lunch."

I returned for breakfast and informed them of my plans to depart shortly thereafter. They expressed their concern that the weather was still unfit, but I reassured them that I'd merely suit up and paddle out to the mouth to have a look. If I then felt it was unsafe, I'd simply return.

Simon helped me bring all my gear down to the shore and I returned to give my farewells. A big kiss and embrace to her bosom from Mary and a strained smile from Joe, for he was going to have a hard morning following all the commotion of the previous day.

"Now you call Joe now, as soon as ya can, for 'e'll be worried sick over ya," Mary called from the door.

"I promise. Now don't y'all go worryin' about me," I trailed off as I turned to skip down to the shore.

Simon sat buzzing away at the gift that I'd given him the day before.

"Now you take care of ya mom now, hear," I said.

"I will," he sheepishly muttered into his shoes. "And t'anks for d', wha's she called agin?"

"A jaw harp."

"Yeah . . . t'anks."

I pushed off, and in turning to head out I heard him holler, "I s'pose ya gonna see d'Mafia when she comes by?"

"What?" I hollered back. I thought I'd come a long way in comprehending the speech in the few days that I'd been there.

"D' Mafia."

The mafia? I questioned to myself. Oh, the *Matthew*! "Ha ha, kid, you're a genius."

The day was spent with my head on a swivel.

A great, following sea awaited me outside. A little unnerving to begin, but a rhythm was soon developed and I was sped along the coastline — which I never saw. A thick, soup-like fog. I could actually feel it entering my lungs; it was like breathing near liquid. There were times when the bow of my own boat was difficult to see.

Occasionally, one of the swells had extra momentum and would roll over. This created a brief crest of turbulent white water which had to be avoided. Constantly I'd have to look back and judge the stage at which the swell would overtake my small craft. Then I'd adjust my speed, many times slowing to let it pass and break up in front of me.

The problem with the skeg days earlier had been minor. A small pebble had wedged itself between the reservoir enclosing the skeg and the metal plate itself. I'd have to avoid contact between the stern and the typical, small-pebbled beaches that the Newfoundland coast provided.

I began to be consumed entirely by the ocean again and all thoughts of the trials I'd encountered while ashore were gradually dissolved. What remained were the sheer challenging thoughts of survival, a simple appreciation of being there, in the present.

My confidence in myself grew, as did my reassurance that uncontrollable fate was motioning me along. Thus, *Destiny* and I slowly struggled through the fog.

A physical check: the two days rest had taken care of the sore elbow I'd developed on the approach to the river; the injury to my forearm had healed remarkably well. I continued to wear the pressure bandage, but it had given me no further grief; my shoulders and neck were quite sore, but to be expected; my digestive tract, on the other hand, was in shambles — days later my intestines were still painfully clogged as if cement had been poured into my system and it had disastrously hardened.

I was unable to go ashore for up to five hours at a time. I needed a massive amount of liquid to try and work it out, but the opportunities to urinate were rare. I vowed it would be a long time before I abused myself with the consumption of meat again. I was exhausted in the evenings upon retiring, so my caloric intake would have to be increased, but mentally I was getting stronger with each passing day. I'd become completely focused, meticulous even, in understanding the adjustments needed for the successful continuation of the expedition. I was surprising myself with how serious an attitude I'd developed towards the trip. I had no other choice.

It was the first day of summer. The faint glimmer of a warm breeze welcomed me as I left the inner harbour. I'd lunched in the cove of a once loved community. All that remained were rubbled foundations and the decayed remains of wharves. Or the wild flowers which had begun to bloom, or the currant bush which had once been the key ingredient to the finest jelly in the cove. It all rests now, overwhelmed with weeds and loneliness. It was in these defunct paradises that I felt so utterly disappointed . . . and alone.

So the ocean beckoned me back and the now clearly viewed cliffs awakened my spirits and enthusiasm again. The heavy precipitation we'd received still glistened off the cliffs' desolate peaks. Adolescent rains cascaded down to rejoin their mother. Birds clung to the shore's nooks and crannies. At times, a caribou or two could be seen grazing on the barrens above, unperturbed by the incredible drop only feet away.

I'd seen a number of whales along the horizon, yet the lone Minke previous to the storm was the only one to have graced me with its immediate presence. Fishermen told me of a pod of Orca sighted during the week — my excitement grew.

I'd been leisurely crossing a narrow, spectacular bay which continued inland as far as my vision allowed. Oh, the treasures it contained I'd wondered, as I realized that to explore the entire coast, with the thousands of coves and inlets, would require just as many lifetimes.

Without warning, a strange upheaval of water began to build just aft and off to my port.

Submarine!

This was still my thought as the mammoth object broke the surface. It was pushing a large wake in front of it. Shit, what a way to go — all that I've encountered in my short life and nature's challenges and I'm gonna get taken out by some fuck's toy . . . this nuclear sub!

It was a few stressed moments of intense paddling to distance myself before I realized its true identity. Not that it affected my frantic paddle speed at all. A Sperm whale! As wide across as *Destiny* was long. That enormous head of his, so seemingly unnaturally adapted for movement through the water.

A splendid gulp of air and he was gone. He'd come out of the long bay and headed straight out to the expansive sea. I sat in silenced awe, my hands still shaking from the close encounter. The surface had once again calmed following the brief, explosive climax. I chuckled aloud. A fine remedy for constipation indeed.

"Mind if I come's ashore?"

"Sure, b'y. Come on, I'd love to have ya," I replied invitingly.

He was a young man I'd met in town briefly, only a couple of hours previously. Matthew was his name. He'd just come in from lobster-catching with his father when I met him coming down the path from the store. Quiet and shy. I'd liked him immediately. I'd asked him of a nice spot to camp for the night. That's where I was, setting up, when he came around in his boat.

"Nice spot ain't it," he said as he approached.

"Have you eaten yet? I was just gonna fix somethin' up, after I get's my tent set up."

I went about deciding a spot and was unaware of Matthew's movements, until I looked up minutes later and discovered he was busy collecting wood along the shore having started a fire already. I was approaching the more wooded area of Bay d'Espoir and the driftwood was becoming much more available along the shore. We'll get along just fine, I thought.

Camp settled, I returned to the beach and began preparing a meal. There was little need for conversation as we both busied ourselves with the chores. It wasn't long before a fine pot of rice, and one of fish stew, was boiling away on the fire. He returned and we sat quietly near the heat, thankful for the relief from the ever-increasing swarms of flies.

"Guess you're glad to be out of school," I began.

"Ye-ah," he answered simply, with a grateful expression.

I handed him half of my orange. "How's the lobsters been?"

"Oh, good, b'y. Fadder an' I got a fine haul dis'marnin'," he glowingly announced.

"Yeah, been good back d' way I come too. They said a feller brought one in with a claw that was sixteen inches. I s'pose he musta got it in 'is lumpnet, ya figure?" I welcomed the conversation following a few days of being alone.

"Fadder got one dat big once, b'fore I was grown enough to get out wit' 'e. I remembers bein' on d' wharf dough an' d' t'ing was as big as I."

"Yeah? I ain't ever seen one that big," I humbly replied. "Must be some caplin aroun' now."

"Yeah, just in d' past coupla day. Seen many whale?" he continued.

We talked ceaselessly.

The rice had cooked and I dished out the grub. We ate in silence, the light wash of a wave reaching the shore occasionally to accompany the frequencies of flies in our eardrums. When we'd nearly finished and the water had been put on to boil, I proudly spoke of his grandparents' generation in the community — when they'd refused to be resettled by the government.

A fine smile appeared and he replied, "Dat was good, wouldn' it."

"I'll say. If we had more people like that today — willin' to take a stand and fight for what they believed in — you and I for sure as hell wouldn't have to leave here to find work or start a family. Those folks never would've stood for the shit the government's pullin' over on us now. Now we got a bunch too lazy to get up off their friggin' couches!"

"Yep," he agreed simply.

I thought for a long time.

"How do you like school, Matthew?"

"Ah . . . don't find much use fer it m'self. I'd radder be out in boat or up in d' woods somewhere."

"But still they make's you go, even though you could be more use to your family if you were say, up gettin' a load o' wood for the winter, right?"

"Yeah."

"Did you feel you were encouraged to develop, ah, to improve on the stuff you were interested in, when you were younger?" I asked curiously then.

"Naa," he quickly answered.

"But to learn your Times Tables or the Table of Elements — the government decided that these were important for everybody there to know.."

"Yeah . . . "

I remembered my own school experience then. And all the young kids like Matthew who I'd grown up with, but who had inexplicably been removed from my environment year after year. How they were ridiculed because they had no interest in reading at the time or couldn't be bothered with knowing the capital of the United States.

Once the school system had broken their willingness to contribute to the society in a way that they knew how, then the system deserted them. The rest of us they molded into a uniform, easily managed group that would become willing workers. The purpose of the school system is not to encourage individuality of character or integrity. The purpose is to demoralize the children like Matthew, who were foreseeable "glitches" in The Machine.

It was the individuals like Matthew, who'd saved the communities along the shore thus far — but every year the pendulum swings a little more to the right; the blind sheep multiply and our culture continues to predictably fall out of existence.

> 6.21.97 I've watched teachers mutate — young, energetic, inspired, overflowing with ideas — as they joined the ranks of the old regime. Within days they've been stripped and degraded, told their methods of teaching will never work. "We're not interested." By the following week they're handing out assignments and sitting mortified at their desks.
> The same sheets our mothers saw . . .
> My children will never be subjected to that lie.

My father arranged a place for me to stay up in Hermitage Bay. A gesture that enabled them the opportunity to keep me in one spot, if only for a day, to give them the chance to come down and reassure themselves that I was, in fact, doing as well as I'd reported. Not until Sunday they'd informed me and this translated into an extra day of relaxed paddling. I'd spend it rounding Long Island.

My body took solace in the easy paddling as *Destiny* and I took a break from the exposed open ocean. My mind however was not granted the same courtesy. The forthcoming visit initiated some questioning.

In the travelling off-island that I'd embarked on for many years, the issues of my genealogical history were never explored in depth. The sheer physical distance seemed to buffer the realities of my past and while separated from the island of my bloodline, it was psychologically easier to simply detach myself from the subject all together. Once home, however, this excuse could no longer be applied. The issue kept popping up along my coastal paddle and I'd be left in a state of frustration, above all else, at the lack of information that I could provide. Was the reason for my constant wanderings over the years a subconscious attempt to block out and avoid the subject?

It had rained all night and I was awakened a couple of times by the force of it. However, once I began the morning's paddle, it cleared and a low cloud cover remained. There were still considerable tides from the full moon of a few days earlier. The timing was ideal for me to eat lunch at the northeast tip before having an escorted journey along the narrow inside passage.

A beautiful day resulted, with little thoughts of anything but my graceful movement through the water. I barely saw a boat. This of course on a Saturday was quite strange. I asked a couple of lobster fishermen earlier in the day and they seemed quite baffled by my question.

"B'y, I s'pose nobody 'aves boats anymore. Dey uses d' road or ain't got no use for one. Is only d' few fellers bees out t' git a few lobsta now, right? And d' few queer ones like ya self, wha'?"

We'd laughed hard at that before they moved on.

What would Matthew's great-grandfather have thought if someone had told him that not long into the future there'd be a day out in Bay d'Espoir during the summer that he wouldn't see a boat? He'd never have believed it possible.

Later in the afternoon I approached four people on the shore, two men out for an afternoon of fishing with their sons. They'd seemed a little distressed from my vantage point, only a boat-length offshore from them, for they were busy swatting the air and waving their ball caps about. One little fella was running around in a small circle, as if being driven mad.

When I approached and asked what they were up to, one of them replied frankly, "Oh, we just t'ought we'd come out an' feed a few flies."

We all laughed good naturedly but I held my tongue, for I could see what awaited me once I came ashore. Dark clouds could be seen surrounding the heads of the four unfortunate souls.

"You must *really* like trout to put yerselves through that torture, fellas," I called as I paddled on, anxious to get moving, for the flies had begun to discover me offshore. Suddenly the exposed, bare coastline seemed all the more inviting again.

6.23.97 It wasn't Sunday the folks were coming at all; it's always a great sign when I begin losing track of the days. There's a holiday — I can't believe this, my mind is still numb — it's because the Queen has arrived on the island! How soon we forget that it was in disgust and contempt for the monarchy that this island was settled. There were thousands here, upon jumping ship and refusing to return to England already, when Britain in all her putrid wisdom and greed decided to claim the island for herself. Now — a quick jump to the present, and while half its populace is scattered unwillingly about the globe, the government, hellbent on obliterating the culture for its own selfish advancement, has decided they need to waste *our* money in recognition and support of an invasion which resulted in genocide; as a "gift" to the people of Newfoundland . . .

Every town I've encountered so far has the people questioning why. Yet, they're slowly persuaded into submission by the incessant onslaught of the television's propaganda. I've yet to encounter a home which hasn't been invaded by this belittling, wretchedly unwholesome device.

Ironic that this "news" would find me within the confines of my first encountered "reservation" community, which the government created in luring/deceiving/forcing the villagers

70

out of their homes not long following Confederation with that glorious nation called Canada.

Here I lay in a warm, comfortable room — yet I'd much rather be snuggled up in some cove, being lulled to sleep by the lap of the nearby waves. Today's paddle was disheartening really, for I've definitely left the pristine splendour of the south coast. All beaches here now are just a mess with rubbish — all coves overcome with cabins. Welcome to Nfld. of the '90s . . . For awhile, I guess, I'd best get used to the interaction and realization of civilization again.

A messy low has begun to move off to the east — gonna fall on those blind blokes in Bonavista. It should leave clear air for me tomorrow. A day off and I'm itchin' to go again.

I'd returned to the gentle rock of mother's embrace. Following a couple of days in protected waters and a half day off, the rolling swell which greeted me on the outer edge of Hermitage Bay was remarkably welcome. It was like reuniting with a long departed friend whose idiosyncrasies you appreciate as much as her finest qualities. Once more the schedule was to be set entirely by the sun and the moon.

I'd come ashore shortly afterward on the outer edge of the peninsula. A beautiful crescent beach had beckoned, created by the slow erosion of the storm ravaged island out in front, which deflected the prevailing southwest swell. I set up camp and had begun a fire when another fishing boat approached.

Two men, one in his late forties and the other a young man the same age as me, could be seen in the boat. The youngest navigated in through the scattered rocks which were then showing with the falling tide. Great skill was involved. It was obvious he'd had much practice and had been instructed well. The eldest waited confidently in the bow with painter in hand until he could jump athletically ashore. I was there to greet them and we pulled her in. We spoke briefly before he headed down the beach.

"Rough day, b'y. Lost a lot o' pots wit' d' sea come on yes'day," the youngest explained as he jumped to the beach.

"I was up in d' bay, never got out this way at all yesterday."

"Yeah. She come on right quick. Johnnie figures we lost o'er half o' dem, das me fadder-in-law," he said as he motioned at the quickly moving speck along the shore. "Well . . . in two weeks 'e'll be," he concluded.

"You're gettin' married, dude? Ah man, that's the shit!" I excitedly exclaimed.

"Where'd ya say you was from?" He eyed me suspiciously.

"Oh, down Notre Dame Bay way. B'y that's grand news," I continued, shaking his hand. "Congratulations."

"T'anks, b'y. I been fishin' wit' 'e now for five year. We'll be busy makin' pots d' winter. Oh, looks like 'e got one, but b'y jeez, we 'ad five up agin dat shore," he shook his head acceptingly.

"You see any boats like mine along this way?" I asked.

"No, first one dat I ever laid eyes on. Where'd ya come from in she now?"

"Started o'er Port aux Basques a few weeks back."

"You never d' like now — in dat?" he promptly said in disbelief. "Wait'll I tell's d' b'ys what we found out in d' bay d'day." He returned to his boat, reached into the box and jumped back quickly thereafter with a lobster in hand. "Take dis now, luh. You'll need a few o' dem b'fore yer done. How far ye goin'?"

"Back home."

He merely closed his eyes and shook his head. "Gotta heave off," he said finally. "Or we'll be spendin' d' night wit you in dat tent."

I pushed him off, with a tinge of envy, and watched silently as he navigated the large boat through the rocks. Johnnie was approaching with a lobster pot slung on his back and an armload of salvaged pieces in the other. I rushed along to relieve him and we walked a stretch of the beach to where his future son-in-law waited in deeper water.

"You'll have a new addition to the family pretty soon," I said feebly as I winced under the strain and awkward weight of the lobster pot, having only carried it a fraction of the distance he'd come.

72

"Oh, 'e been family a long time now. I 'llow 'e's d' best buddy I got," he proclaimed honestly.

He swung himself up over the gunwale of the high bow, seemingly unaffected by the mile long burdensome trek he'd just completed. As they turned to head out, I could hear him being briefed on the tale of my trip's beginnings, over two hundred miles back along the coast. And their harmonious talk followed, only to fade from earshot as they slowly idled out of the bay, ever accepting of the hardships on which their friendship was based. It was as unquestioned as the setting sun's descent into the sea before me. I marveled at how rare and precious such a strong relationship as that, between males of two generations, was. And how rarer still those relationships were becoming.

I'd received mail from afar and there was wholesome food to ingest. My entire family's arrival had also meant the welcome of a fine crock of Mom's legendary stewed beans, a needed switch from the now bland, tiresome repetitiveness of vegetable pea soup.

The day developed into a beautifully star-filled evening. Normally I'd been retiring before dark and with an early rise the majority of my day's paddling would be conducted in the morning before noon. Midday usually saw windier, more unsettled conditions and the unforgivably powerful rays of the sun. But I broke with routine and enjoyed an extended evening of campfire thoughts, a letter to my friends on Vancouver Island, and some time spent gazing skyward.

I'd entered Fortune Bay and, theoretically, the south coast was behind me. Here I could be greeted with less dangerous swells from the south. I was moving along, yet so was the summer.

The extended campfire resulted in a late rise and I found myself tested with a late morning, eight-mile crossing of Connaigre Bay. It had been foggy, but the ocean broke with tradition as well and the sea built up in recognition of my tardiness. Following lunch I was still feeling strong and boldly set out on a 13-mile crossing. Conditions seemed to be improving and the barometer was steady. A dream-like paddle ensued.

The fog remained for two-thirds of the crossing, a faint, silk-like haze enveloping me. I could not make out any landmarks, yet the sun shone through in a thick, other-world subtleness. A massive halo around it filled the sky. It seemed to permeate the hull of *Destiny*, where it reemerged with such brilliance as to create a golden aura around me. The sea calmed magically, until it became a dense, unbroken mirror.

I felt the need to expose as much skin as possible to the cool, inviting light. I removed my lifejacket and the bandage which had protected my arm for so long. I inhaled the thick, moist air deeply into my lungs, until I became intoxicated with its soothing effects. The only sound was of my paddle, as it effortlessly penetrated the virgin surface.

I'd become so in tune with *Destiny* that she was no longer a boat — she was an extension of myself.

As I'd practiced religiously upon entering her, and again before I withdrew, I touched her holy liquid to the centre of my forehead.

This was my chapel, *my* immortal beloved.

Seeing the Burin Peninsula so close as I was paddling up into Fortune Bay was very tempting. To make a long crossing would save time. Yet, I realized at the end of my journey I'd perhaps have regrets of not visiting the last community inaccessible by land on the southern side of the island. And then there was the sea monster.

During my training period in early spring there'd been excited news that fishermen up in Fortune Bay had seen a strange animal: a massive horse-like head with long extending horns and large-scaled, reptilian-like skin. One man refused to ever go out on the water again. How could I pass up the potential encounter with a creature such as that?

It had been a day of fierce winds, the strongest in fact that I'd encountered thus far, easterlies coming off the land. There was little swell and by this stage my body had pleasantly adjusted to the rigors of constant work. It was unseasonably cold and light rain was falling. I pulled up to the slipway and quickly headed up to the store. There weren't many folks around. Once inside, I welcomed the soothing heat from the wood stove;

the 27th of June and everyone still had their stoves crackling away. The couple of patrons and the lady behind the counter eyed me quizzically.

Huddled up next to their stove, I decided to calm their uneasiness at being confronted by a bizarre looking drenched dude straight off the *Pequod*. "Little chilly out dere dis mornin', ain't it?"

"Ain't fit. Now where's ya come from dis marnin'?" she asked as the two others quickly left. She looked around in the hopes of being reassured by some more familiar faces.

"I just come across d' bay. Doin' some kayakin' for d' summer."

"Sure d' b'ys ain't even been out t' check der pots dis marnin'. Whadya say you was in?"

A tall man in his fifties entered the store before I had a chance to explain further, and gave me a warm smile. "Mornin' Maggie," he chirped quickly before returning his full attention to me. "I got me house up back o' d' hill and saw you come in. B'y, she's a fine rig out in d' wind, ain't she? Come up for coffee now, when you're done 'ere — just follow d' pat' along-gin d' brook and you'll see d' white house wit' d' flag pole out front. Me name's Phil, by d' way." He extended his hand. A first.

"Yeah, I'll be up after I gets a few things . . . like d' didgits in me fingers workin' again," I jokingly responded.

"Right y' are," he answered with a mighty jerk of his head and a blink of his eye before leaving. *That* was the official greeting I'd grown accustomed to.

I bought some chocolate (I didn't even like chocolate), and said goodbye to Maggie, who'd quickly warmed up to me following her unburdened participation in the conversation between Phil and me. The gestures, smiles and nods that she'd contributed saw her just as much a part of the exchange as he.

"You take care now, love." Then she groaned, "Oh my, if me son was out doin' d' like o' dat, 'e'd 'ave me in d' Waterford."

I began my walk back to the slipway to pull *Destiny* up above the tideline and was amazed at the scene before me. I couldn't see her due to the crowd of people that had gathered. I thought someone must have collapsed and started in to help, before I realized it was my boat that was in the centre of the mob.

"What're y'at, b'y?" This was the first statement to hit me before a tidal wave struck.

"Yeah, 'e come aroun' d' islan' in 'er, wit' 'e's paddle all goin' snakey."

"Sure, 'e's sittin' right in d' water . . . Lord dyin'!"

"B'y 'tis d' queerest t'ing ever I saw."

"No chance a gettin' I in som'in like dat!"

"Wouldn' git in d' bat'tub in she sure . . . "

It was as if I wasn't even there, they were still so overcome with *Destiny*. Over the excitement and merriment I felt a gentle tug at my pants and looked down. Before me was a little girl, wide-eyed and runny-nosed. "Is you in d'Olympics, sir?" she asked bravely.

"Nahh. Olympics don't come around dis way," I said to her, crouching. "So I turned 'em down, told 'em I'd rather come see you instead." She gave me a wide grin and returned quickly to the protective space in front of her mother.

It was still a miserable day, yet there were dozens out to see the queer boat.

"Now, crowd. Let d' man t'rough, right," ordered a senior representative for the welcoming committee who was standing along the outer limits of the nucleus. The crowd consisted of men, women and children — all shapes and sizes. Some were properly dressed for the conditions, while others in their haste to come see remained aproned or slipper'd or stood sleepy-eyed from their midday naps.

"You'll 'ave t' come up t' d' 'ouse for a lunch now, won't ya," demanded the inviting, portly face of a woman.

Oh, the scoff of toutons that I envisioned as my mouth watered. The pan-fried, flattened patties of white flour bread dough are the outport Newfoundlanders' impoverished equivalent to the native people's bannock.

"Ya welcome t' stay up t' d' 'ouse fer as long as ya like," came another call.

"You guys are the grandest," I said finally. "The finest reception I've had yet and look at d' weather! Phil's invited me up to his house already but thank you all. I'll have to return for another visit." My spirits had reached another level as I scampered joyously up the muddy path, never missing a puddle.

The stay at Phil's was a dandy one — his wife was in St. John's.

"So I ain't much use in d' kitchen," he admitted as he looked naively into the fridge. "I s'pose ya likes bologna now, right?"

The bottle of rum was magically produced and I was expected to mix it as I pleased. A good time later into the afternoon we were still at the table with a couple of bologna sandwiches and the same glass of rum.

"B'y, I 'spose ya can drink up a bit," he good naturedly suggested, eyeing my glass disapprovingly. "I won't be tellin' on ya, I swear."

"No, b'y. I ain't finished me paddlin' yet and I'll get up d' shore a ways b'fore I calls it a day."

"Ya knows now ya can spend d' night if ya likes. We'll keep sockin' d' bologna to ya," he laughed.

I explained that the summer was getting on and that I still had a ways to go.

"Ah, yes," he said. "I was young like you too once. You stick t' ya goal, son. From what ya been tellin' me, ya got the will. By God, I can see it in yer eyes, you'll do it yet."

"God willin', sir," I answered, as I downed the last of my rum-tainted Coke.

"Aiee, ain't dat d' trut' b'y . . . ain't dat d' trut'."

> 6.28.97 . . . Phil was a fine fellow and we had a glass
> of rum. I'd time to wait out the southerly which had picked up!
> Did finally set off and had a fine crowd on hand. As I turned
> to bid farewell, in unison dozens of hands went up — it was
> the real shit . . . had me smiling for miles. On a day that
> didn't look too productive, I may have covered quite a bit of
> coast. Got to where I'd planned at the start of the day at
> least. But not without its mishaps. Seems Phil's drop of rum
> worked a little too quickly and I ended up having an accident.
> I pissed myself. Filled my boots I did and was none too
> pleased as one can imagine. But what can you do?

And wet my pants I had. The weather was of the bone-chilling variety to begin with, and it certainly didn't make things anymore comfortable. But there was a brief period leading up to the climactic moment (and once I'd finally resolved myself to the inevitable outcome) where it was an emphatically powerful experience, where all social ramifications were unimportant, where I was expressly my own entity.

The shore represented our struggle to keep ourselves within the confined, set practices of the society where we had to stop at a red light, regardless if there was anyone else there, or we had to buy our kids Nikes because the pressures from other parental peers was too great. Or we had to kiss the Queen's ass because we were simply told we must.

Like the majority, I fought and struggled to reach that shore. I altered my course and went in agony to keep myself socially acceptable in a society which has evidently gone insane. I knew, though, that if I simply relaxed and accepted myself and my ideals, the social shackles which I knew to be false would no longer exist for me. I realized I was struggling along to keep up with protocol, before realizing that I had the power to question why and the ability to take responsibility for my own actions. No one was going to make the rules for me. *I* wasn't going to burden myself with the formulating of rules . . . because there weren't any.

I stopped paddling and slowly drifted in the windswept downpour. No longer in a mad struggle, either upstream or down. And simply relaxed and relished its warmth. As Orwell wrote: "It was a blow struck against the Party. It was a political act."

A short time later I paddled into a cove that I'd decided would be a good spot to camp for the night. Like all coves now it seemed, there were a few simple cabins built along its protective shores. There was smoke coming from one and a boat was moored offshore. They'd spotted me by then and a man walked slowly down the slope to the wharf. I paddled towards him.

"Nice evenin'," I began.

"Yeah, 'twould be alright if you was a duck, I s'pose," he jokingly replied. "Come on up b'y, we gets ya some tea."

"Ahh . . . " I stumbled. I'd be smelling a bit ripe for an evening of socializing, I felt. "It's gettin' on dark. I'll go over cross d' ways and set up camp, an' get into some dry clothes before I heads over." It seemed like a legitimate decision to him and he left me to it.

The only spot I found was terrible: a sponge-like riverbed that was a haven for flies. If the rains were to increase during the night, I'd be swimming by morning.

I was a sorry sight in the failing light. Naked, shivering and crouched in the brook as I rinsed myself off. The rains subsided and the flies murderously descended onto the bounty of exposed flesh. Shortly thereafter I returned to my boat, relieved that I'd prepared myself for bed, and paddled over to visit with the folks.

The scene was beautiful: two couples who'd come out to spend the weekend in the company of each other. A simple room without electricity or phones or schedules. I only stayed for a short time, but a lunch was readied for me — tea, biscuits and jam. We spoke of my journey and my hopes of crossing to the Burin Peninsula the following morning. They had the look of such contentment.

It's a phenomenon found throughout the entire island, as nearly every family has a basic cabin in the woods where they can escape on weekends or for their typically allotted two weeks of holidays in the summer.

That evening while paddling back to my camp, I paused in the middle of the cove and looked back at the warm glow from the oil lamp shining out over the stillness of the water. If that was where we all felt the most content, why were people subjecting themselves to an existence of frazzled lifestyles in the mere quest for material possessions? The "American Dream" had only recently invaded the shores of this island, yet remnants of the earlier, more substantial lifestyle still remained in all of us. And, like so many others, those folks didn't miss any of the things that they were later informed were essential.

I'd now been paddling for nine days straight. My body was weary and I knew I had to stop and rest for a full day. When I left the cove the next morning, I'd full intentions of merely crossing up into the bay, to the community on the other side, for an easy six mile day.

Weak armed, I surveyed the conditions once I got outside. Winds steady from the northeast. To cross over to the town meant a difficult sidewind. To head downwind meant another long day, but with accommodating conditions and definite progress. I headed for the far distant headland. A 17-mile crossing was what I'd set myself up for.

Six miles on course and I began hearing a steady rhythm of horn blasts. I ignored them initially and continued on. Again they could be heard. Five long blasts of a fog horn, only clearer. I glanced behind and the coastal boat had altered her course and was headed straight towards me. I kept paddling for a long time, still not believing that it could be me she was heading for.

She was certainly a little faster than me so I continued on course. The conditions were fine, but I was still three miles from the nearest uninviting shoreline. I wondered why she'd be coming for me. By the time she'd overtaken me, I assumed that someone at home had taken ill and they'd tracked me down. I turned about and slowly came up to her starboard before the captain swung his vessel around likewise and headed her up into the wind.

"You got an EPIRB on board?" I heard one of the mates shout as she was swinging around.

Finally, we were in position to communicate effectively. All the passengers had gathered around the man in the stern as he began again, "You alright? We got a call from d' Coast Guard, said someone's EPIRB been goin' off in Fortune Bay. We seen you down here and figured it was you, so we come t' check on ya."

An EPIRB is a radio device that, once activated, sends out a steady signal that can be tracked by the Coast Guard, one of the many high tech gizmos available to mariners. For reasons equally economic and personally based I opted against one.

"No, b'y. I'm fine," I shouted back. "Haven't seen anybody else out that would have an EPIRB on board though. Sorry, wrong guy."

"You sure you's alright den?" he repeated.

I reassured him and he went to report to the captain. Before they picked up steam again, I said to a lady who was looking down on me curiously, "Sorry 'bout the delay I guess I caused you."

"What?" she replied. "No trouble me son. B'y, dis here been d' best boat trip I ever 'ad! Be d' most excitin' ting'll happen t' me all summer I 'llow." And she waved gratefully.

I continued on and eventually pulled myself ashore, exhausted but very content. I'd officially touched down on the Burin Peninsula! Healthy and in good spirits, for rarely did my unquestionable fears for the island's future interrupt my thoughts while paddling. The ocean had become my escape, my sanctuary where all evil ceased to exist.

I found myself in a quaint sandy cove, with a few cabins interspersed with some older homes that had been kept up. As I looked around, content just to be standing and at rest following the longest crossing I'd yet encountered, two figures could be seen descending the small hill out behind the cluster of houses. I walked up to greet them.

"Hello m'son," the man announced heartily. "We was up on d' hill and we seen ya comin' wit' me spy glasses. Couldn' figure what ya was fer d' longest time. Now, I ain't right sure yet what ya come in." We were joined soon after by his wife and then we walked together down to their cabin.

"Now," he said finally, as we sat out on the bridge. Then he paused and called out over his shoulder, "Mudder, put on d' kettle dere too, luh, before ya comes out. She's 'ot d'day, ain't she, b'y? Might get our week o' summer after all." He went on, "Oh, but I wouldn' leave 'er, b'y. Not a chance. We used t' live 'ere . . . now, 'twouldn' yes'day, but we 'ad a fine life 'ere. Use t'ave d' garden o'er 'gin d' cliff dere. D' spuds we 'auled outa dere, by God. An' when d' caplin' come well, d' kids'd be into it up t' deir waist. B'y d' fun dey 'ad wit' d' fish we'd 'ave t' burn d' close afta . . . an' mudder'd cuss, but you 'ad t' let 'em go, sure."

My contented smile reassured him that I was enjoying his reminiscing. His wife joined us and she continued as if, over their long life together, their minds had beautifully merged into one. "I rared up seven youngsters in dis 'ere cove, an' we done it wit'out d' 'elp o' d' gove'ment. Now, dey all near gone t' d' mainland. Dey all fergets now from where dey come," she finished sadly before returning quickly and unexpectedly into the cabin.

We spent the remainder of the afternoon there before I left them to their memories. They'd been coming home every summer since they'd been forced to leave. Looking forward to it throughout the winter was the only thing that "kept 'em goin'," they'd told me, "since d' kids was all gone."

> 6.29.97 . . . Smallwood moved them out 30 years ago and five of their seven kids are now in Ontario . . . and so the story goes everywhere along this coast. It's a bloody exodus and all because of the fucking government and greed. Now what have we got? Imported poison for food, imported entertainment to rot our minds.
>
> A generation of kids growing up that've had drilled into their heads by morons that education is the only way, while they can't fix a decent meal, knit a pair of socks, tie a bowline, or dance a jig for the life of them. We were even interrupted at lunch by two dumb droids in a speed-boat — fisheries officers out enforcing "the law". Didn't even wave, or have the decency to shout hello . . . the swell-headed flakes.

I came ashore on a fine point of land not far beyond and prepared myself for a beautiful relaxing evening. The sun would set majestically into the ocean before me and I was alone again to transcend all unpleasant thoughts and to anticipate a day of rest. A calm aura surrounded me as I lay in the late afternoon sun and basked in its warmth. All was still.

Slowly I detected a faint buzzing. Then I realized the distinct annoyance of a "bog-bike's" whining engine. The silence was broken. I rose and walked up over the bog-covered point to the adjoining beach to the south. A bog-bike was indeed fast approaching. My heart sank even further once it came to a grinding stop in the virgin sand that it had raped and degraded.

Where on this earth did I have to go to rid myself of these clowns? For below me stood the unmistakable body of a party member, regally clad in untarnished khakis. A subtle bead of sweat had developed on his brow from his arduous journey. He saw me before I had a chance to retreat.

"Well hello, didn't think I'd find anyone else way up here. See a spot where I can get this bike up there?"

I was standing on bog, on a very exposed point on the Burin Peninsula, on an island in the North Atlantic. It had probably taken several millennia for it to develop to its current state. It would probably take a number of seasons for my footprints to disappear from the fragile ecosystem. That shmuck wanted to get up here with an All Terrain Vehicle. A government employee.

"Naa . . . can't see a way. Why don't ya leave it there on d' beach?" I suggested.

He kept peering around and apparently didn't hear well. In a few minutes he was by my side after scampering his way up the bank.

"My name's Joey." He presented his hand.

I looked deliberately down at my own and then boldly held it up in the air. "Sorry," I said valiantly, "just finished cleanin' a cod fer supper."

With a look of bewilderment he paused briefly and then continued on with his mission statement: "Been sent in to prospect up the river. My degree is in geology, but the government is considering an ATV trail up this way to attract the tourists."

It all didn't seem to connect. Then again, I thought, it was the government — it didn't have to.

"I'd like to get the bike up here. I thought I'd camp out on this point and I got a lot of gear."

"I'll leave ya to it den. I'm camped down on d' beach on d' other side," I said as I backed away. "Drop down for tea, once ya gets set up."

I returned to my camp. Resigned to the fact that all tranquility had passed, I began reading from the book which accompanied me for the duration of the trip. The air was once again overcome with the noise of the ridiculous machine. It drifted out of earshot before eventually returning, this time in full force as it wove its trail of domination upon the barren above. I stood and, in horrified disbelief, watched as Joey drove his machine down onto the untarnished land, which until that day had never been exposed to the greed-driven ignorance of its "saviour."

Joey descended onto my camp later that evening following "paperwork" that he'd had to complete. We sat around the fire and I offered him my cup to drink from.

He'd finally picked up on my air of uneasiness for what he was doing and tried to make amends. "That's a fine boat ya got. I did a little m'self up in the park. I tried to persuade them to give me one to use for work such as this. Too time consuming, they told me."

My furrowed brow and a skeptical look told him it hadn't worked. "Wha's all the stuff on your belt?" I asked him, to make conversation.

Revealing the grandest toy, he proudly announced it as a GPS. "With this instrument you can find your location, to the nearest 165 feet or better, anywhere on the earth. It uses an advanced array of satellites."

"Most times I dig not knowin' where I am," was all I could muster.

"This is quite an adventure you've embarked on. I guess you've gotten pretty good coverage from the media."

"No. I wanna keep it as low key as possible. Then I've only me own expectations to fulfill and I get a much more genuine representation of coastal life when d' folks aren't informed of my arrival beforehand. I figure if someone wants to show me hospitality it should come naturally and from deir heart. Not because dey feels obliged, 'cause I'm seen as a travelling accompaniment t' some Caboto farce . . . and it's expected of them."

I had to take care.

"I noticed you writing in a journal when I came down. You're taking lots of pictures along the way I'm sure." This was projected as more of a rhetorical question to continue conversation, to give him time to comprehend what I'd just said.

"No. Couldn' see a need for it on dis largely unexploited coast. The grandeur of this land would be degraded with a picture, and then it just creates a snowball effect, the end result being some despicable scene like we've got at Niagara Falls. I believe there should be some places on this planet that human eyes should never see, and, just as importantly, beautiful regions that are solely appreciated by the few who actually make the efforts necessary to get out and experience them. Moments like this sunset before us . . . it's unfortunate that we humans want to try and duplicate it, which we could never do. But we're stuck in this world now where everything has to be recorded and preserved, captured for eternity without basking in the glory that what we're witnessing, right now on this small beach, will never, as long as the earth spins around the sun, be reproduced again."

I paused. "It took me awhile t' figure that out," I said finally, as I reflected on what I'd only moments ago said.

He appeared utterly baffled, as if his entire belief system had suddenly been shaken. I reassured myself then that within the man's eyes there was a faint ray of questioning for truth. There was hope!

As he rose to return to his tent for the night, he took notice of the book lying beside me and simply remarked, "*Nineteen Eighty-Four* . . . never heard of it." Then he slowly retreated until the darkness once again enveloped him.

6

The next morning I saw Joey briefly before he headed out to "survey" the river. He dropped down for tea again and our conversation was far less philosophical than the previous night's. I suggested that there was no need to rush, yet he looked at his watch and said he must go.

"Perhaps I'll see you up dere at some point. I'm gonna drop up for a bath and wash some clothes," I called out to him as he climbed up over the bank. Curiously enough, he decided not to use the bike for the trip back down the shore to the river.

My day was spent on a relaxing walk up the river as well. I marveled at its clarity and unaltered shoreline and swam occasionally in the deep pools. A warm day developed and I was delighted to have the opportunity of spending it without the restraints of clothing. Barefoot, I slowly meandered upstream and took delight in the many small schools of darting trout that would catch my eye. "Rejoice, my friends," I called to them. "I won't have t' eat you today!"

I returned as the sun began its slow descent into the sea once more. A fire started and a fine pile of wood collected for the evening saw Joey's return. He was flustered and overheated from his hike and large patches of perspiration dampened his khakis. "Come join me for supper. It'll be Indian tonight," I hollered invitingly.

"Oh, I can't take your food on ya, b'y. I'll bring mine though and cook it down there." With that he trounced tiredly toward his tent.

I readied subjhi, a pot of rice, and even made chapatis, for I'd been in such high spirits and was fully energized following the day of rest. He arrived with an armload of gear and sat down.

"Well . . . not sure I can compete with the spread ya got goin' there. Smells good."

"What've *you* got?" I asked happily as I licked my spoon.

"They gives us army rations for our field work. Tonight? Macaroni and cheese," he replied forlornly as he read obediently from the package. He kept eyeing my bubbling pots and seemed none too enthused.

"Man, you ain't gonna eat dat shit here while I made a ton o' stuff for both of us, are ya?" I joked.

"Well, if you say you made enough then."

"Now, how was your day?" I continued, that settled.

He remained quite vague and merely said that it had potential. I cut in eventually, having become somewhat braver after testing the waters the evening before. "Now take our conversation o' last night, and put it in context wit' d' river that we both experienced t'day. Weren't d' waterfalls and cascading pools all d' more appreciated and understood after we had t' hike through d' difficult brush t' get dere?"

I didn't wait for an answer.

"As opposed to a full access boardwalk where folks all goes in, stands at a lookout and yawns, 'cause dey already seen footage of Angel Falls on the Discovery channel the night before. Then they take a picture and simply leave. It ain't understood, if we provide wilderness areas to the public, Joey, so that they can go in and not relate to it, anymore than if it glared up at them from a book or a television screen. We've got a generation of kids now that think the woods grows with boardwalks and signs and outhouses. Hell, they don't even comprehend any longer that the cellophaned package of minced meat at the grocery store was once a living animal.

"It's because the government's turned these areas into petty amusement parks that we've lost the respect for them that they deserve. And the populace becomes so detached — they no longer have any connection to it — that it's destroyed without any guilt whatsoever.

"But then it gets even more despicable, and they pay people like yourself," — still struggling to remain tactful and objective — "to go in and be the catalyst to start it rolling, 'cause they sit on their fat asses all day in St. John's, and try and put it over as some 'wilderness trail for the public'. And in the end, their minds just see the hydro dam that can be constructed on it, or the bottled water plant they can cash in on to sell to the Mexicans."

There was no response.

"Hey," I apologized, "neither of us needed *that* following the fine day we've just had."

"No," he said finally. "You're right. These things you're sayin' are probably right. But most of us ain't got d' guts t' think it, much less say it . . . and I got a wife and a kid and I gotta do somethin'. I jus' don't know."

And we both sat forlornly gazing into the fire.

The day's rest had been sufficient and the ones to follow were gloriously spent.

The peninsula had a much different geography than the south coast, which I watched slowly fade from view until I realized I'd rounded an inconspicuous point and left it behind completely. Now the shoreline elevation wasn't so drastic and places to land were more frequent. I'd also spent long periods of paddling alongside the immediate shore as it slowly curved around the "toe of the boot".

The ocean had calmed and a very slow moving high pressure system remained for many days. The sun became ruthless, hitting me from all angles. I'd developed a substantial burn on my forearm where the bandage had previously covered it. I learned quickly that the sun could be as dangerous a hazard as the wind or the sea state. Maintaining a sufficient water intake still posed problems; with the continued inaccessibility of the shore, there was nowhere to urinate. If I was to suffer from heat stroke out there, the results would be devastating. I kept those thoughts well in mind.

I began seeing many more seabirds and their arrival would always brighten my spirits. I began studying their habits and flight patterns, and even made up my own names for many of them.

Sally Anns were always seen in large groups flying very close to the surface. Their vibrant beaks would contrast brilliantly with the muddled greys of the shoreline and dark depths of the sea. The YinYangs who'd accompanied me along the entire coastline thus far seemed to find some interest in me, and nearly always flew a tight circle around me before continuing on their original flight pattern. I'd seen only a few Gannets, yet they fascinated me. They have an incredible wingspan to support the substantial mass of their bleached white bodies, which flows into a mystically golden-smoked neck and head. A futuristically long and beautiful grey beak completes the masterpiece. I'd grown up on the island my entire life and had never seen one before. They were well worth the wait.

They were spooked easily and rarely flew directly overhead. Upon speaking with many people about them, they informed me of their brilliant dives from as high as a hundred feet in the air, to slice directly into the water after unsuspecting prey. I waited patiently for my chance to experience this sight.

    29.5 nautical miles Sugarloaf Rock to Blue Beach Cove
  <u>331.5</u> nautical miles so far
  361.0 nautical miles in 18 days of paddling.

     7.2.97 Very tired and unsettled in a fine spot looking out of the harbour, but I've landed on a steep, pebble beach with a direct swell. Arriving finally I discovered that the skeg was once again jammed (third time) — small rocks, just big enough to bar against the skeg well and the plate itself, have once again caused me grief. Spent over half an hour at least, exhausted. Yet with the help of two new friends, I finally got it free — but with the cable breaking free of the plate! I'd brought the spare and I'm confident I can get it installed pretty easily, but I just left it until morning.

The paddle today was very hot, with little or no breeze until late. A lot of seals and some very shallow and rugged coast again — just a mad section if there was any kind of a sea on.

My thoughts were definitely not on paddling though and I made a couple of judgement errors resulting in wasted energy. And with nowhere to land following Lamaline (translation: malignant, evil or wicked!), I'd gone the whole day and over twenty miles on little more than a bowl of cereal. Finally found a spot beyond Lawn Head, a mad little rock beach about thirty feet wide, inside the cliffs. Many caves there also but I was exhausted and the swell was up at the time. Managed to wolf down some food and make a daring escape before it got too hairy. It was there that the skeg problem occurred.

I walked into town after setting up, hopeful to find a shower and a good meal. I was rewarded with the news of $5 washings at a motel (I'm not sure if I'd pay that for someone to hand scrub me!) and a meal of deep-fried chips, shrimp and scallops. I'd have been better off eating nothing — the digestive system's already feeling the effects. The lady was swell though and we chatted for the duration. I used her phone and she gave me the meal!

And so ends another long adventurous day. I'll sleep well.

Entering into Placentia Bay resulted in my quick reintroduction into the hazard of fog. This climatic condition and the bay are synonymous with one another. I welcomed it with open arms. By this time I was being baked like a lobster — every part of my skin had to be covered and sunglasses were a necessity. The soothing effects of the fog were magnificent; it was great for my confidence and kept my mind solely on the sea and its beauty, and I'd just myself, the birds and the reassuring sound of the horns to help me along.

Placentia Bay encompasses a massive area. It is sixty miles deep and to cross from its outer points is forty miles. I'd been warned of the frequent high winds that blew onshore to its eastern coast. This was the extent of my knowledge upon entering.

It had been a long morning and strong southwesterlies had begun to develop when I came ashore in the quiet cove. Within its tiny protection there were a number of elaborate stages, or suspended fishing sheds, and the low tide revealed their forest of stilts. A few old homes were nestled smartly up against the lee of a cliff.

A strange thought overcame me with the deathly silence: that some bizarre chemical warfare had resulted in everyone's annihilation, apart from myself; that my protection within the fog had somehow prevented my vaporization along with the rest of the planets inhabitants.

I was having a lunch, comfortably leaning against the door of the stage, when four strange creatures descended the hill — so I wasn't alone.

Atop their heads were white coverings of some sort, which the strange glow of the fog seemed to accentuate. They were clad in full-piece suits of bright yellow and white. They walked toward me, seemingly silent until an immense chatter became audible. They were laboratory experts of some sort — from another planet — having picked up on their sensors that this strange human had somehow withstood their dastardly scheme to obliterate the entire population. They'd been impressed and felt that perhaps I must be some fellow galactic traveller who'd inadvertently been stranded on earth. "Why, look at his strange ship." They were coming to welcome me into their clan. I'd be given eight maids-a-milking as a penance for their sin and all my long suffering. I stood to greet them.

Alas . . . they were merely gossiping females, strangely clad albeit, in fishplant garb — off to the graveyard shift at the plant in the next town. My maids-a-milking denied, I inquired about the location of a store as a sobering consolation.

"B'y, ya missed d' town over d' 'udder way. We's walkin' dere t' catch d' bus. We'll show ya."

So down the road we went, off to work at the fishplant.

"Where's ya come from now? I didn' see nar bo-at dere," said one with her hairnet protectively pulled down over her ears.

"Oh, I come aroun' d' shore dis marnin' headin' up into d' bay now, love," I answered. "I come in a kayak. I s'pose ya blinked an' missed 'er."

"Well, for d' love o' God," shrieked another. "I seen one o' dey on d' TV. You need's ya 'ead checked!"

The others agreed and we walked for awhile in silence. This was only brief of course, before they quickly resumed the four-part symphony of garbled chatter. This seemed to be a universal trait of woman as well. I marveled at the routine subjects yet complex structures with which the conversation was conducted and was content to simply listen.

"What was dat dere?" I questioned quickly, during a brief millisecond pause for air. I motioned towards a scarred waste area to the side of the road as we descended a hill.

"Use t' be d' dump b'fore we all protest an got 'em t' take it out. All d' women in d' cove, sir, we wouldn' gonna put up wit' d' likes o' dat. Dere was days, luh, when ya couldn' get out o' d' 'ouse when d' wind be westerly. D' smell, b'y, 'twould turn ya stomach, right?" The rest agreed solemnly as they recollected.

"D' youngsters' clothes 'ad t' b' t'rown in d' garbage, dey reeked so bad," contributed another.

"An' y'all told 'em ya wouldn' have'n it, an' dey come an took it out?" I asked.

"Only afta we 'auled d' kids from d' school. We keep 'em in d' 'ouse 'til dey agreed t' move 'er," answered the earless lady.

We all walked silently as the sight passed before us. None of them turned to look at it as I did, for it seemed to hold memories for them of a hard struggle that had required much effort, of something which they wished they'd never had to endure. They were forced into action when no other alternative was available.

If there is any hope left for saving the culture and lifestyle of this island, it lies largely in the hands of those women. The mothers of children. The children of the rock. They alone have the power, influence, determination, grit, stamina, and wisdom to know what's right and just for the survival of their families. They all know how much is being lost and their hearts ache. To see their children leave, for good, is something no mother should have to bear witness to.

Those ladies took a stand when they saw no other option. *That* last resort for our existence here is upon us.

This has become a plea to our mothers.

7.3.97 . . . In returning from my walk with the ladies, I'd finally roused a few of the local people out. I'd sat down to eat supper before packing *Destiny* and heading out to find a place to camp (it was already late, as I'd not left in the morning until after I'd fixed the skeg. Had little trouble, but it took awhile).

So . . . following supper I'm just about to shove off and the gentleman living just above the beach comes down with his dog, introduces himself and is noticeably a little wary and uncomfortable at first, not quite knowing what to think of the peculiar-looking bushman on his beach. He'd tell me later that he thought I must be a "pimp or som'n"! I explain who (or what) I am and that I'm looking for a place to camp. He lights up and the next half hour is spent upon the hill, reminiscing about growing up on the island across the tickle from where we stood.

I'm told that's the place I should camp. But, "would ya come in for tea before ya goes?" This led to an invitation to spend the night, a grand car tour, drinks of whisky and ice water, stories of homebrew, the sea, the state of the people, and dozens of others.

It's pretty late and we've only now retired. I'm exhausted, yet very content once again, and thankful that I've met more new friends. A good wash, clean bed and enough stories and scenes in one day to fill a book. What more can I ask? I am so very blessed.

7.4.97 I guess the craziest thing I've yet to see on this trip came yesterday evening. They took me out for a drive — as is the case where ever I go, it's off to see the "new" homes where all the droids live: the golf-green gardens and yards, garages of useless junk, the assembly-line rows of houses that they have no more connection with, or input in producing, than merely shopping in a book and then selling your soul to the bank!

But she was merely stalling and said we'd see the "Heritage Site" after it had gotten dark to see "the lights". The lights being a ridiculous display of ornamental Christmas-like silhouettes plastered to a cliff for the tourists. What a bloody circus. A freakshow the fucking government's turned us into. There were bright-green glowing codfish upon the cliff, a dazzling herd of angelic caribou racing up over the bank, gulls in the trees, and of course everyone would expect "our" beloved *Matthew* replica to be represented.

Like Simon asked me up the river, "Ya gon see d' *Mafia* when she comes t'rough I s'pose, eh?" He hit such a streak of irony that I've laughed ever since.

Awakening this morning, there was a little northeast breeze on and much fog again. Over smokes, eggs and toast they assured me I didn't have to leave. By this time they'd accepted my revolutionary talk and obsessiveness for the old times and it was a fine parting. All were out to see me off and I promised to return.

So for the second day it was foggy. Nice though, there was negligible wind. No boats. Saw another gannet and many great sights of SallyAnns flying about. Spent time in a field with some sheep at lunch.

I'm in a fine spot here, with a good view looking to the northeast. If it happens to clear I'll see the nearby islands that I'll be hopping to. It's raining hard now though. Brothers at the weather centre called for gale warnings, 10-15 foot seas and rain until tomorrow noon. No sign of those winds thus far in here though.

Physically I'm quite well. Food is becoming quite monotonous. Potatoes, turnips, carrots and onions . . . only so many things can be done. Not much luck fishing lately, and energy levels could be higher. The arms have settled in nicely to the daily routine and workload, yet the muscles in my neck are at times extremely sore. My enthusiasm could be a little higher, but it's all the people and insanity that's got me down. I must have patience as I've discovered many times.

7.5.97 The worst of the storm went through at about lowest tide last night: heavy rains and much wind. Memories of the storm spent following my injury come back to me.

It's near noon and I've eaten little since lunch yesterday. Can't seem to stomach another meal of onion soup mix, vegetables and vegetable protein. I'm looking forward to a couple of days in St. John's and meals of tofu, beans and spinach . . .

Been reading all morning but am now becoming impatient and I'll get out and fix a meal, check out the scene of the sea, the little that *can* be seen. Welcome to Placentia!

— later — the pressure's dropped 8 points in the last 4 hours. Currently at 989 mb. I hiked over to the cove facing southeast and checked out the swell — isn't too bad and I've definitely spent days out in worse. I'd need to take today or tomorrow off anyhow, and this low can't last too much longer.

— 1530 hr — A fine feed of split pea soup. Fine weather, if you're a duck.

I found myself in big seas. The biggest, in fact, that I'd encountered on the entire journey.

I left the sheltered harbour which had seen me endure my second extended storm in isolation. This required the most physical exertion of the entire day. Once I'd made it outside and headed downwind on my desired course, the morning's paddling conditions were clearly realized. The first five miles were a quick crossing to the channel between two islands. The swell was largely contained outside them, but it was at that stage that the challenge arose.

Before me lay large, imposing swells, ten feet or more at times, coupled with thirty knot winds. It was an intimidating scene yet there was no turning back.

Again, once a steady rhythm was established and with periodic checks behind to watch for the occasional cresting wave that had to be avoided, it was merely to keep the paddle moving. *Never stop paddling.* It is in the motion of the stroke that balance is maintained. It felt immensely rewarding to be out in such a sea and to be in complete control, to feel a growing confidence in my skill.

There were times when a roller approached and I found myself optimistically paddling harder in an effort to surf down the clean face of it. Then realizing that I was completely and utterly alone! There was no one on shore watching — hell, shore was five miles away. There was no one who knew I was here. No audience. No competitors. The freedom felt in doing that is unexplainable. Words cannot do justice to its power.

In approaching Long Island I decided my safest course would be along the outer shore. I was currently in the unaltered swell and was doing fine but it was tough to predict how the conditions would be affected upon hitting the southwest point of the island.

This meant giving the island a wide rounding. The sight of those monster ocean swells barreling in on that immoveable wall of rock was breathtaking — and I'd the only seat in the house. A half-mile away I could still hear its ripping crescendo smash and see the brilliant sprays of aqua-white as it was sent into the mist-filled air.

Hours later, I tucked in behind the first point of Marticot Island and scampered up onto a small rock shore and collapsed from fatigue and mental exhaustion.

I casually glanced up from my prone position on the beach. It must have been the subtle change in the acoustics emitted by the deflecting swell into the cove which caused me to look up.

"Oh shit!" I groaned as I stumbled to my feet.

Immediately I knew I had to get out of there quickly. The tide had receded to a point where a large rock was now awash with each wave. It was directly in the middle of my only route out. This passage was only just wide enough, so that when each swell rose over the now partially submerged rock, it created chaotic white water across the entire width of the channel. I watched in amazement as each swell worsened the conditions. I'd come in *over* the rock upon entering. How long had I napped?

"No time — gotta go!"

It was going to be a tricky maneuver. The low tide also created a steep slope down to a head-high wave curling onto the sand. It dropped off so fast that the undertow was quite evident. The problem was the newly exposed rock only a boat-and-a-half length beyond it.

"I have to go in facing the wave," I thought quickly. "There's no room to turn once I'm in and I gotta go out through that mess facing it." I scampered into my gear and hauled *Destiny* down to the sand, brought her around and stopped to rethink.

"No. I'm on too much of an angle. I won't be able to straighten up before the next wave comes in and puts me sideways back up on the sand, but hopefully not on my head."

I dragged her fifty feet along the sand until we were dead on centre with the approach of the wave. There was less water now between the shore and the rock. It would be tight.

I'd not worn my life jacket since the Golden Fog experience of weeks earlier. I quickly grabbed it from its position up in front of my cockpit. Down to the churning water we went. I had to get as much of her bow in the water as possible, yet sustain her heading into the swell until I was able to climb aboard.

"Quick. Get the skirt on before the next big one comes. Here it is!" It pulled me into the undertow and I fought just to keep her straight.

I was in! Then I had to counter the affect of the surge onto the shore without going forward onto the rock.

"Over a little," I strained out as I struggled to jockey her around into position. I had to wait for the next swell to rise up over the rock and give me the opportunity to jet through.

Now! GoGoGo!

I broke up over the crest of the surge and quickly out into the clean water just beyond. I looked back at the position I'd only moments ago been occupying. It had been an uncharacteristically large swell and it would've pummeled me backwards onto the shore. I thought no further of what the aftermath may have been.

"Woohoo! Kh-rist . . . That was the shit! Ha-ha . . . didn't even get me feet wet!" I hollered into the air.

The man was high on life!

Less then a mile later I was paddling joyously through the tickle, still adrenalized from the re-entry only minutes before, and I began my tour along the shore of an old village with a couple of newer-style cabins among the old houses.

I remained on course for the distant head, confidant now that I'd get a fine paddle in for the afternoon, when something caught my eye. It looked like a water tower of some sort up behind the houses, unlike I'd seen anywhere else. Perhaps an inquisitive inventor of yesteryear had fabricated some fandangled device.

I turned to go in and investigate when I heard the clear pitched clang of an iron bell coming from the tower. It was an old church steeple but the building structure no longer remained. Somehow, the tower had stood erect. I saw there were people at the base of it once I got closer. I slowly made my way into the inner cove and pulled ashore. A number of kids were down to greet me and some folks were up on the hill looking on. My enthusiasm that afternoon overflowed into everyone else and we all had a swell time.

They were all past liviers, or residents, of the community back to prepare for a reunion that was to be held the following weekend. They'd only returned the bell to the steeple the previous day, in anticipation of the forthcoming celebrations. I was the first one to be welcomed into the cove by the bell in forty years. It was a fine omen I felt, and we spent the remainder of the afternoon in the company of one another. There were gifts of freshly dried cod and caplin to see me on my journey, the first flake I'd seen since I was a child. There were complimentary pictures of everyone around the bell and then again down at my boat. I eventually bid my friends goodbye. There was an invite for Jig's Dinner, which I graciously passed on and set out again.

In all the commotion, I'd nearly forgotten about the conditions that would welcome me outside the sheltered tickle. I quickly put all things behind me and concentrated on the sea. All thoughts again were focused on safely getting to the evening's camp. Things were going well when I rounded a point and set my course along a very intimidating stretch of coast, known by locals as simply "the Wall".

Suddenly a large humpback whale surfaced briefly off to starboard. My first! "Wow," I uttered humbly. How would he react to my strange and nearly silent presence above him?

Then the surface broke only fifteen feet off to one side. A mammoth gulp of air. My mind was blank. I was still dealing with triple-overhead swell when a goliath of a fluke emerged from the sea next to me, before it ceremoniously retreated back into the wine-dark depths.

Directly below me the haunting blackness suddenly became white. "Oh, brother," I pleaded with him. "You're feedin' underneath me? Oh shit . . . please take care."

The cliffs and shoreline fifty feet away were filled with shrieking, noisy and obsessed birds. The caplin must've been everywhere. The spectacular tension was only enhanced by the murderous sounds.

Then he broke again and the absolute stench of whale breath filled my nostrils! I glanced back to view the mist he'd created as it glistened in the air of the light from the falling sun. He surfaced for a final time between me and the cliffs, before disappearing mysteriously as quickly as he'd come.

I always seem to be drawn to graveyards. The history of families and the makeup of a community that can be discerned from a visit is astounding. And thankfully they're always peaceful and uncrowded.

I found myself before the long forgotten grave of a young girl, Anistasia. The stone had fallen over years earlier and the lichen and growth had nearly overtaken it completely. She had been twelve years old.

I sat quietly and concentrated for a long time to picture how her life must have been in the late 1800s, in the small community of homes nestled closely together consisting of merely a few separate families. The interdependency amongst them would've provided an incredible network of warm kitchens and welcoming laps for her to be subsequently raised. The freedom she no doubt experienced is a far cry better than the scenario that overwhelmingly haunts children today. Quite often they are subjected to the stifling woes of constant supervision from completely uninspired guardians, with their vast array of "educational" videos as bleak substitutes to nurturing parental and community exposure.

The remoteness of her upbringing was directly influential for the charming wit, intense resourcefulness and complex imaginations which molded how and why Newfoundlanders evolved as they have. Yet her world undoubtedly is frowned upon as being repressively dull and monotonous compared to that of the average 12-year-old of today — whose 400-channel television sets, video games and movement obsessed parents,

I'm sure, would've seemed to Anistasia as the quintessential manifestation of an overwhelmed schizophrenic's nightmare.

I'd only wandered onto the graveyard, the path leading to it from the once proud community was now undetectable. Yet there's always a graveyard. I scoured the hillside until I found it. The ages of the other deceased attested to the challenges of life in that time, in that place as well: 36, 42, 48, 52 . . . An old sea captain who'd survived well into his 70s. Admittedly short lifespans for today's time, yet undoubtedly filled with more vivacity, richness and colour, no?

And then there was Anistasia, the girl who'd been twelve.

Later that morning I found a path that led to the adjoining community. The warm smells of the earth and new growth on the trees was a welcome change to those of the vast expansiveness of the coast. The thick air, untouched by the ocean's coolness, was strangely unfamiliar. I sang my praises to the comfort it provided and contentedly strolled along the path. Approaching the shoreline again, I was curious as to what would be remaining of the homes and surrounding land. As I emerged from the trees I found myself at the rear of a giant structure.

The remnants of a church. It stood skeletal and remorseless. It continued to impose its authoritarian superiority upon the cove, which was so desperately struggling to reclaim its untarnished grandness. Its ostentatious display of needless waste lay heavy on my heart, for my thoughts returned to Anistasia and the others who'd been subjected to *that*. For my God could be found out in the woods that I'd only moments ago walked through, more reverently than He could beneath the richly ornamented ceiling of *that* building.

My steadfast views were only reconfirmed when I investigated a little further and discovered the rusting, decayed pile of an automobile! The good Reverend had seen it beneficial in the Lord's eyes to purchase an automobile. An insurmountable amount of money to the people in communities such as this — to drive his pompous posterior between the two towns, while his parishioners went without and obediently every Sunday gave their donation to the collection plate out of fear, pure fear, created by the church to suppress the people into faithful "lambs" for its own despicable glorification. As a display of protest and disgust, I proceeded to relieve myself on the filth and quickly retreated into the forest to seek forgiveness for my hateful thoughts.

Later that afternoon upon returning to *Destiny*, I swore that the little girl's life would not be forgotten, that her dying under the oppressed condemnation of organized religion had helped set me free. I then readied myself and solemnly slipped *Destiny Anistasia* into the undying reservoir of Mother Earth's tears.

Heaven is as much under your feet as it is above your head. — Henry David Thoreau

7

7.8.97 The hottest day yet, with light winds throughout for the most part; won't be long now and I'll be taking swims in the ocean. Yet, thinking of this, it's gonna get a lot colder once I round the bottom of the Avalon. I'm looking forward to seeing my first iceberg — won't be long, for I've reached the shores of the Avalon Peninsula!

I continue to find people less friendly. Along the south coast not a boat passed that didn't alter course and come say hello. Even guys out fishing dropped their gear and came to have a look. Here, there's puffters out in their speedboats on vacation who don't have the courtesy to even wave.

I made an effort to eat more during the day today, and it made a difference — soup and caplin before making the big crossing tonight. Waited until after 1700 hr to ensure that the winds weren't going to pick up. Makes me wonder how much I could accomplish if I'd fine meals to digest every day.

It was inevitable that *the* boat and I would cross paths somewhere along my journey. Of course, I attributed the gale winds, my inability to come ashore and wetting myself again to the decidedly bad karma that would surround the thing like a black plague.

Strong southwest headwinds arose in the late morning and I was forced to land on the now inactive (radioactive?) U.S. military base. A gnarly, land-filled and unforgiving shoreline of large boulders greeted us. It was high tide when I awkwardly staggered over the cursed rocks with the boat.

I was exhausted from the long paddle upwind. I had to stop for supplies. I prayed it would be a successful and rapid journey, and that my foray into John Cabot's Five Hundred Year "Discovery" Celebration would be minimal. I set out across the expansive tarmac in the direction of town, bidding farewell to my beloved companion. When I returned she'd be many feet above the waterline; getting us back into the water was going to be an adventure entirely in and of itself.

I'd suspicions that the base was off limits to the public, but there was little I could do in the situation. My only concerns were centred upon my exposure to whatever bizarre substances lay lurking beneath my feet. It *was* a newly discarded wasteland that had been occupied by the U.S. government after all.

The nearest town still looked four miles away. It looked unpromising as I slowly made my way over the desolate land. In the distance, to the far edge of the runway and amid the shimmering heat radiating from the tarmac, I saw a large dumptruck. I'll be sleeping in this nuclear dump if I don't make a dash for that truck, I quickly thought to myself.

I began sprinting across the pad, but soon realized how weak my legs had become with the lack of exercise they'd received. The weeks of upper body paddling had left my lower half soft and unconditioned for such acts of endurance. What'll they be like by the time I'm done, I wondered. I eventually reached the truck and the lone occupant seemed quite taken by my arrival.

"How far t' d' closest store ya figure?" I greeted him breathlessly.

"A store? Well, you miles from any store dat I know for. Where in heaven's ya come from?" he asked.

"I had t' come ashore back on d' point, accordin' d' wind but I gotta get some grub."

"Well, 'ead toward dat buildin' way up d' slope, dat'll git ya t' d' road. Ya can try an' t'umb ya way from dere," he suggested quietly and then paused. "Ah, hell . . . git in, we git's ya part o' d' ways. Can't see 'em bein' too pleased wit' you bein' out 'ere. She be top secret, right?"

"Don't intend t' be 'ere any longer'n I gotta be," I replied once we were moving.

"Ah right," he said once we'd come to the end of the pavement, "Dis is as far as I goes — up over d' hill dere, 'alf a mile an' you comes t' d' gate. Take care now, b'y."

I thanked him kindly and began the brisk walk a little more optimistically, following my first conversation in many days. Approaching the gate, a man descended quickly upon me, clearly distraught and befuddled.

"How'd you git in here? Dis is private property — U.S. Government. We can't 'ave folks walkin' aroun' on dat stuff in dere . . . dere still might be mines an' stuff about," he frantically whined.

"Hey, brother, I don't wanna be in dere anymore den you want's me dere. I was forced t' land on dat wretched shore due to d' wind, b'y."

"Well y'ain't goin' back den," he stated matter of factly.

"Excuse me?" I demanded. "Me boat is still back dere on the shore. I gotta get to a store and then I'll be back t' get outa ya hair. I'm sorry, but nobody owns d' land — not *even* d' U.S. Government. Although they do a fine job of messin' it up. Again, I'm off it as fast's I can."

I began walking along the stretch of road, leaving the poor dude to scratch his head. You really shouldn't have barked at him, I chastised myself. He was only doin' his job . . . I continued on. Still the road was deserted and quiet. A couple of cars passed going in the opposite direction — I merely received puzzled looks of mistrust. An hour later and I was still walking the road. Cars had passed. Many, full of tourists in strange celebratory Caboto regalia. It was bizarre that no one seemed willing to help. I felt baffled, rejected and utterly alone. I'd spent nearly a week in complete isolation, only to be welcomed back into "civilization" like this. I walked on, dejected.

My friend who'd helped me out on the base eventually pulled over. I climbed aboard. "Ain't 'ad much luck, eh. Ah, dem's too busy wit' dat friggin' boat, b'y."

"Yeah, I s'pose," I mumbled.

He drove me to a junction and said there was a store only a fifteen minute walk in. We parted ways and I set out again. I didn't even bother to stick out my thumb, I'd reached such a low.

The store eventually arrived and I entered in anticipation of some fruit and vegetable juice. I spent an extended period in the cool confines of the back of the store, having begun my ten-mile paddle at sunrise and then standing in the sun since mid-morning. It was late afternoon and I still had to get myself back to the base and paddle who knew how long before my day would be finished. I collected all my items to be purchased and brought them to the lady at the counter.

"Can I use ya phone, ma'am?" I asked her. As I dialed the numbers I tried desperately to pick up my spirits a little.

"Hello?"

"Hi Mom," I said, a little too enthusiastically.

"Where ya to? We haven't heard from you in so long. You're alright are ya?" she questioned closely.

"Yeah, I'm good . . . bit of a rough one today, but I'm over on d'Avalon, so dat's good. Just wanted to call and let ya know that I'm alright . . . Everyone fine home, Ma?" I managed to ask.

Home seemed further away than it had ever been.

"We miss ya. How ya doin' for food?"

"Alright. It'll be good t' get t' Town for a few days."

"Dad's not here; he'll be sorry he missed ya."

Home seemed so far away.

All the people in the store were watching me. It didn't matter. I just wanted to be able to pull myself through that phone for a hug. Just some small form of physical contact. I was starving . . .

"I'll call again soon, Ma. Don't worry 'bout me, please . . . I'll see you soon . . . I'm fine really . . . " I choked. "I love you, bye."

I felt I must have reached the lowest chasm of my journey that evening. I'd arrived at a point where I could no longer relate to anyone or anything except the ocean. And this was sure to be the death of me if I remained in the frame of mind that saw me setting up camp that night. I lay in my tent, the steady force of gale winds in fierce competition with the stream of cars rolling blindly along the road, only a quarter of a mile away.

The greatest travelling celebration the island had ever witnessed was taking place nearby, while I cursed every one of them for their shallowness. I lay in the darkness, shivering, while I waited for my body heat to warm the small cavity of my sleeping bag.

The darkness. Light. Darkness. Light. Occasionally the lights from a passing car coming around a turn would illuminate the inner realm of the small tent which had been my home, my humble abode, for so many years.

Darkness . . . Light . . .

There were reasons for such hardships, I told myself. Have patience. I prayed that night that it wouldn't be too much longer before these reasons became known to me.

I awoke early the next day and quickly descended into the water. Conditions remained just as challenging, yet the exposed, steep beach that I was on would not be a welcoming spot — another gale warning had been issued. I had to find shelter before it arrived. I struggled into the wind and a number of large swells broke over the bow on top of me. Seven miles later I arrived at a sheltered cove and thankfully pulled ashore.

It took some serious motivation to get myself thinking objectively. I congratulated myself for overcoming the many challenges of the past day and realized I'd bypassed the shenanigans relatively unscathed. This seemed to work and I began prioritizing the duties which needed to be accomplished in order to set myself back on track and lift my spirits.

Clothes. I needed clean clothes and a bath. There was a river in the cove and it was going to be a warm day onshore. I gathered my things and headed in.

The river fell down into a long field which had been cut for grazing years before. There were a number of peculiar buildings along the road that dipped into the clearing as well, before continuing along the coast. I headed inland, spirits already improving with the warmth of the sun and the promise of a needed bath in the river. I passed one house which appeared to be inhabited, or was until recently, yet all the windows were boarded up to some degree.

There were bizarre looking cattle in the river, like none I'd ever seen before. Small and passive, they had long, Great Dane-like hair and the males had wild horns that jutted menacingly from their skulls. I approached quietly until I was certain of their mellow nature. They seemed content to stand in the river and curiously look my way occasionally.

The water was cool and refreshing. I sat for a long time and simply soaked the encrusted salt from my arms and face. I relished in the near religious experience of the grime washing from my body, enough to discernibly taint the colour of the water that flowed solemnly downstream into the mouths of the seemingly spiritually presenced cows. I cleansed and purified myself of the tribulations which had fought to suppress my quest for clarity, truth and freedom. Some time later I began my walk back to the shore, invigorated and optimistic once again.

108

It's incredible how some things that are often taken for granted can become so substantial and appreciated when one goes without them for a time. A mere bath in a river saw me emerge with new hope and determination. I'd been down, but by no means was I beaten.

Approaching the apparently abandoned house once again, I'd even struck on a tune and was contentedly singing to the air, when I noticed a man out in the rear. I walked up, hopeful for a forthright conversation like the ones I'd enjoyed at the beginning of my journey. Naked from the waist up, he grabbed a shirt from the line and retreated quickly into the house. I found it quite strange as he'd definitely seen me, for there I was leaning casually up against his fence.

What to do? I couldn't very well leave after approaching the man's property, I felt. So I sang out a clear hello and waited. I was turning to walk on when he emerged slowly from behind the door. "Oh, hello. I t'ought you was one o' d' kids from up on d' hill," he said sheepishly. "Don't get many friendly visits dese days."

"Sorry, I didn' mean t' startle ya when I come up," I apologized. "I just come from d' river for a wash an' t' clean me close. Wha's wit' d' weird cows down dere?"

"Well, b'y," he began as he warmed up to me and approached,. " 'tis like dis . . . dem cows, from Scandinavia dey is or somew'ere like dat. Dey belongs to a feller up on d' hill. It was one o' 'is kids I t'ought you was. Well, dey and all d' buildings ya sees — d' barn dere and d' ones agin d' road — d' works o' dem, apart from me 'ouse ere, belongs t' 'e. E's a greedy ol' bastard an' wants no one 'ere in d' cove but 'eself! But I ain't leavin' s'posin' it kills me . . . just t' piss 'e off!" he continued heatedly.

"Me name's Bart, an' dat's Brian up on d' hill. Ya probly seen 'e on d' television wit' 'is buddies in Sinjohns. 'E's in wit' d' gove'ment crowd, right. Well, dey give 'e more money o'er d' years, b'y ya wouldn' believe, fer d' crazy stuff like ya sees b'fore ya. None of it ever come t' nudding. Git's a few stamps fer 'is relations, an' 'is son — check out d' car when ya goes o'er d' hill. And 'tis you an' I get's t' front d' bill." He stopped briefly as I looked quietly around the cove.

"Wha's d' new building dere agin d' barn, boarded up? Sure it ain't ever been used, have it?" I asked.

"Oh, dat was d' slaughter 'ouse dey come in an' put up oh, six, seven year ago. Ain't a t'ing been done wit it since."

"And d' ones up by d' road on d' udder side, Bart?"

"Cream'ry. Like I said, 'is clan comes in an' gits enough for d' pogie. Sure me 'ouse!" he hollered then. "Can't keep a goddamn window in 'er, d' man's so nuts. Dey cut down t'ree o' me flagpoles. I 'aves t' take me mailbox aboard d' pan o' d' truck whenever I goes sure, feared 'is kids is gonna make off wit' 'e!"

I didn't know what to say. I couldn't tell then whether or not the brother was nuts himself. "B'y, sounds like you ain't been 'avin' too much fun, 'ave ya?"

"No, b'y," he replied quietly. "I come 'ome from d' mainland, oh, ten year ago now I 'llow, 'cause I 'ad enough of it. Dis is where I was reared up. Me folks' is gone now but I can't seem t' leave it, even wit' d' loonie on d' hill dere. D' gove'ment b'y, dey can't stand seein' a feller live peaceful-like 'cause dey lives s' bloody crazy deyselves."

His quieted tone told me he'd finished. I looked over his shoulder at the weathered house of his parents, his childhood, at the chickenwire and boards covering the windows, at the wearied and watery eyes of the man before me, and knew he spoke the truth. And I realized then that I'd best toughen my shell a little further if I hoped to weather the many seasons that this man had trying to beat the system. I'd managed to keep it all at a safe distance where it only affected me to a very minute degree, and I was letting it eat me from the inside, while this man found himself daily . . . hourly . . . continually haunted by the garbage — and still he fought on. Civil disobedience indeed.

"Oh, but ya didn' 'ave t' 'ear all dat now, did ya. Where's ya comin' from, b'y?"

"Just come from up d' bay kayakin'. D' winds on dis shore is fierce b'y, I 'ad t' 'aul up in 'ere dis mornin'."

He brightened a little with my recognition of the winds. "Yeah, she been known t' blow a scatter time."

"How far t' d' closest store? I'll go up fer a walk dis afternoon. Ain't gonna get any farder in boat I figure," I said.

"She's pretty far, 'bout six mile I 'llow. If ya wants, sure I can give ya a run up afta lunch."

"Sure, Bart, if's not too much trouble."

"Ah," he scolded, "no trouble, b'y. 'Ead back 'ere when ya wants t' go and we'll dart ya up."

I thanked him and left to return to the shore to set out my clothes for drying. It was obvious I was destined to encounter all these troubled tales. It was essential I learn from them but refrain from letting them affect me so personally, or it was going to result in getting me killed out on the water. I had to remain focused.

I returned following lunch and Bart was there, waiting, when I went up the lane. I hopped aboard and glanced into the pan quickly before we set out. Sure enough, there was his mailbox resting on its side, looking like some dead animal being brought to the butcher. His disposition had improved and we spoke of my journey as we drove the stretch of highway along the coast. I studied the coastline, this being the first time I'd have a preview of what lay ahead.

It was also very strange to be moving so fast. It was as if I'd never driven in a car before, the foreignness was so intense. I cringed when an approaching vehicle passed, in horror that we were going to strike against one another.

We arrived and the store was a small room in the basement of a lady's home. She was up having lunch but quickly came down to let us in. "Ya still 'avin' troubles up d' cove, Bart?" she inquired as we entered. He remained at the counter in conversation while I went to the back.

"Love, ya sell d' beer separate by any chance?" I called out.

"Yes m' trout, no problem. Open up d' case an' take what ya needs. No trouble t' find a place fer d' udder ones, lad," she jokingly hollered back.

I didn't even like beer. It had been a long, strange trip indeed.

A few more folks had entered when I came up to the counter, and we all joked lovingly about the ship which had so thoughtfully graced us with its presence.

"I s'pose you made d' trip up to see d' Matchew, did ya?" one fellow asked.

"Not likely, sir. Sure we all seen 'er bein' towed up d' bay by d' Coast Guard. 'Den she gets outside o' d' harbour just outta view, d' tourists be all gaddered, and she comes off and sets up 'er sails all smart like. Whadda fuckin' farce," another fellow bitingly exclaimed.

"B'y, I'd be surprised if she didn' make d' trip across in d' guts of anudder ship."

"I t'wouldn' step on t' she when she's tied up t' d' wharf," chortled an old fisherman, "for fear she'd sink!"

On the return trip I asked Bart if the caplin had come into the cove yet, and whether or not he'd gotten a few meals.

"Yeah, dey was in, but Brian an' 'is sons was down dere an' dey wouldn' let me come near d' beach." As he stopped at the top of the lane to let me out he said, "I s'pose you'll be alright down dere on d' beach d'night. Yeah . . . 'e's in Town and 'is sons won't bodder ya, seeins' y'ain't come from 'ere. D' way 'e is, 'e'd p'robly be d' nicest kind t' ya, 'e's dat queer of a stick."

I invited him down for a beer yet he declined and seemed unwilling to approach the beach.

"T'anks for ya help, Bart," I said in parting. "As long as we're 'onest wit' ourselves, b'y, we'll survive. 'E'll get wha's comin' to 'e in d' end, don't worry." I gave him a quick nod and a wink of my eye, and as he pulled away I got one last glance at the perished mailbox, lying dejectedly in the pan of his truck.

7.10.97 . . . Shortly after returning I'm visited by "the other side." The three sons seem nice enough and stay awhile. As they're leaving, their mother comes out the path and I can see her screwed up face a mile away; she gets in the car without even a wave.

Not about to let any of this bother me anymore, I settle down to a fine meal of multi-bean soup, a bottle of Dominion and enjoy my fire. There's one house still intact but abandoned out behind me which was fun wandering thru the rubble. Got Dad an old extendable shaving mirror that may work again once it's cleaned up. And found an October 1971 edition of *National Geographic* with major article on "Mother Ganga".

I'll rise early again tomorrow; hope to plug at it a little more yet it calls to rain tonight, strong SW again tomorrow.

When I stand before thee at the day's end thou shalt see my scars and know that I had my wounds and also my healing. — Rabindrinath Tagore

7.11.97 — 0945 hr — I awoke early at 0445 hr to rain and huge gusts hitting the side of my tent, blowing from SE or maybe just getting looped around in this cove. Regardless, I feared that the two cross poles would be snapped — the tent was being doubled over me.

I quickly got out in the mess and got her turned into the wind — returned to bed, nothing more to do. Didn't sleep well. I'd opted to place the tent down on the beach next to my boat and gear, after hearing all Bart's stories yesterday. The beach drops off quickly, so even a small wave rolling in makes for a loud lullaby.

Looking out this morning, there's low lying fog and wind's higher than yesterday's. Maybe it'll drop off this afternoon/evening. For now I remain. I'll cook a breakfast and visit Bart to thank him again for yesterday's ride with the remainder of my caplin (I've had enough), and probably write a few more cards, or see if I can salvage my last three. They got wet some days ago.

What possessed me that day in making the decision to leave is still unknown. Perhaps it was the idea of having Brian returning with the likes of myself still on *his* beach that sent me out into that sea. Regardless, following an early lunch there I was with camp dismantled and *Destiny Anistasia* packed and ready. The worst of the storm had passed on, yet the winds remained and the onshore swell and quick drop-off would make for a difficult, demanding and very brief entry.

I was observing the swell and deciding my best course of action when a car pulled into the lane overlooking my position. A young man in his early thirties got out and, prospector's tool in hand, walked the short distance to where I was standing.

"Hey, little rough day out there, idn' it? You just come in?" he asked.

"No, just gettin' ready t' go out. It's good ya come, I guess, so you can fish me out in case I get's me skull cracked!" I answered jovially.

"Which way ya headin'?"

"Aroun' t' Sinjohn's by next week I hope. Well, wish me luck."

I decided the only way to make the entry was bow first. The skeg was bound to get jammed, but the paddle was directly into the wind and swell so I convinced myself I'd be able to accommodate it, if it were to happen.

I positioned myself as close to the breaking shore as possible and tried to maintain her bow into the swell. I climbed in quickly and began fastening the spray-skirt around the cockpit. Suddenly, the backwash of a wave began to drag me into the undertowed drop-off. I had to abandon the skirt for more pressing matters. A thick, overhead whitewall of a wave came crashing in on top of me when I was barely afloat in about an inch of water. I shut my eyes and ducked my head into the wall as it overtook me. Punching through it, I emerged on the other side and began assessing the damages: half the cockpit under water, jammed skeg and one damp, chilled paddler.

The lad on the beach was holding his head in disbelief.

"I'm o.k.," I shouted. "If you'll excuse me, I gotta head t' d' office." I gave him a wave and left him to his rocks.

It was only upon reaching the point that I received a true indication of what I'd set myself up for. I was greeted by steady thirty knot winds! I set my course and quickly realized that the swell was not going to allow me to land for at least ten miles. What followed was the most physically demanding six hours of my entire life. Once I'd made the decision, I simply had to keep going because the coast, along with the wind and swell conditions, completely prohibited my option to land.

I struggled on. Slowly. I'd reach a point of land — and there'd be another one, miles further to take its place. The strain was incredible. My eyes focused solely on those points of land. There was no enjoyment, for I made myself suffer heavily. There were times when I wondered if I was making any forward progress at all. I pleaded agonizingly for the winds to abate some. It was like paddling through hardening cement. For four hours, the entirety of my thought processes was: "STROKE, STROKE, STROKE, STROKE . . . "

Finally I saw a faint hint of hope, for down the coast loomed the blanket of an intense fog bank. If it reaches me, I prayed, there has to be calmer air within.

Slowly. Slowly, it began to drift towards me. I had newfound hope and a visual finish line to my agony. In the dramatic eternity of a slow motion film reel we struggled toward one another. At the last point of land it finally enveloped me and slowly . . . slowly, the winds began to ease.

I set my course for town a little more than a mile inside.

It was a godsend, I soon began to realize, for the fog bank's approach saved me from an extremely dangerous situation. The winds beyond would've been entirely too strong after the struggle I'd gone through.

As I gradually adjusted to the lightened paddle, a sense of euphoria overcame me — so strong in fact that I began to question whether or not I'd met some sudden demise and this final paddle through sun-tinged whiteness was now a passage toward another realm. The calmness of the water, my effortless movement through it seemed all too surreal. Had the six hours of ceaseless torture so suddenly ended? It didn't seem possible.

I must have brain hemorrhaged and drowned, I thought to myself. The endorphins released were like that of the culmination of a thousand orgasms. I felt immortal.

7.12.97 . . . speaking with some of the men, I learn there's a store and hotel just over the hill where I can get a shower. It's getting late and the lady's sweet and gives me a deal. I decide to treat myself — a night at the hotel, sweet conversation with a girl, fine shower and meal as well . . . I hung out with a band from Town, in to play at the pub for the weekend. I sat for the first set, then dragged my ass home — exhausted yet content that the world is a playground and as beautiful and stimulating as I choose to make it.

8

One step ahead . . . one step ahead, I thought as I awoke the following morning. If I continued to remain one step ahead of "them" through life, then "they" wouldn't be able to corrupt me and succeed in destroying my will to think independently.

The struggle through those remarkable conditions of the previous day had triggered a catalyst for a fundamental change in my attitudes. The sea's teachings of perseverance through even the most challenging of circumstances had given me strength and determination to overcome the selfishness of "the system," the social hierarchy, the "powers that be." I'd fought with this nagging injustice the entire voyage, and it had festered like some cancerous growth until it was prepared to assault me with its mightiest of challenges.

I'd survived and it had made me stronger. The harder "the system" tried to impose its lies on the people, all the more we were going to awaken and realize its truly frail and unethical make-up.

I remained ashore that day and the people around me could sense my re-established enthusiasm and joy for life.

The band had invited me to venture out to Cape St. Mary's with them if I remained in town. I declined with the reasoning that for my inaugural introduction to the reputed splendour of that particular section of coast, I'd wait a lifetime if need be to experience it under my own power and from the seat of the vessel that had gotten me there.

I relaxed in town and spent the morning walking along the stunning cliffs and ragged, blistered shore. As I headed back towards the hotel, I wandered down onto the wharf and was welcomed into the rear of a TransAm for a beer. It was Saturday afternoon and the young men were relaxing, patiently awaiting the festivities to be created with the live band playing at the pub that night.

They had already heard of my arrival during the gales of the previous evening, so there was no need for me to introduce myself. Instead, we mainly discussed the benefits and frustrations of our growing up in a small coastal town, the lack of privacy it sometimes amounted to, and the limited amount of peers, especially female interests, that we'd been exposed to. But most notable was our discovery of how much freedom of movement we had as kids — that our respective towns were ours to explore and we'd not been unduly restrained by the ever watchful eyes of our parents, as kids in other environments seemed to be.

More importantly, that afternoon we were simply content to be in the company of different faces, enjoying the loud music and basking in the lackadaisical pace of a warm Saturday afternoon with nothin' t' do. After some time I bade them farewell and returned to the store to thank the owners for their much appreciated help and generosity.

"Hello," I said enthusiastically as I bounced into the store. "I can't thank you enough, love, for the room last night. It was a welcome change from the past month's accommodations. Sure, I'm feelin' like a new man dis mornin' — ready t' take on d' world. She's gettin' on in d' day already and I'm gonna hang ashore for d' night's gig anyway. So thanks again fer ya help."

The lady to whom I'd spoken the previous night was then joined by her husband, the owner of the hotel, and she replied, "Oh, 'twas nothin' sure. Ya certainly are lookin' a bit more lively than ya was last time I seen ya. Glad we could 'elp. 'Tis some trip you're doin', wa?"

"Yeah, she's kept me busy, but I still got a ways t' go. D' summer's still young d'ough. Well, t'anks again," I said as I turned to leave. I'd retrieved all my gear and was now heavily laden as I began the walk down the hill to the wharf. I set out happily in the midday sun.

"Hey, buddy," I heard someone call out from behind. I turned and it was her husband standing in the doorway. "Come on back fer a sec, luh."

I laid my gear down next to the road and walked curiously back to the store. He'd re-entered only to return moments later with a key in his hand. "Sorry, b'y, wha's ya name?"

"Michael."

"Well, Michael. D'ere's no need for you t' be camped out down on d' wharf b'y. Ya been paddlin' hard, I figure, so here's a room for d' night. . . on us, we got extra sure. 'Ave yaself a nice break for d' weekend.

I didn't know what to say. "I don't know what to say, b'y," I stuttered out. "But you're a fine man and I'm indebted to ya, sir."

"Not at all b'y. Now git, and 'ave yerself a good toime tonight."

"Oh dat'll be arranged, sir, don't you worry," I grinned enthusiastically as I turned to skip back to my gear.

I'll always remember the generosity and kindness of the people along my journey. Through these acts my long struggle proved worthwhile. I returned to the shoreline shortly thereafter and praised her for all she'd continued to bless me with: the challenges, peacefulness, reassurance, new friendships, and hope. The eternal hope that goodness and truthfulness could transcend all else.

I gazed out over the rippled swell and a scallop dragger, wildly surfing her way back to port, drew my attention. I envisioned myself far up in the stem of her as she accelerated down the face of the swell. *That* was why we chose to risk our lives out there everyday — for that sheer essence of freedom, which for some could never be suppressed within the confines of a cubicle under the watchful eye of a supervisor.

This was the catalyst as well behind our giving nature. Up until very recently in the island's history, the majority maintained an inseparable bond between sea and self and understood the fine line that this created between life and death. A race of people evolved who recognized the more relevant, essential aspects of life, and we were richly blessed as a result.

Lifestyles were based solely on family values and community. The importance of friendship was intrinsic in the survival of the coastal livier, where giving of what you had was as unquestioned as the tides which brandished the shores because tomorrow there'd undoubtedly be an occasion where you needed to receive the same help in return from your neighbour.

This land can be ruthlessly unforgiving. The fundamental principles of the Christian philosophy were instilled into the people who settled here out of necessity and natural order, long before the religious sects arrived to overburden and manipulate them for secular purposes. To survive here, the people did unto others as they'd have done unto them. This was not required "teachings" by the brothers of some "faith." This was simple intelligence required in order to survive such a hostile environment.

7.14.97 . . . I went down to meet them and they were a grand bunch from the other side of the bay. All hands were pretty impressed with my current journey and I received incredible amounts of respect. The skipper gave me a pound of scallops and I fried them up on board. Fine eatin's and grand company. For drinks, we all had a glass of the hot "liquor" from the Jig's Dinner they were cooking.

I'm so blessed and as always, when times get a little frustrating and tough, through perseverance I'm rewarded even more.

Saturday night's festivities went long and hard, well into the morning. They began just after I'd left the new room to walk down and check on the boat. I took in the fine sunset and was approached by a drunk 16-year-old who'd gotten the courage to approach "the paddler." I was brought over to his

120

hidden case below the telephone company shed and given one of my 6 donated beers of the day.

Five minutes later, I'm picked up by the TransAm Trio and we went up to their shed to yarn and drink beer before heading down to the club. A fine time and many new sorts were met. Even one of the lad's 80some-year-old grandfather was out to tell a few lies and carry on. I invited him to the club with us as we were leaving, but he declined and I felt terrible leaving him there alone. The last glimpse I saw as we were leaving the driveway (dust flying) was the silhouette of a man in a bedraggled suit, pouring himself another mix of whiskey and beer, alone in a bare-bulbed fish shed surrounded by mounds of rotting, unused gear.

In a flash, our "TransAm of Love" finds us navigating the cove and up over the hill through the fog which had moved in. The club is alive and there's folks arriving from all directions. The next three hours are a maddeningly entertaining succession of bold and marvelous scenes:

— the expected shyness and questioning looks as I entered the joint.

— the drink at the bar with a shy fellow who, by evening's end, is loaded and prepared to make me his blood-brother.

— the donation of a stiff drink by a hulk of a man. "Of course I'm an Irishman, what else would I be?" As we part he leaves with the words, "Watch out fer yaself, kid!" And in his slurred and deadened speech, I've still yet to determine whether it was sound advice re: my trip, or a warning that he'd decided he didn't like me and that I'd better watch my back.

— the band had begun to play and I was anxious to just jump around and seek release through the dance, yet ...

— there were invites to the lounge where a stiff lineup of serious looking pool players were embarking on silent games of mental intimidation. An older guy and myself ended up scraping thru one game (the winners being bought a beer each) with little help from my play, and we lose the next one after I sink 4 in succession.

— my TransAm buddies approach and the following dialogue occurs:

"You toke?"

"Excuse me?"

"Do ya toke, b'y?"

"Oh yeah, sure," I said glowing. I'd not heard the expression in years. A quick wink and head nod for the door. It was all so covert. I loved it. Once we'd gone around back I inquired, "Don't s'pose ya got much trouble wit' d' cops aroun' here do ya?"

"Cops? No b'y, never sees 'em sure. 'Tis Mudder ya got t' watch fer b'y. If she knew we was up t' dis . . . B'y, I'd radder deal wit' d' Mounties, I don't know 'bout you!"

— the dancing was hilarious — bad cover tunes, yet nothing to do but relax and go with it. By the end of the evening I was chanting along to AC/DC with the rest of them. I guess I caused quite a stir with my "unorthodox" style of dancing.

— halfway through the last set, the girl in the band encourages me forward as everyone's retreating back to the security and comfort of the ill-lit extreme limits of the club's interior walls. "This here's our new friend, Michael, come all the way home from Vancouver t' paddle aroun' d' island. He's a fine fellow and it's great to see all the hard work he's doing. If ya get a chance t' talk with him, he's got a lot of great stories . . . " She's a sweet girl and I guess I had a fan, but she shouldn't have done that. It felt nice to be recognized a little though and I noticed a great many more smiles my way, many handshakes and introductions. Hopefully I can keep my fame restricted to the local pubs.

— the girls were all very shy and unapproachable, but I had little interest concerning them this evening anyway, contrary to the fishermen's warnings of the scallop's aphrodisiac capabilities!

— 0230 hr Following farewells to band members and other friends that I could find, the party began to break up and I headed for home a smile on my face, a spring in my step and with the hopes of a clear and inviting morning in my melon.

As a fitting truce and solemn invite back to her company, the sea was remarkably docile the following morning. Despite the lack of adequate sleep and the previous day's binge of booze, one quick glimpse of the glorious conditions and it wasn't long before I'd readied my gear and eaten a breakfast. I found myself down on the slipway not long following sunrise.

Two retired fishermen whom I'd spoken with upon my arrival only thirty hours earlier must have been watching for me, and they wandered down over the hill shortly after I did.

"Y'up early t' git a crack on 'er, eh son? B'y you'll 'ave a fine mornin' t' round d' Cape. She's some rare b'y, t' git one's as civil as she be dis marnin'," welcomed one of them as he approached.

"Yeah . . . you'll need 'er as she is, goin' aroun' in som'n like dat! B'y, I still be amazed ya come as far as ya did. You're a brave lad," complimented the other.

"She's goin' pretty good," I agreed. "Once I get's aroun' d'other side o' d'Avalon, I figure she shouldn' be as rough goin'. I'll be in d' lee most times, and she ain't as 'ard t' come ashore down my way."

"Yeah, yeah. I 'llow you're right, b'y," they both agreed.

Before we had a chance to continue our conversation, there was a great squeal of tires and a mad looking boat of a vehicle came barreling down the hill to the slipway. "I knew dere was someone I forgot to mention in my journal," I whispered to myself quietly.

Upon us unsuspecting early-birds descended three young fellas in their early thirties. The biggest and leader of the motley crew was a guy I'd met briefly and exchanged a few words with the night before at the pub, that went as follows:

"Daas some triip ya got gooin' on dere, b'y . . . congratulations . . . dat broad in d' bannd . . . she muust bee (hiccup) your gi-irllfriend."

"Nope. Just met 'er las' night actually."

"Yoouu 'ad 'er lass' night d'ough . . . didn' ya?" his slurred baritone of a voice yarbled out at me.

"Listen, I should be go. . . "

"Wait!" he cut in excitedly. "I know's yoouu . . . seen ya b'fore I 'ave. Noww where was I to . . . ?" he uncomfortably whined, as his eyes rolled up in his head to hopefully try and retrieve the fabricated knowledge that may have been floating about in his brain. "Jail!" he spit at me finally.

"Jail? Brudder, I ain't never done time as far as I can recall, d'ough I'm sure one day I'll probly be given d' opportunity t' experience dat too."

"No . . . no. 'Twas jaail I seen ya," he insisted. "Kingston . . . a few yearrs . . . (hiccup) back."

And so it went, until I finally had to pull myself away from the truly riveting conversation. But there he was again — still standing. Still alive. And faring much better, it was apparent, than one of his other buddies who was by this time in the process of dry-heaving his duodenum up into his nasal cavities over the side of the slipway.

They arrived in such an intimidating fashion, that I was quickly left to tactfully weave my way through the encounter alone — my two elder wharf mates were soon seen exiting the premises. I hollered out a farewell and simultaneously worked out a scheme that would have me in the water as undisturbed as possible.

"You guys still goin' since last night? Das hard core, man."

"Las' night?!" shouted his other mate. "Wee's been goin' at 'er . . . since about '84, right? Ohh, das d' las' toime I'm drinkin' dat shiitt . . . "
He'd changed topics, realms, personalities, sex, and a couple shades of grey

in mid-statement and was now clinging to the shirt of my "jail mate," pleading for mercy from his discomforts.

"Your love is like (hiccup) bad medicine . . . ," crooned the now formerly retching soul, lying prone on the slipway.

I'd tried.

"Sorry guys, kills me t' leave all dis fun, right. But dere's an ocean dere beckoning."

I quickly gathered all things together and slipped deftly into the water. Being detained from what was to follow by such a vulgar scene on the slipway was riotously silly.

"See ya in Kingston," I hollered back as I instinctively touched a tear to my forehead, which was more for the benefit of the three lost souls that I left behind than for myself that morning.

Conditions were remarkable. And as my earlier wharf mate suggested, it was advisable that they were for an attempt to round the head of land separating Placentia and St. Mary's Bays. It was a sheer wall, weathered round and smooth at its peak from eons of constant exposure and an ice age, which had long since created the bare, stark landscape of the Avalon Peninsula. Averaging four hundred feet, the cliffs were a brilliant backdrop to the morning's voyage along their shores.

Surprisingly, I felt little effects from the previous day's abuse of my system, and the negligible swell and winds were certainly accountable for my pleasant disposition. Above me, the upper limits of the cliff could rarely be seen under its cloak of dense, low-lying cloud.

Two miles before reaching Cape St. Mary's itself, I was crossing a small bay. The inner limits of its shore were only a mile away, where I caught a glimpse of a whale rising for air. A long, concentrated blow followed and, viewed from that distance, I immediately knew it was a species I'd yet to encounter. He was travelling in the same direction and I surmised that if he were to maintain his course and I continued on mine, our trajectories would meet as he followed the shoreline; the approach to the cape would be the location of our rendezvous.

I maintained my regular speed and twice more the whale came up casually for air. My excitement grew as I became aware that the creature was of mammoth proportions. As our paths converged, I discovered that this whale was something entirely unique to my journey thus far. "My God, it must be eighty feet long or more!" I exclaimed.

Many minutes passed. Ten, fifteen, and there was still no sign of the giant. My spirits sank as I counseled myself that the brief, distant encounter with the animal would be just that, all too brief and from a distance all too disappointing for my inquisitive self. As with many of my previous encounters with the depths' inhabitants, the sea was vast and there were no rules which these beings had to follow. They certainly didn't have to meander about for the sole enjoyment of a mere human. I'd have to be satisfied with the scene I'd witnessed, for how many others currently alive on the planet had witnessed such an occasion?

Then I nearly capsized from the next unexpected occurrence. A boat-length off to my starboard, the gargantuan creature slowly broke the surface, and a vast expanse of whale began to perform its process of entering my world for another breath of life. Slowly his eye became visible over the short distance that separated us, and he looked deep into my soul and was reassured of my peaceful nature. The vastness of his eye — its clarity, its calm, is a vision which will remain in my mind forever.

There were no overzealous whoops of joy. I was humbled into a calm, refreshed understanding with this mightiest of creatures. His curiosity must have overcome him as much as mine had. Without any fear I slowly guided myself closer to him. In an act of solidarity, we slowly, side by side, escorted each other to the cape. I'd never felt such a powerful connection with another being. Each time he resurfaced, his eye would remain fixed on my own.

There was a hint of sadness in his as well. We were both very scared for the world which had evolved around us. I wondered how lonely *he* must feel, he being one of the last remaining individuals of his kind. He had to roam his world in search of a mate as well, yet his probably no longer existed.

We continued on and separated a little to give ourselves a comfortable berth. All else concerning my surroundings had little comprehension for me, until we slowly began rounding the awesome headland. The sea was so giftedly calm that I approached to within a boat's length of the cliffs walls and gazed awe struck at the array of crags and ridges.

The birds. Never had I seen so many. Gannets. I'd seen only six the entire journey, but before my eyes was a colony of thousands! As we reverently proceeded through the paradise, they all began leaving their nests and places of perch on the rock face.

Before me, a massive orb of life began to form in the sky. The top of the cliffs remained shrouded in fog. The sky offshore was clear, and it was there that the spectacle took place. A stunning swirl of soaring birds — it grew dense and magical as swarms continued to leave their roosts and join the gathering in the sky. It developed into a continuous ring, like those surrounding Saturn, and I was merely on the edge of their orbital plane. It stretched over a mile out to sea and remained unevenly dispersed; the majority, a thick nucleus of life, came around to make their approach every eight minutes.

The audible soundtrack of my journey could never be duplicated. There was no sound emitted from the entire population, other than the slow, graceful wing movements as they occasionally sliced sharply through the air. Like a crow flying directly overhead in the stillness of a morning, yet slowed to the rate of a gannet's flight, and increased in decibels to the point where it was like placing your ear directly above a colony of termites.

The smell of ammonia was thick in the air. The cliffs were spottled white from centuries of nesting birds. Occasionally a barrage of waste would descend like droplets of gelatinous paint onto the surface of the water surrounding me.

My earlier companion remained stoicly by my side. Gradually the sight of the forthcoming headland came into view; there was a mile stretch between us and the point. I looked on in stunned, disbelieving wonder. How was it possible that this tantalizing glimpse of Nirvana could be improved upon? Before us lay yet another remarkable sight. A pod of thirty or forty Humpbacks lay in our path, casually feeding and breaching. From the shore extending almost a mile off, it was a literal minefield of mega-ton sea mammals.

What to do? I couldn't hold up and simply wait in the hopes that they'd disperse. After all, I was in the process of rounding one of the most exposed, dangerous headlands on the face of the planet. The ocean had calmed to permit me a safe voyage. Who's to say when she'd awaken to put a few disrespectful *homo sapiens* in line?

My guardian angel beside me continued, unperturbed, towards the group of Humpbacks. It was elementary that I was expected to follow. Slowly we approached the outer fringe of the pod, and, while a thousand gannets continued to soar overhead, one of the largest animals ever to grace the planet and I entered the party. Incredibly, we were permitted a respectful passage and continued on, unhindered by the group of feeding whales around us. Where once they had seemed immense in their size, they were now dwarfed by the gargantuan mass of my escort. Surrounding us, the pod seemed unaffected by the faint interruption to their early morning feeding.

To have encountered this pod alone would've been an incredible event. The environment I found myself in that morning was nothing short of miraculous and, without question, one of the most spectacular paddling experiences anyone has ever encountered. Yet the experience was not yet complete. Once we'd navigated through the thickest section of the group, we periodically encountered others as we crossed the entirety of Golden Bay. There were many spectacular displays of tail flukes as they descended into the depths for an extended dive.

We were rounding a small island to set my course for the final point and I felt the pinnacle of life had been left behind. I turned and looked back toward the cape. The majority of the birds had returned to the cliffs, and the pod of whales had continued their feeding. As many as twelve blows could be seen simultaneously, as the rising sun emphasized their mist-enshrouded surfacings from the distance we'd put between them and ourselves. I turned to proceed, an overwhelming glow in my heart, and quickly found myself back-paddling as I focused on the scene before me.

I'd nearly paddled into an incredible, baleen-filled mouth as it came forcibly out of the water. Dozens of caplin broke the surface with the whale's head. Displaced water and fish were being thrown high into the air as I stopped completely and marveled. A mother and her calf were before me and I soon discovered that she was teaching her young one to feed. I watched in continued wonder as she dove deep and then reappeared straight up, mouth wide to catch all the caplin that she'd schooled together. She did this three times and then following a quick turn to herd more fish together, she was joined by her calf.

I simply waited and enjoyed, confident that fate would decide all things. This early morning tour would be completely uninterrupted without any concerns of impending weather, a place to land, a girl to marry or even a government to denounce.

I felt so incredibly privileged that I soon discovered tears were streaming down my face. What had I done to deserve such remarkable displays of love and nurturing compassion from the earth? Blurry-eyed, I remembered my faithful companion throughout the entire experience and realized that at some stage, while I'd marvelled at the female with her young, he'd silently slipped away.

Later, as a fitting bookend to wonderfully contain the entire experience, I was surrounded by a small pod of harbour porpoises, silently slipping energetically above the surface. Their size was as remarkable as that of my morning companion's. It would have required perhaps forty of them to match his length. A friend I'll never forget.

I came ashore once the inevitable high I'd experienced had subsided a little, to be replaced with the realization that I was dehydrated and sluggish. I immediately set about preparing a meal for the mid-day break. This broke from the routine of eating a leftover portion from the previous evening's supper, which had developed since the trip's inception. If I was to continue that day, which conditions suggested I should, I had to replace needed fluids and regain energy.

I contentedly rambled about on the beach while I waited for a pot of soup to cook. To the left of the beach was a brook and on the other side of that, the bank rose sharply to where one house could be seen. Not long after noticing this, I saw two figures crossing the stream and slowly walking along the stretch of shore toward me. The energetic sprints to the water's edge and back revealed that one was a small child. As they came closer I saw it was a young girl with her father. She ran well ahead of him and approached unfrightened.

"Hi. We seen ya come in and we come for a visit," she said in greeting.

"I'm certainly glad ya did. Is dat your house up on d' hill?"

"Yeah. Dad built she when I was a baby. I'm seven now. How old is you?"

"A little older, twenty-two," I replied as I handed her half of my orange. "You got a pretty spot."

She thanked me for the orange and swung her frayed pigtails behind her shoulders as she reached for the gift. They'd nearly come apart from her morning of obviously enjoyed activities. Her cheeks were flushed from the running and she hummed contentedly as she swayed to the tune that was in her mind. Her enjoyment in eating the fruit was contagious and I watched her happily. She sang unreservedly once she'd finished eating and explained that it was a song which she'd learned at camp.

"Can ya sing it agin an' I'll join ya, so's I can learn it?" I asked hopefully. We sang the little rhyme twice through before her father approached to find us sitting in the sunshine and singing. He sat down with us and waited quietly for us to finish.

"Well, I sees ya met Jackie. She don't mind strangers as ya can see, 'specially dem dat comes ashore in bright little boats," he said warmly. "Ya come aroun' d' cape, did ya?"

I gave them a brief account of my remarkable journey that morning and Jackie remained with us for a time, before she wandered down to the shore and contented herself with the little lop that splashed in.

"Ya got a fine view from ya home. You're a lucky man, my friend," I congratulated him.

"Yeah, we loves it o'er dis way. D' kids, dey never in d' 'ouse sure, deir foreva out playin' in d' garden or down 'ere agin d' sho'."

He paused for a time, while he looked proudly upon his little girl playing happily in front of us, then he continued, "She's gonna be 'ard t' leave, b'y. Ain't 'ad no work since las' fall. D' 'ouse be up fer sale now but I 'llow we won't get a t'ing fer she . . . too far from town I s'pose. But I gotta go anyway. We's goin' t' Brampton two weeks from now . . . gonna stay wit' me brudder 'til I finds a job."

The intense despair in his face was difficult to behold, for, like him, I looked at the little girl at the edge of the water and remained silent.

"Brampton . . . ," he said finally. "Wha kind a jesus place is dat t' raise me kids? Sure, I'll 'ave t' keep 'em locked up in d'apartment like some friggin' hamsta. Don't make no sense, b'y." He shook his head in defeat.

Shortly afterward Jackie returned, unaware of the grief her father was bearing, and presented me with a small stone. It was weathered completely smooth by the storm-tossed sea. A gift, she said, to keep me safe out in my boat. I thanked her dearly for it, along with the song she had taught me.

They turned to leave shortly thereafter and I called out to the man. There had to be something I could say, I thought. "Good luck, my friend," I called out. "Perhaps one day, God-willing, we'll all get t' return . . . and we'll grow old on d' beaches like we're s'pose to. One day, we'll get 'er back, b'y one day . . . "

He gave a wave and didn't seem too convinced.

I said a prayer for him and his family as I watched them slowly walk back to the brook. He'd gone up to his thighs in water in coming across to talk with me. He must have supported his daughter across it as well. I wondered how many times he'd wade through a brook once he arrived in Brampton. Leaving that beach with the child's rock pressed reassuringly against my heart, the journey continued. But it was no longer for myself.

Following the spiritually enlightened paddle of the morning, the talk with Jackie's father was like a massive anvil being dropped on my psyche.

The swell increased and it helped speed me along up into St. Mary's Bay and likewise helped to keep my mind free of the anguish I felt. Arriving at my destination, I was chilled and anxious for dry clothes. As I rounded the point of land my spirits rose when I saw a boat leaving the beach where I intended to land. They never saw me as I tucked inconspicuously around the point but I saw what they'd left for me.

A fire remained burning on the beach where I would come ashore. This encouraged me and I set up camp below a bank of dozens of nesting terns. They were all frazzled with the commotion of the last party, and at times they made daring dives at my head in defense of the nests they had in the grasses above. Their undaunted dedication to the unborn offspring was remarkable. All nests consisted of little more than soft dried grass, molded into saucer-sized cups in the tall grass, with two eggs of light beige and speckled brown.

To watch these fine acrobats skimming bat-like across the water, jetting down and plucking a krill from the surface was a daily occurrence. To experience this new aspect of their survival scheme helped me understand them all the more. Like the other creatures I'd encountered that day, all their actions were conducted for a reason. I wondered at humanity's incessant will to do things without any practical purpose. We were the only animal I could think of who did so.

9

7.14.97 . . . I've nearly all preparations for bed readied and am warming my leftover soup on the fire when two men approach from further down the beach. They're quickly accompanied by their enthusiastic wives, and formalities are conducted. They're from the town in which I'd spent the weekend and laughed heartily when I relayed tales of my previous night's escapades. I was invited over to their fire for a drink (they are camping in tents, yahoo! in the next cove down) and they left to gather firewood on the way back and gave me time to finish my sparse meal. Getting an armful of wood, I joined them later and a beautiful night was spent — warm and cloudless, funny tales and no flies, many cigarettes and a wiener roast with all the toppings. Finally I bid my farewells.

Following a day of paddling over 34 miles on a hangover and about 4 hours sleep, I'm exhausted. They understood, but I was not allowed to leave until I promised to join them for breakfast in the morning. I'll sleep peacefully on a thick bed of moss, surpassing any hotel room known to man.

. . . It was following the blood pudding that I felt I'd accommodated quite enough. I needed a little time to straighten out my thoughts and, even more importantly, to show some mercy to my poor belly, whole digestive system, entire being!

Today's intake (this is no joke) consisted of 10 eggs ("fresh from d' 'ens ars'ole, lovey"), a heaping mound of freshly cut-from-the-pig back bacon, 9 slices of heavily buttered bread, and 4 cigarettes (for breakfast!) and for a "stopper," as Dad says, about 7 biscuit-sized pieces of blood pudding for lunch. I'm amazed my heart is still functioning!

A thunder and lightning squall has just passed — the rain's on my tent, inviting me to sleep.

There is *so* much to write of . . . all in due time.

7.15.97 – 1000 hr The sea she be angered today and, like all, her pent-up energies must be released at times. I'm content where I am. I've much in my head to spill forth, time now to nurse my abused body back into top form and fine food from home with which to do it. So on with my tale . . .

There's a bit of wind on in the morning — yet no trouble for the first leg, as I'm in the lee of the island all the way to town. Yet there's no sign of smoke from the cove of my past night's friends and I sleep a little later. In an hour, arms laden with wood and still 60 feet cross-wind of the camp, I round the point on the beach and can smell the unmistakable odour of scorching pig. Looking to the sky for forgiveness, I join in with the merry bunch. To follow would probably be the maddest breakfast that certainly this kid has ever encountered, and God-willing will never have to be an accomplice to again.

2 hours later, and with the majority of yesterday morning's intake already finding an unwelcome place in my belly, I bid farewell one last time and waddled back to break camp and set out for the town, 3 miles away.

No longer than an hour later, I find myself before a similar spread in the home of a retired sea captain. On his walls are many pictures of his schooner that he once sailed. Stories of fishing off the cape in her kept me in awe for hours. Then Smallwood's name came up in our conversation and he'd personal ties to the nincompoop, so I said little about my views and we quickly headed for his shed out back to show me his boats.

He now builds miniature scale models of his schooner and other ships, but it seems there's a dollar to be made at it now and his sense of pride and detail have diminished. He's currently making 6 at once for a lady in Town — "She wants 'em in t'ree week or not at all, an' dat was two week ago!" he told me incredulously. They pale in comparison to his first model — truly a work of art. So much of this I've seen all over — India, Egypt, the west coast with the native artwork, and now here. Why does money destroy people's sense of pride in craftsmanship so easily?

I called home and found out that Sis was in Town, and was pleased to discover that she'd make the run down off the highway. Translation: goodies from home!

While waiting we worked on the boats and his nephew arrived to hang out as well. He'd just returned from caplin fishing down in Notre Dame Bay!? I looked to the god-like framed picture of Sir Joseph R. Smallwood that he had hanging reverently on the wall of his workshed and thanked him ever so kindly for what he'd created. We've resorted to a caplin fishery. Jesus, how stupid are we? We've raped everything else, so we might as well take the bloody bottom of the food chain out with us as well!

Sis arrived and she was given the full tour of the sheds as I was, then we left for the boat which was down by the plant and spent a little time talking. I was caught commenting on the weather when she cut in, "Listen to you, sure. My brother sounding like a rugged, old sea captain himself."

"Aye . . . guess I found me calling, girl, is in me blood now, s'pose it always was," I smiled and took a deep breath of sea air. I told her of some of my sea adventures — all good ones of course — and we spoke in an honest and relaxed style that I'd never reached with her before and it felt very fine. She even said she may get out to camp with me in August.

Mom had prepared loaves of bread, two kinds of stewed beans, a peanut loaf, date squares, 8 big cloves of garlic, and a partridge berry pie — which I took up and shared with my hosts.

The winds were still very high, so it was also nice to see that I'd wasted no time in hanging ashore for the day, which was getting on and Sis had a long drive ahead. She came in only for a glass of water, as the missus was preparing supper. Looking back now, I think she expected her to stay and prepared a serving for her as well. So of course, I had the privilege of consuming an extra portion! Good on ya, Sis. For on the table before me lay a heaping plate of pan-fried biscuits of blood pudding. I'm still amazed I ate them — cleaned off the entire plate!

The weather glass had fallen considerably and I'd only 3 hours until dark, yet I simply felt the urgency to move, to be alone to sort out my head — and the thought of another meal of such sickening degrees was too much to bear. I knew the weather was going to get messy. This one time I prayed I'd be spared only long enough to find a safe spot to camp.

I bid my farewells, for they'd certainly been a generous and lovely couple, and the skipper brought me down to the beach. They'd invited me to stay (and I knew I should). He felt wary of my leaving under the current conditions, yet I reassured him I'd be fine and if I got to the point and it was too bad, I'd return. This seemed to calm his concerns and minutes later I was off.

It seemed the minute I rounded the wharf and breakwater, conditions deteriorated. I'd have a workout and probably be soaked before arriving anywhere — and all I could think of was getting as much of the vile shit out of my stomach as possible.

Shoal Bay Point certainly lived up to its name and I could've been toast a number of times. I rounded it a little too close and was amazed to see 10 foot waves building in front of me, and there I was in only about 18 feet of water. Only clean, hard, consistent strokes allowed me to pull away from the breaking water behind, and up over the ones which were about to break in front. The point behind me and once again in deep water, I let up a little and reserved my strength.

How far would I have to paddle to find a safe landing and would conditions remain favourable?

Shoal Bay itself had a beach which was receiving the full force of the storm. No dice. The wind was veering a little more southerly — the swell still SW — but the inner edge of the bay leading to the next headland would be blocking the wind somewhat, I told myself. That would be the closest and most likely of spots. I headed for a grey outline of a pebble beach about a mile and a quarter ahead, and slowly made my way. Large seas yet not unlike many I'd been in before, but would I be able to land?

Arriving, my hope brightened when it did look approachable, the drop-off not too sudden and a point just
upwind which was breaking the sea down a little more. I
waited just briefly for a break in the larger swell to hit and
glancing back, saw my chance. Before I knew it, I was up on
the beach and the landing had gone smoothly. Incredibly I'd
only even gone over one boot. I'm hauling my boat up above
the hightide mark when a mad set rolled in, and I shuddered
to think . . .

Next on the list of priorities was to empty my stomach
of the filth.

How's this for a scene in the 10-part, epic mini-series,
NBC late-night docudrama, starring the latest heart-throb,
bad-ass Hollywood progeny in his first ever "serious" television role? I'm on my knees, shooting up puke while blacken-
ing sky and raging sea imminently approaches. And the
adventures continue . . .

Once comfortably within the tent, the rest of the
evening is spent writing (first time since hotel room), reading
the mail stash that Sis brought, and eating a few wholesome
biscuits lovingly made by Mom. While outside the storm
rages. Thunder fills the air and my tent is emblazoned in
awesome white light every few minutes.

It's already past noon and the winds have not abated. I
just went up on the hill and they say there could be 50 knot
winds this evening. It is clear one hour and pouring rain the
next. I'm content to write and patiently wait it out — get
myself back in top form with Mom's beans and bread and
loads of water, so I'll be able to get a jump on it in the
morning.

The effects of a day's abuse are still greatly being felt: tight bowels/intestines of steel, stomach pains, heartburn and headache. For the second time of the trip, a suppository may be needed.

"Take Care of Me!!"

 37.5 nautical miles Shoal Bay to Meadow Point (Trepassey)
 27.5 nautical miles Trepassey to Chance Cove
<u>539.5</u>
604.5 nautical miles in 30 paddling days.

7.17.97 Thursday — I must be off my bloody rocker. I can't believe I've paddled that much in *2* days. All thanks to Mom's beans and home cookin'. My stomach muscles are definitely feeling the miles.I'm exhausted, so all pertinent details of the past days are sure to go unwritten. It's damp out and I'm pooped, I must sleep.

7.18.97 Friday — I've just awoken and haven't even looked really at what the sea is doing. The rains have held off and the glass is steady. But regardless of the conditions, a meal must be eaten first.

Wednesday's conditions upon awaking were quite inviting — from the beach. The previous day of course had gale winds from the SW, then by evening I had to turn my tent and construct a driftwood windblock. 50 knot winds did develop, from the north!

I made the decision and entered the water. It was a mess all day; until rounding Cape Freels it was a struggle just to maintain a straight course. At times I thought I must have lost the skeg, or I'd put too much weight in the bow, the current was *so* strong . . . This is why I'm so amazed that I covered so much distance by end of day. I'd certainly no expectations of it.

Upon passing St. Shotts, conditions were very welcoming to round the cape. I'd thought there must be somewhere to come ashore along the cliffs on the other side, so I kept going even though it was well after supper. There was no place to land. All I could do was press on — until well after dark. Yet a near full moon lit my way and I made it into Meadow Point and ashore safely. Twice I'd wet myself that day and this was not a time in which I wished to deal with it. I set up camp, ate a sparse meal and collapsed.

Yesterday's conditions were nothing short of another Karmic gift for putting up and struggling through the chaos of the previous day.

It was past noon before I'd left the harbour. My adventures there included:
— the boycott of a large supermarket for the small, privately owned store immediately next to it. I bought toothpaste and prune juice. She'd no pens to sell she informed me, as she sat with her inventory sheets behind the counter. God love her, she gave me her own.

— hung out with a gang of just finished high school kids who were working (I use this term loosely) at the town's museum, an old house built in the '30s and lived in by the area's first nurse. I was in a room upstairs where reportedly over 120 children were born. There were 6 of them, standing around bored and nearly useless. The two males being the worst, with no more initiative than to park their feet up on the desk and pout because I'd come in and probably made them look like the lazy fools that they were in front of the girls. One girl though, who's to do nursing in the fall, showed genuine interest and was nice to talk with.

— before leaving I was invited up to a factory, I believe for light fixtures (!?) and given coffee. Made a call to wish Pop happy birthday. He was 88! One guy there was amazed I'd been paddling yesterday and came around Cape Pine —

they'd an 80-foot cargo ship anchored off for the past 3 days which didn't leave until that evening. I'd seen it beginning to move as I was entering the harbour, but didn't give it much thought.

But like I said, seas yesterday were ideal. A gentle swell and no troubles. I was even in the boat for over 6 hours without an "accident".

Took a leak in the wildest place ever — just beyond Cape Race there's a deep crevasse in the coast. It went in over 80 feet and was no more than 2 paddle-lengths wide at the opening. Deep inside I could see a pebble beach, yet no wider than the kayak itself and surrounded by towering 100 foot cliffs everywhere! What a trip!

I'd noticed the water temperature getting noticeably cooler over the past couple of days; my heels while in the boat, took on a similar feeling of numbness that I recollected from my earlier days of training in the spring back home. I'm approaching the Labrador Current.

This truly became apparent with the encounter of my first iceberg! — but off Cape Race of course. And, as if it were all written well beforehand, it slowly disintegrated over the hours that I paddled by.

Conditions are looking good for a continued push down the shore. I've passed the most southerly point of my journey — within days it'll be the most easterly point of the continent.

Tourists! Why do people seem to lose 40 percent of their I.Q. when they suddenly find themselves on vacation?

As I emerged from my tent dwelling that morning, this is what I was faced with:

"Oh, you started in Port aux Basques, that's where we arrived on the ferry. How long that take you now — a week?"

"Like, how much is that boat you got there?"

"Yeah, paddled a lot myself (sniff), ain't nothin' like a good Eskimo roll in the morning, to start your day off, right kid?"

"We're from Texas. You got a beautiful country here but Jesus, don't you ever get any sun?" Etcetera, etcetera, etcetera . . .

I remained polite and answered all the questions that I could, some being so ridiculous that I couldn't help but be left with my mouth hanging open and wondering, huh?! . . .

The small group that had gathered about me was then joined by Chad, a local who gave guided whale tours out of the cove. We spoke of the weather and whales that we'd seen before we were joined by his son, a young man still in high school who helped out his father during the summer months.

"How's d' business been?" I asked as we gazed optimistically out of the cove for signs of improvement.

"Aghh, slow, b'y. Tons o' whales, most I seen in years. We figured she'd be a great year, wit' dis celebration goin' on, but Christ, dey's all off chasin' dat bloody boat aroun'," he answered dejectedly.

"Yeah, and dere, d' bloody gove'ment got a jesus monoply on all stuff concernin' d' t'ing, and d' locals sure ain't makin' a dime off it. I passed right on by, m'son — I'll 'ave nudding t' do wit' it. I 'ad t' come ashore wit'in a coupla mile o' d' racket. You'll never believe d' shit I saw in d' ditch, b'y, when I walked t' d' store. D'ose bloody pull tickets . . . emblazoned wit' d'jesus Mafia all over it! Gove'ment, b'y . . . on top o' d' whole pile o' shit, dey continues t' git d' crowd home 'ere addicted t' gamblin'." I pulled up and told myself that I'd ranted quite enough. No sense getting myself all flustered again.

"B'y, she's a bloody farce, but d' lot of us is too lazy des days t' kick up much of a fuss," theorized Chad as his squinting eyes tried desperately to see through the thick fog which had settled in the cove.

"Well, enough o' dat. I'm goin' out on d' water where dat stuff can't touch me," I replied enthusiastically.

"Yeah, looks t' me like ya figured out d' secret t' stayin' young, b'y."

"Dat I did sir, dat I did."

They helped me transport my gear down to the shore and watched as I paddled out.

"Be careful now," shouted Chad. "Der callin' fer a suderly, right? She'll be wicket for a toime if we get's 'er."

I'd not given it enough thought, I realized once I arrived at the point, a mile away. It was some of the thickest fog I'd been in and very stiff southerlies had begun to blow. Within minutes a sharp swell had picked up and I quickly made the decision to head back. Coming about, I had to take another compass bearing just to make it back to the beach. I could barely see the stem of my boat.

They were still at the shore when I arrived.

"T'ought we was rid o' you."

"Naw . . . 'ad t' come back an' shit on d' gove'ment a bit more, b'y," I grinned as I pulled in.

He invited me up to the shed he'd constructed as an office/shelter/ change room/tea house and we spent the afternoon tellin' yarns.

He'd been a fisherman until the fishery closed down and stated simply that the sea was all he knew. "I was still s' young, right," he grinned proudly, "that I 'ad t' find som'n else. I wouldn' movin' t' no jesus mainland. 'Twas lucky d'ough. I seen it comin' an' we sove up an' I started dis 'ere. I loves it an d' whales is som'in I always liked. D'ere's no money in 'er d'ough — d' season be too short. Me wife's 'ad t' go back t' school. Oh, but she's wort' it, b'y t' look out in d' marnin' an smell d' ocean . . . d'ere's no price can be got fer dat."

"Hear, hear, brudder," I said as I clapped my hands. "Amen t' dat."

He was also a diver and on the wall was a poster of the known ship-wrecks that were reportedly around the coast. I was amazed. It was plastered completely with ships that had unceremoniously met their end along the shores I'd been paddling. He noticed my interest and stated, "Da's a poster me buddy an' I put together, took a bit o' research as ya can imagine. Amazin' what ya can learn wit' a bit a toime in d' winter."

I realized then, looking around at Chad's shed, that with a little intuition and energy he'd continued a life for himself and his family there. The benefits of his efforts showed in his face, his speech and the ways in which he spoke with his son. He'd not plopped his posterior down on the couch and grumbled while he awaited the government handout, like so many others had done. As a result, he'd remained where he knew he belonged and it didn't matter whether he was a materialistically rich man or not.

He invited me back to his home for a shower and supper. Wary of a bad onshore storm, he took his boat around the ten-mile stretch to the protection of the wharf, while his son and I travelled in the truck back to town. He rejoined us a short time later and we spent a late afternoon at his home.

As he was preparing bologna burgers for us, I took note of the artwork that adorned the walls and was particularly struck by one of them. "Dis guy's a genius, Chad," I called out to him as I marvelled at it. "Must be a Newfoundlander is 'e, dis Gerald Squires?"

"Yeah, b'y, 'e's a buddy o' mine. Lived fer a toime down in d' Ferryland lighthouse. 'E give me dat one year," Chad hollered from the kitchen. "Some job, wha'? I'm surprised ya never 'eard of 'e."

Where had I been? I realized then, looking at that painting, how much I didn't know of my own island and how much I'd been responsible for my own ignorance, for I knew more of Andy Warhol than I did of that man, Gerald Squires. 'There's much to learn,' I lectured myself, "and the rest of my life in which to do it."

7.19.97 Didn't get out of Chance Cove until this
morning, yet the thought of wasted time is inconceivable. I
had a brilliant time ashore, for which I'm forever indebted to
my new friends.

Regardless of how late I'd gotten to bed, I was up and
on the water by 0830hr. — a little sluggish yet I'd feared
much worse. I'd help from 3 young friends who gave the most
jubilant waves and shouts goodbye from the shore.

Conditions all day were excellent. A fine swell from
behind and steady wind to push me along. It's neat to see
how comfortable and productive I am under these conditions.
I may become a competent paddler after all.

Writing of paddlers — I encountered my first kayakers!
A couple from France (she being originally from Halifax).
They were in Ferryland camped out. They'd left Witless Bay
in a double and they'd gotten spooked a few times with the
swell the day before. They've rented a car and are now going
to drive to Cape St. Mary's. She was beautiful and so
refreshing to speak with. She translated for him (what a place
to come and try to learn English!) and we had a grand chat.
Mostly they were pretty impressed with my trip and boat.

If I get another day tomorrow like this one, I'll be in
Town quite easily — a shorter paddle than today.

A tidal wave had hit the coast where I slept that night in '66. I inquired with the locals about it, to little satisfaction, so I went to the
source. Unfortunately, no ghosts visited me that night to retell the tale and
I slept soundly. I awoke in the morning to more fog. I was anxious by this
time to reach the northeast shores where this hazard was less frequent. I'd
navigated through it quite well up until that point. This day would see the
end of that streak.

As I quietly slipped into the water and left the security of the granite rock beneath my feet, I'd little awareness that it would require a 23-mile marathon before I touched once again on the steadfast shore.

The early morning's paddle was welcome, with frequent visits from humpbacks. Most often I'd be greeted with the sounds of their breaking the surface for air around me, as their presence visually was lost in the thick veil of secrecy. I'd become quite comfortable with them around me by this time, since it was very apparent they were more aware of my position than I was of theirs. Many times one would alter course and swim close beside me, curious about the craft which moved so quietly through the sea.

Arriving outside of Bay Bulls, I was still feeling strong and anxious to move forward. The decision to continue on translated into at least another two and a half hours aboard *Destiny* before I'd reach an inviting shore. The swell was high, yet the winds were northwest off the land.

"050°, 9 miles to Motion Head, 2 hours 15 minutes ETA," I repeatedly told myself aloud, so as not to forget.

I set my watch and settled myself into a rhythm. The cliffs were less than a mile away to port but were completely shrouded in fog. In beginning the leg, I could see the distinct white line of the swells hitting the cliffs, then slowly the sound of its crashing diminished, along with the sight of them . . . The shoreline subtly drifted away from my course. I was enveloped in stark whiteness once again. I glanced at my watch occasionally and dead reckoned my position along the route. From this I began envisioning the shoreline in relation to myself. Such is the required procedure for travelling the coast of this rugged, marvelous rock.

An hour later and the cliffs began once again to slowly draw nearer, as they and I continued on our desired routes toward the same destination — Motion Head. I predicted the time when I'd begin to see the distinct outline of the cliffs awash with swell. Shortly thereafter they did in fact come into view. My skills tested, I relaxed a little and eased in closer. Gradually, gradually the cliff became more distinguishable. I continued to approach, in preparation to round the headland.

"Not long now," I thought, "and I'll be around the head. The chart shows a couple a rocks just off it . . . Aha, there they are! A little further and I can make the turn."

I was about a quarter of a mile offshore when I rounded and slowly began to turn in. "Oh, shit! D'ere's more land! I should've known with the motion of this water. This is all just backwash from the cliff. Damn, I must be two miles from the Head yet!"

Once I'd discovered my mistake I was already in the chaotic mess of jumbled sea that results when a large ocean swell hits a wall and rebounds back into the rest of the swell that's approaching. In my anxiousness, I'd given little attention to the estimated time that I was to have arrived, which I'd set at the beginning. Once I saw the cliffs and rocks, I'd merely assumed that I was approaching the headland, when in fact it was an entire two miles further up the coast. I nearly paid dearly for the mistake among those unforgiving cliffs. A large lop from the shore almost capsized me, when it quickly twisted my boat at a ruthless angle into another approaching swell from the outside. So close to those murderously volatile cliffs — within ten minutes I would've been smashed into the sheer wall. Undoubtedly another dot on Chad's chart.

Once I'd made it safely into the calmer waters offshore and finally to Motion Head, I was greeted by strong north-northwesterly winds. This combined with the southerly swell created very sharp seas and I nervously maneuvered my way through, following the near disaster only a short time before. The swell was deflected shortly thereafter and the 40-knot winds ironed out any that were remaining from the opposite direction. So to add to my woes, I embarked on a grueling three-mile paddle into those winds before finally dragging my wearied body ashore — twenty-three miles and nearly a lifetime later.

Where I was forced to come ashore was a sand beach created by low tide. There were young children and an older couple sunbathing and playing in the afternoon warmth of the summer's day. The winds were practically indiscernible here, tucked so closely into the lee of the cliffs behind, which rose more than a three hundred feet above us. They frolicked playfully in the water, unaffected it seemed by the cold temperatures of the North Atlantic. "A hearty breed we got here," I boosted my spirits with, as I began to appreciate again the warmth of the sun which had eluded me all morning.

I pressed on later that afternoon for one reason. Once they'd all left and the tide rose to the point where I had to relocate regardless, Town seemed so close and one of the young girls reminded me so powerfully of a girl whom I cared dearly for on the west coast. I was aching for some conversation with her as a result.

I pictured the telephone booth quietly awaiting my arrival at the waterfront. For some twisted reason, the conversation had to occur from *that* phone booth. I envisioned the bliss I'd feel upon entering the Narrows, where the promise of an extended rest and city life would be enjoyed for a time. The food I would cook; the old friends I would see; the music I'd drown myself in. The temptation was too much. The thought of another night in a cramped tent and, worse yet, the idea of another pot of cabbage soup took me over the edge and I headed out again.

The winds, if anything, had increased.

I didn't care. I *was* going to find myself in St. John's that night. I had to.

10

The rounding of Motion Head had been only a practice run. The seas awaiting me at Cape Spear were . . . disturbing.

I quickly found myself in a very fast following swell on the starboard side. I put a very substantial margin of error distance between me and the cape — including rebounders would've been too much to deal with. It was the fastest moving water I'd been in. I'm still unsure of the reasons. It required incredible concentration. I arrived at the stage where the winds would become a factor. In preparation I told myself, "They're gonna tighten the swell up. It's inevitable that some of 'em are going to break."

The proximity of the lighthouse to the city made it a popular spot for tourists and locals alike. That evening I could see the shoreline scattered with bodies. They'd evidently been enjoying the bold display of power the sea had decided to grace them with. That night they were doubly blessed, with my exploits for entertainment as well.

I was adamant that of all times this was *not* going to be the occasion when I went in. It was the most devilish stretch of water I'd encountered thus far — fittingly, the most easterly point on the continent. Someone must have felt I'd need assistance. The Coast Guard helicopter hovered around overhead for quite some time. I suddenly had an audience? For weeks I'd paddled without hardly encountering another human on the water, and there I was, finding myself under the watchful eye of dozens from the land *and* air.

I blocked them all out and studied the water instinctively as it approached my craft. Boat and man had become one. Eventually I rounded the most challenging section and once I felt I was out of danger, I cheered and hollered for I could finally see the Narrows.

An intense workout remained, however, for the gale winds were steady and direct. Not long into my grueling uphill battle, I was approached by one of the city's tourist schooners. The guide was well involved in his tour spiel. I wondered how many times he'd repeated it, nearly word for word.

"Now ladies and gentlemen, from the right side of the vessel you'll see we're about to approach the famous lighthouse of Cape Spear," his amplified voice rang out over the water to me. "It is the furthest reaching, oh, if you'll all look to the left of the vessel now passengers, we're approaching a kayaker. He's probably been out for an afternoon's paddle to the Cape, before he returns to the city. Everyone wave to the paddler now."

They'd been given the O.K. and everything was on cue — immediately dozens of hands shot up in unison as the ship effortlessly cruised downwind. I couldn't help but laugh, regardless of my strained push into the wind. And I'm thinkin', finger or hand, finger . . . or hand. "Ah, what the hell," I said, and I brazenly began flapping my hand back and forth. They seemed delighted with my recognition of them and retaliated accordingly with increased enthusiasmm, until it got quite silly and I simply shook my head and continued on.

The Narrows loomed a little closer and slowly the city became visible. For an ironic prank on my soul — though more likely completely contrived — the provincial government building, Confederation Place, lies directly in view of all the vessels entering the city of St. John's. With contempt and betrayal in my heart I entered the city's protected harbour. That battle they had clearly won, for now. But with all the force they could muster that evening, they tried to blow me out to sea. It simply made me more determined and conscious to continue the struggle against them.

"Ya know, it's not the claustrophobic feelings of bein' in a city with all the people so close together that get's me feelin' like d'ere's little hope," I said to my friend, John, the next day as we were walking to the park. "It's d' fact dat dey often have's little or nothin' t' do wit' one another. I s'pose dey're all just caught up in dere own lives, dat dey ain't got d' time." I was in very unfamiliar and bland territory. We had to cut through a residential area of manicured gardens and perfectly sectioned-off plots. I'd a guitar strung over my shoulder and strummed it quietly as we walked.

"But if you was t' meet some fellow Canadian, never mind Newfoundlander, overseas somewhere," I continued, "b'y, 'e suddenly becomes some long lost soul mate, some siamese twin other half that's long been separated. And it's nearly expected o' ya to automatically be 'is best buddy."

To which John thoughtfully added, "Yeah, and if you were to meet the same brother back on the street in any right-wing, conservative town back here, chances are ya wouldn' even receive a recognition of even existing from 'im."

We walked on silently.

"Hello," I sang out kindly to a lady who was washing her car.

Nothing. No response as she quickly turned her head away and pretended she'd never even heard. I sighed deeply. My efforts had failed.

"Folks are just scared these days," offered John sympathetically, "or like ya said, too busy."

"Too busy for *what*?" I snapped at him. "To smile and say hello? Scared of a guy strolling down the street singing? Christ, if this is what we've reduced ourselves to . . . " We walked on. "Comin' in d' harbour last night, wit' dat much hate for what goes on up in dat building up on d' hill, ain't any better I know an' it's too exhaustin', an' I got better t'ings t' be doin'. An' all any of us seems t' do d'ese days is rant and roar 'bout how shitty it is."

"But what can we do, b'y?"

"Ain't sure yet — but hatin' 'em don't do me no good . . . and ignorin' 'em don't do anybody no good . . . an' I sure as 'ell ain't gonna join 'em! I donno, b'y, but dis ain't d' way folks should be strivin' t' live," I said finally from within the suburban utopia.

We walked on.

A small group of young teens, in large clothes and each carrying skate boards, slowly passed us.

"Hi, guys," I said simply as they did.

"Fuckin' hippie," muttered one of them.

shot Shot SHOT **SHOT.**

Everyone *was* scared, so they shot out blindly toward anything they could reach, anything they couldn't understand, anything they could belittle to make it through the day, anything to elevate themselves. Then who was I to judge? While I took shots at the government, the church, the school system — because I was scared of them. Those were things I had no use for. But there were others who had no use for music or literature or the ocean. This didn't make these things that I held sacred any less significant, did it?

We walked on. As we did I began to change, to seek understanding with all beings. Even with those who ridiculed me, even with those who hated me. Even with the big man up on the hill, behind the large desk with the view through the Narrows.

We're all different, some more than others. There weren't many who would take to the ocean as I had, just as I couldn't take to a life among the rows of houses. This is what makes the world such an interesting planet to live on after all.

"The less shots I take, the freer I become." Immediately I realized I wasn't as scared anymore. To rant and roar would get us nowhere. Only through our actions could change take place.

> *Oh yeah, we takes d' pogie so easily,*
> *Yeah, we takes d' pogie for free, for free,*
> *Yeah, we takes d' pogie,*

'Tis makin' slaves out of we,
Yeah, we takes d' pogie, for free.

Oh may we rant and we roar no more, no more,
May we rant and we roar no more, no more,
Oh may we rant and we roar,
'Til we even's d' score,
Oh may we rant and we roar no more . . .

This began to spill forth from me as we entered the park that day. I sang it beneath a tree, after having discovered the most valued lesson of the entire journey. It came at the furthest distance from the ocean that I'd been, in the most unnatural and unpredicted of environs.

Let's see, I thought calmly. Nietzsche, no. Steinbeck, no. Tolstoy, no. I was in one of my favorite places, a used book store. I'd one final task to accomplish before my stay in Town was complete — a new piece of writing to sink some thoughts into. They were all excellent choices but I needed something less . . . jaded. Perhaps Orwell had been a little too close to the mark for settling myself down every evening.

I needed something relevant, yet comfortably enjoyable. I was on an adventure after all. This was always a very pleasing and wildly exciting task, choosing a literary companion for the forthcoming moons.

An adventure . . . A long pause as I scoured the shelf. Ha ha, I knew destiny wouldn't let me down. I gladly paid my $1.90. My task complete, I confidently bid the lady adieu and, book under arm, headed for the door. It was time for *The Odyssey* to continue.

7.25.97 One can certainly never come close in predicting what the next day will bring. With my new found dedication to become far more accepting of those on a different path than myself, I left the Narrows with optimism. Whatever, will be. I simply must push on in spite . . .

How ironic again. I'm set up here, in my own little shack that the boys invited me to use, courtesy of the

Premier himself!! Though I'm sure it's unbeknownst to him. It's some office down here by the water, used by DFO. I guess. So it goes.

I was only just settled in when a couple of ladies from the town dropped down with bologna sandwiches for me, and since then there's been fine people and grub all around. I'd been anticipating a quiet evening or two, out camping alone — guess it wasn't in the cards. There's dozens of new folks to meet and with it, complimentary beers to drink. I can't get away from them! A young friend and I took a hike this afternoon to the top of a hill for a fine view of Conception Bay. I'm still buggered, not a single sailboat *all* day. Great winds and little swell; perfect conditions for sailing, and not a dedicated one in the bunch. He was also responsible for providing my lunch. Connors. From off the wharf! He's visiting from Nova Scotia. I didn't have the heart to disappoint his thoughtfulness and efforts. Definitely not the best eating I've had this trip.

It's nearly 2300 hr and there's still a mess of wind on, yet the forecast calls for considerably less tomorrow. There's another tropical storm raging up the coast below us apparently, so we may get the tail end of that. It would be good to get a few nice days together now, to make my way around and off the Avalon — then I'm pretty much home free and even the bad weather days can be utilized. Not like a day such as this has been ill-spent though.

I came ashore on Bell Island the next day for lunch. I'd left many new friends behind that morning, with a tinge of sadness. What was it, so deeply ingrained in my soul, that caused me to yearn so relentlessly for movement? Perhaps it *was* genetically linked, I again suggested to myself. I sighed and wondered if my theory would ever be tested.

"You see caplin dere aroun' ya anywheres, sir?" called one of the two boys standing on the beach where I was to pull in.

154

"Yeah, dere's a few small school. I jus' missed 'em, did I?" I returned.

"Yep, dey come ashore 'bout 'alf 'our ago I 'llow, eh Jimmy," he replied as he turned his attention to his buddy.

Jimmy had a discontented air to him and stood whacking a stick against the sand. He looked wildly out of place on the beach in his proudly displayed hockey jacket and basketball sneakers. He uttered a quick agreement and then continued his abuse of the sand.

"Das some boat ya got. A kayak she's called, right?" exclaimed the more approachable boy. "How far ya come now in she?"

"Started in Port aux Basques over two mont's ago."

"Brudder," he said. "Das a fair 'aul, ain't it?"

I agreed that it was and we carried my boat up a few feet. They were both thirteen and the boy with whom my conversation was conducted was named Peter. He'd a fishing pole in hand and was gloriously content there on the beach in his rubber boots and windblown hair. He proudly displayed his grocery bag full of caplin. He'd collected most of them when they came ashore at the height of the tide. Now he returned to the nearby rock outcrop and was happy to pluck an occasional one out of the water with his line.

"If ya likes, you can take a few wit' ya when ya goes. Mudder says she won't 'ave anymore brought in d' 'ouse," he said with a wicked grin.

"I sees ya got a fire goin'. Per'aps I'll roast a few fer lunch b'fore I goes. How far t' d' store, ya figure?"

He explained the way and before I left to walk, I retrieved the grill from my boat so they could use it over the fire.

"When ya comes back," he said, "I'll 'ave a pile done right good fer ya."

It was a pleasantly warm day on shore again and I enjoyed the extended walk into town. There were many friendly waves as ladies hung out their clothes or as the men worked at the few gardens that I encountered. With Peter's directions I soon found myself at a crossroads where the store was situated. It was a deep green sectioned-off part of an old home. I entered quietly and the friendly jingle of chimes tied above the door announced my arrival.

"G'day, love," I said as an elderly lady entered from her home in the adjoining room, "we got a fine one out dere d'day."

"Well now, where'd you come from, soundin' so happy-like? S'pose I ain't died an' gone back forty years, 'ave I?" she smiled warmly.

"No ma'am, just figured der's no sense usin' d'excuse o' someone else's sad state t' decide me own. An' dey says it takes more effort t' frown den it do t' smile anyways, right?"

"My, my, we got a smart one 'ere and ya manners is in d' proper spot," she continued. "If you was only a couple a year older, sure, I'd get rid o' d' man I got now an' ask ya t' marry me!" She laughed generously at her joke then, before she settled her arms comfortably down and leaned onto the counter.

The room was warm and inviting. The smells of aged wood and lye soap filled the air. "Bay" music could be heard from the adjoining room. My spirits grew to a feverish pitch from the setting, and as I turned to ask her a question, a horse-drawn cart caught my eye through the dusty paned windows of the front of the store.

"Excuse me, love," I apologized as I quickly returned to the door and gazed out. I'd had to look and reassure myself that I'd not hallucinated the fitting image to accentuate the setting. A horse-drawn cart had indeed passed in front of the shop. The horse was then slowly trotting down the street away from me, its five youngsters and an elderly man lurching mildly along to her efforts. The world had suddenly slowed to a more peaceful and harmonious pace.

"Ah, life shouldn'a evolved past that stage," I solemnly whispered to myself. "We coulda sustained ourselves forever on dis beautiful planet, if we'd only been intelligent enough t' keep like dis." I looked longingly at the cart and everything it symbolized. I'd not noticed she'd joined me at the door and stood quietly looking as well.

"Now, where'd ya say you was from?" she asked, taken aback by my interests and comments.

"Notre Dame Bay," I said, still lost in my thoughts.

"Wha's ya surname?"

"Paul."

"Ain't none of 'em round d'ese parts."

I returned to the present and resumed my pleasant chat with the lady. "Ah, d'ere's not much relevance d'ere anyway, girl. I be a bastard's son, I'm afraid."

"Oh . . . ya was adopted, was ya? And ya got a fine fam'ly now?" she inquired.

"D' best kind. I was a lucky one, d'as fer sure," I remarked as I scoured the shelves for natural chocolate.

"D'as all dat matters den, love. Looks t' me like ya been reared up proper."

I stood at the counter then and continued, "In India, 'tis not uncommon fer a woman in d' village who been blessed wit' a number o' children to voluntarily give one of 'er own to an'udder who's been unable t' conceive. Often d'ey'll be livin' in d' same garden. D'ey does it t' strengthen d' community as a whole I figure. As long as d' kid be loved, don't matter sure, really where 'e comes from."

"Yeah," she replied, as she paused to digest what I'd said. "Sound's like a good t'ing t' me. I'm sure ya mudder gave y'up 'cause she figured you'd 'ave better toime of it. Pretty near d' same t'ing, ain't it?"

I reasoned that it most certainly was. "Now, love, I got me a fine cravin' for pea soup when I comes ashore d'night. Ya got any carrots?"

She proceeded to open a bag of them for me and I was instructed to take the amount that I needed. For a turnip, they were all huge so she handed me a knife stating, "Now, ya cut off what ya like, no trouble, sure. I'll just use d' rest fer dinner t'morrow. And ham sure — ya gotta have a few slices o' ham t' put in 'er." She quickly shimmied over to the cooler and proceeded to cut off two thick slices. "Now you take dat stuff now and uh, uh . . . " I'd reached for my purse. "Don't you t'ink o' puttin' ya 'and in dat d'ere pocket!" she ordered. "Dis one's on me, fer takin' d' toime t' come visit me d'day. Now, 'ow long b'fore ya sees ya mudder again?"

"Oh, less den a mont', I 'llow."

"Fer d' love o' God," she said as her eyes shot heavenward. "Well you take dis now."

She firmly kissed me on the cheek and escorted me to the door. We parted warmly and the last words I heard as I rounded the corner of the house were, "Sure, look at ya, you ain't nudding but a bag o' bones. Wish I 'ad ya 'ere wit' me fer a week, we'd fatten ya up."

When I'd gotten a ways up the lane I realized I didn't even know her name, so I quickly ran back. "Ma'am," I said quickly, "I don't even know ya name — and you've been s' kind."

"Mary, child. Me name's Mary."

"Have a good one," I smiled.

"You too."

I skipped out and made a note of her name and that of the store in my note pad. A warm wave of calmness overcame me. "I gotta be doin' som'n right," I said to myself as I headed for the shore.

Peter and Jimmy were sitting around the fire when I returned.

"Had a bit a trouble," Peter began apologizing as I approached. "Dey keep stickin' t' d' grill — got 'em all burnt up sure."

"D'as no odds, sure, we'll eat 'em d' way dey is."

Jimmy seemed unamused and poked clumsily at the fire. Peter and I took a fond liking to each other. We laughed openly at ourselves once we'd gotten into a fine state over the charcoaled mess. During our chat, I mentioned the lovely visit I'd had with Mary, and Jimmy cut in with, "Dat ol' woman? Sure she won't let none of us in d' door no more."

Peter explained, "She been 'elled up a couple a toime in d' past year. She pull a gun on 'em d' last toime. Sure, dey even made fun o' 'er on dat comedy show from SinJohn's. She's always nice t' me d'ough," he said finally, before adding, "I s'pose she 'ad enough."

I left shortly thereafter and bid the two boys goodbye. I saw a lot of myself in that kid when I was his age. I wished them good luck and set my course. There was hope for us all I thought. I'd once played hockey as well.

11

7.27.97 Sunday — Once the caplin were consumed
(well over 2 dozen) I once again bid new friends goodbye
and headed out. Had a lovely paddle — yet I'd not left the
island until after 1900hr. and quickly realized it would be
approaching dark once I found an adequate place to land. No
moon this time. My first real darkness paddle. I was blessed
with an incredible amount of phosphorescence — wild
strands of blue light would stream off my paddle with every
stroke. From nearly 2 miles out I began to hear live traditional
music being played from a town.

Saturday night and they must have been having their
Come Home weekend. The temptation to join them was great
— the music so alluring — but I just needed to sleep in
peace, without any alcohol in my belly for once. I headed for
a point (these newer charts continue to frustrate me and are
inferior to the old ones) which consisted of nothing more than
sunkers and rocky, jagged shore. Retreating into the cove, I
even struck in the darkness. Luckily there was little swell. The
flashlight setup to my souwester that I took the pains to rig

up proved very useful and coming ashore at the beach was no trouble. I'm sure I probably spooked a few folks if they were looking out of their windows.

It's a silly cove really, full of swank houses and although many of them are occupied and within view, I've yet to see any welcoming faces. Too busy being Christians . . .

There are strong winds (and cold) from the north this morning, forecasted to die down, so I'll make my soup and check it out from there.

— bedtime — They didn't die, so I remain. I've had a terribly upset stomach all day though and I'm not sure I'd have left even if the weather was suitable. Walked a bit to try and work it out and napped for awhile before making yet another pot of pea soup (minus the ham!).

Finally saw a few of the local folk (from the older part of the cove) and went for a visit. One gentleman even gave me the use of his store to sleep in. It's dry, roomy and with my bed of a pile of 2x4s, more comfortable than last night's bed of crushed rock. Above all I pray I'm feeling better tomorrow so that I can get out on the water.

I'd been travelling on a challenging sea all morning. A large swell was following to starboard. Maintaining balance was crucial as it combined with a strong southwest wind to my back. Physically it wasn't demanding, though mentally it took a heavy strain.

I came ashore for lunch inside a small breakwater and pulled up on a slipway adjacent to numerous boats, which had remained bottom-up and unused for many seasons. I was joined sometime later by a retired fisherman who'd come down to do some work on his boat.

"Gonna fix 'er up a little I 'llow," he told me. "She ain't been out in a few year, but d'ere's talk d' gov'ment gonna open d' food fishery for a coupla weekend. B'y, I ain't 'ad a good feed o' cod in some toime."

He wandered down to have a look at my boat. "I sees ya jigger dere agin ya seat," he remarked. "Watch out for ya self, b'y. Ya knows it's d' law dat ya can't even 'ave 'em aboard, right?"

"Sir," I replied respectfully, "I ain't too much worried now, whedder dey t'inks I should catch a fish or not! If a man can't go out an' jig 'eself a fish t' simply keep 'eself alive like I been doin', well . . . if dey t'inks dey gonna take me boat fer dat, dey gonna start a war, sir. An' all due t' d' greedy buggers t' begin wit'. No sir, me jigger'll stay right where 'e is, an' I don't care who sees it!" I stood there for awhile, amazed that it was me who had just finished speaking. It was becoming apparent that I'd formulated some opinions on more than simply the art of paddling along my journey.

"Y'ad no trouble wit' d' sea comin' down d' shore dis mornin'?" he questioned, in an effort to change the subject.

"Oh, she was a little 'airy out dere, b'y, but it keeps me on me toes and I makes good time when she's like she is," I answered, thankful that he had. "I'm gonna head out an' make a run for d' Tickle d' once."

"I'd be careful, b'y, she can be a rough spot down dere. Den again, ya come dis far I s'pose."

"Whadaya figure, she's eight mile or so t' dere I 'llow, eh?" I questioned him.

"Yeah da's right. Now ya got a nice town dere too, t'ree mile in," he hinted casually. "Y'ever been dere? B'y, d' cove is still full o' boats, lovely sight. One time dere was as many as a hundr'n fifty boats moored off in d' one cove. Das what dey says now. You should make a stop in dere."

He insisted that I head for the community just inside Baccalieu Island and the tickle, to the point where I was nearly driven back into my boat for relief. I thanked him for the swell chat. I'd still an ample supply of energy and set a goal of rounding the major headland by that evening.

I settled into the challenging paddle and made my way downwind. My course altered a little and the swell now approached from directly to starboard. Within an hour I was fast approaching the most conspicuous and intimidating of headlands, just prior to the approach of the tickle itself. The seas had grown larger. The winds from my back had become much more of a factor, as each stroke of my paddle distanced me further from the shore I'd departed. I grew a little wary, yet was confident that once I'd made the turn into the tickle I'd cut off the factor of the winds completely and it would be an easy paddle from thereon in. It was only to get there. The head drew closer and I felt I was far enough off. The swells now were ten feet high and building.

I suddenly saw a boat approaching from the southeast, riding the swell cautiously as it headed back into port. The swells had grown so high that the boat itself became a hazard, as I was unaware if he'd be able to see me. I'd considered heading for the town only briefly prior to that point, and the boat was to pass very close in front of me. Only briefly could I catch a glimpse of her as she approached, before I was lost again in the trough of a deep swell. She arrived and I had to slow up to let her by. The two men onboard were caught with stunned, incredulous looks, as they encountered the unlikely vessel and her sole passenger out on the most riotous of seas.

They'd just passed and I had resumed full speed when I found myself in frighteningly devilish waters. I saw the thick wall of a cresting roller fast approaching. It had developed too quickly. I altered course and paddled hard towards it, to get myself there before it became a chaotic avalanche of thunderous white water. I reached it in time, but there was no chance to relax, for when I'd reached the summit of the two-story high wave, I'd the dubious view of a vast sea of like-minded rollers that were close behind. The itinerary immediately changed. I simply had to get ashore!

I swung back around in the direction my seafaring buddies had taken only minutes before. To travel directly down those swells would've meant disaster. I immediately realized I'd have to zigzag back and forth along the swells so I could see them clearly, heading up into one sharply if it began to crest too quickly. It was nearly a reverse tack-like routine that I'd decided was safest on several previous occasions.

I looked longingly at my life jacket strapped loosely on the deck ahead of me. Why hadn't I worn it on this tricky leg? No amount of wishful thinking would make it magically appear on my shoulders — and there was no chance of reaching for it then. Emergency procedures began racing through my head. What would I do if I went in? I continued on and finally made the decision to switch back, to face the head again.

In a fraction of a second a thunderous force hit my shoulders and I was buckled over into the churning water. Somehow, I'd instinctively braced enough and the well-centred weight of *Destiny* brought me back upright.

"Hare Krishna, Hare Krishna . . .," I began chanting.

My face had been in the water. I kept my composure and continued on. The tacking was murderous on my psyche. To be so close to the breakwater, yet to safely reach it meant many more drama-filled passes ahead. I struggled nervously on.

I finally reached a point where I felt I was in far enough to cut down across the swell a little more. The first wave nearly sent me somersaulting over and face-first into the sea. It came over my shoulders in a dense crash of white and collapsed the skirt around me, filling the boat with sea water. To refrain from jack-knifing over, I found my head resting on the rear deck of my boat. The stem of her was a three feet under water! We got pummeled over the tip of the wall and miraculously stayed upright.

"Hare Krishna, Hare Krishna," I continued.

Twice more similar situations occurred, yet each one was a little less life threatening as I got further inside the head of land. The sea was churning and frothed. My concentration never waned until I'd slipped quickly around the edge of the breakwater. I paused and sat there.

I was still alive.

No whoops. No hollers.

I'd made it ashore. ALIVE.

I got to see all the moored fishing boats after all.

How could I have been so disrespectful? I lectured myself harshly. "Jesus, you can't just relax because you've left the windward side. You're just as vulnerable on the last leg going into the bay back home as you are anywhere. You fucking goof — you'll *never* see home if you act cocky like that again. Man, you were sixty-five feet from that cliff when you nearly went in."

I was being ruthless, and deservedly so. I sat on the slipway and gazed out at the tumultuous sea that only minutes before I'd found myself in. I was shivering and completely soaked. My self-inflicted rebuke finished, I calmly waited for my heartbeats' return to somewhere bordering on normal. I deeply inhaled the moist, mist-filled air. Pause.

"But brother, you are alive and well!!!" I suddenly shouted. "That was *the* shit, man! I'm off my bloody rocker but shit, it feels good!"

I sprang to my feet. I had attained a heightened, enlightened plateau of consciousness. I immediately began to appreciate all things surrounding me — good and bad, yin and yang, light and darkness. For without one, there *is* no other.

I'd been awakened further.

I'd given little awareness to my surroundings leading up to that moment. It *was* in fact a beautiful cove. The hills were scattered with homes as they sloped down on all sides to the shoreline. It was there that *Destiny* and I found ourselves. I quickly knelt before my girl and touched her glistening skin to my salt-encrusted forehead. "I'll forever be indebted," I whispered softly.

Changing into my warm and inviting clothes was the next priority. I was well in view, yet the stage had arrived where this became crucial. I respectfully crouched beside a nearby shed and stripped the chilled garments from my body. Donning the awaiting clothes had become a most pleasurable experience at the end of each day's paddle. That night it was like reentering the womb.

I returned to the slipway singing and joyous, for there was much cause for celebration. I reached into my stash of chocolate rations and divvied out an extra dose of the sweet treat. I'd developed a routine of rewarding myself at the end of any extended, grueling leg of my journey with a small morsel to encourage and congratulate myself. In that situation I felt it was doubly warranted. I was enjoying it on a near erotic level when I heard a voice from behind state, "B'y, I seen ya come in and 'ardly believed it. I 'ad t' come down."

"Hey, brudder. Aye, she's a fine day out dere now, right," I joked.

"Come on over to d'ouse, b'y, we'll get ya some tea. Ya must be froze."

"Sounds lovely, b'y."

I quickly sealed up *Destiny* from the elements and caught up to the young man. He lived alone with his dog, and it wasn't long before the kettle was whistling away on the stove. Many cups and sea adventures later and we'd developed a fine friendship. He quickly invited me to use the spare room and I thankfully obliged as the weather grew worse outside.

During my stay I was shown the utmost respect and his hospitality was impeccable. And did he have visitors . . . It was a constant stream of new souls to meet while I was there, all shapes, sizes and philosophies — and truly refreshing to see. His kitchen was an assembly for folks coming from all areas of the entire peninsula. The amount of understanding attained there among people with varying ideals and beliefs was incredible. I wondered how much more integrity, dignity and respect was displayed within my friend's simple kitchen, compared with that of the church on the hill.

The following day there were similar scenes. There was complimentary tea for breakfast again and I contented myself with frequent strolls around the cove. There were countless conversations with the local folk as we all awaited the strong southwesterlies to diminish. A considerable amount of time was spent in the company of a number of the fishermen of my grandfather's generation. They gathered, almost religiously it seemed, on the bridge of an old weathered store that overlooked the cove below. I'd stumbled onto their gang when I stepped out to check on the weather. I'd strolled out to the store's ideal vantage point when I saw them contentedly relaxed in one another's company. Like myself, they patiently gazed out over the water's surface, ever entranced with the mysteries it bestowed. With a spry and deliberate jerk of his head, I was silently invited by one of the gentlemen to join them.

"Y'aint afeared o' bein' out dere, son?" asked a white-haired, stoic man who sat quietly with his hands clasped together on his knee.

I felt richly honoured as they all shuffled a little to make a place for me. It also gave me time to formulate an answer to a question to which I wasn't quite sure how to respond. There was little feeling of urgency among them. I realized I felt more comfortable and at ease with those men than I did around those of my own generation.

"Feared?" I began. "No, I s'pose I been out dere long enough now dat if it boddered me like dat, I wouldn' keep at 'er. I been learnin' t' respect 'er d'ough, and dat she don't allow ya too many mistakes."

Many nodded slightly in agreement, so I continued: "Ya can't fight against 'er or she'll swallow y'up right quick. An' dere ain't a day out dere . . . no, ain't an 'our dat dere ain't som'n new she be teachin' ya. I t'ink most folks'd prob'ly make it t'rough som'n like I come t'rough yes'day outa sheer will t' survive I 'llow."

I looked out across the sea then and contemplated. "D' true test o' ya spirit is gettin' up d' next mornin' and goin' out dere again."

12

7.31.97 Thursday — Leaving on Wednesday morning, conditions were acceptable; still high winds from the SW but with little swell and with only 3 miles to the tickle. A warm farewell to my gracious host and I was off early.

Reaching the tickle, I was rewarded for my patience with very close views of two adults and a young humpback feeding in the calmer waters.

All along the leeward shore was fine going. Following another pissing myself session and coming ashore on a small landwash to cleanup, the barometer dropped 8 points and I'm caught in a rain squall and increased winds. It's no trouble rounding the point and slowly making it to the slipway. Ideas of making more progress that day were dwindling, and I was drenched. I'm not ashore 10 minutes before I'm up at a kitchen table, yakkin' yarns with warm tea, and slippers on my feet and awaiting two big bowls of turkey soup. The couple were so kind and interested in my travels, an hour later it's as if I've known them forever.

It's comforting to know that with the people along the coast, their eyes are instinctively drawn to the water and we've always folks watching out for one another. Incredibly, following lunch we look out and a few boats are heading out for the crab. It's all blown off! Clear skies and not a whitecap to be seen. An hour earlier I was preparing to find a store and settle myself down for the week.

Pressing on was definitely in the cards and the afternoon paddle was wonderful — low winds and such a welcome change from the past days. Arriving at the next town, 6 miles up into Trinity Bay, the couple are there to greet me! They'd followed along in their truck and we chatted again for some time. Before leaving she breaks out the camera and photos are requested. I oblige.

Returning from a short walk to the store, I'm greeted at my boat by three fellas, two of whom I'd met at my buddy's place a couple of days earlier. The youngest has got a board and he hangs out on the government wharf and skates most days. "Well Jesus, b'y, dere's nudding else t' do, and I sure as fuck ain't gonna sit 'ome and glare at d' fuckin' tube all day. All d' fellers minds t' do dese days is fuckin' smoke dope, drink beer an' eat! Sure dere's a new ballfield been put up agin d' hill just d' past year. T'ink ya can git a bunch o' fellers t'gedder t' 'ave a game o' ball? Shit. It ain't been used since, 'less dere's a tourn'ment or som'n."

Before they leave, they inform me that there's surfers another 5 miles up the shore. Surfers! Damn, who would have thunk it?

I'm feeling *so* good as I make my way to the reception that I know will be waiting for me, for surfers are universal — at least the legit ones are, as these guys must be I tell myself . . . to be hangin' out in Newfoundland!

The paddle leading up to the surfers reception was wildly intoxicating. Never again could I question the undeniable fate of all things, and the gloriousness of waking with each new day unaware of the joys and kicks to follow.

I approached the slip as a grand, motley crew began to assemble on the shore. There were hands to help me pull *Destiny* above the waterline before any conversation was conducted. It was as if I'd been an integral contributor to the dialogue all along. I'd simply stepped out for a short time and was unquestionably reinstated into the flow upon returning.

"We were in the store, drinkin' our butts and smokin' our coffee . . . the usual mid-afternoon scene around these parts, and I said to Johnnie, 'Will ya look at the point, why's it lookin' so odd?' And we were all stumped with the sight, until you came closer, headin' straight for the slip. We knew you must be a like-minded soul, comin' to visit. Come on up to the pad before you entertain us with some tales. The name's Phil," he said, extending his hand.

We walked the short distance to his home, where I immediately felt at ease. "This is an old store I been fixin' up, with the help of these guys. Been comin' up here for four years now. That outer point you just came in around," he stated as he pointed through the large bay window before us, which provided a stunning panorama of the entire cove, "has got the longest rides on the eastern seaboard at times; she breaks off that point with a nor'east swell and, my friend, fifty-second rides are possible."

We settled into a fine conversation and all the others were properly introduced. There was a young couple, both from the town who'd just finished high school that year, a lady who lived up the road who was a regular visitor and good friend, and another surfer from Massachusetts, who'd also discovered the pleasures of coastal outport life as I had.

"Some fellers I met down the shore told me you was 'ere, met 'em over at Tom's a few days ago," I informed them as I obligingly, for the sake of cultural integration, rolled a cigarette from the generous bag of tobacco which had slowly been making its way around the small group.

"Ha, ha," roared Johnnie. "You 'ad yer run-in wit' Tom den. 'E treated ya well, no doubt."

"Ya know," I assured him. "D' brudder, sure 'e gits more folks t'rough 'is kitchen den d' fuckin' Pope at confession."

We laughed heartily at the memories we'd all accumulated. There was a lengthy segment of sea tales to be relayed. Phil had a fine chart of the entire coastline on the wall facing me, which acted as a great impetus for my recollections.

"B'y, listenin' t' you talkin' and seein' you dere, I'd swear you was d' same feller from up d' shore," commented Johnnie at one point as he turned to his girlfriend. "Don't 'e look d' spittin' image o' Eric Blaire up Plum Cove?" She agreed wholeheartedly. "B'y, ya swear ya was brudders at least," he added.

In an effort to change the insoluble subject, I took notice of the collection of Phil's books that were lying around.

"Y'ever been t' Walden Pond, Phil? Ya got a fine selection o' literature."

"Nah. Some Eagles shmuck decided he'd throw his flaked mentality into 'preserving' it as a memorial to the man. Ends up turnin' it into another plastic theme park and degrading everything the man ever stood for to begin with. Just another example of the Capitalist trash that seeks to milk the life out of every honourable tit that country's ever produced," he responded passionately.

"Ah . . . s'pose I could've assumed as much," I said, disappointed, yet happily noting the man's awareness and apparent grit. I looked forward to any and all private conversations that we would have. The others had quieted, being removed from participation in the segue, so I quickly brought it back to common ground. "She's wonderful-grand, b'y, to see a home wit' no television."

This somehow had the least desired effect, and I found myself surrounded in conversations of "old school" sitcoms. I played along and did my best to remain coherent and audibly active. At times I was completely content to simply listen to the speech of each individual, rather than its content, and I found myself becoming much more tolerant, passive and at ease.

I was developing in ways I'd never felt possible; I began to take notice of even the smallest details in every situation which could bring me pleasure. I was now developing awareness of the endless positives surrounding me — whereas previously, the opposite was true. With fish, my dory was now half full.

It wasn't long afterward that the small store was nearly overflowing with young locals from various communities along the shore. Our friends from Tom's, who'd only hours before informed me of the locale, arrived and the glorious news of a "tear" happening at the "surfers' shack" rippled quickly up and down the shore. There was much merriment and good cheer and Phil pulled me close at one point and remarked, "Seems your arrival's instigated the first official party at my place for the season. Welcome aboard, my friend."

We raucously clinked our coffee mugs together and winked knowingly. We were a number of years older than the massed gathering. We looked around the warmly lit room and relived our own days, when the absorption of mass quantities of alcohol improved one's confidence and sexual prowess, and it was understood as an obvious rite of passage into adulthood by our own misguided culture. We smiled — for without mistakes, we'd've never learned a thing.

Once the influx of testosterone had abated and the room had ebbed to a more intimate number, I found myself sitting beside a beautiful girl. I marvelled at how much I appreciated merely sitting beside her. Having gone without the company of a female for so long, I experienced faint pangs of giddiness and healthy nervousness, which I'd not felt since I'd been in high school. It was delicious. We joked and smiled.

Smiled. She smiled at me and I received nearly as much pleasure from the experience as if eight maids-a-milking *had* in fact seduced me and had all given themselves obediently to my erotic desires. I knew then that the remainder of my existence on the planet would be gloriously spent in spectacular wonderment of all things around me. I suddenly felt the need to be outside. The evening's activities, surrounded by so many people, had been a little too uncharacteristic of my past months' environs.

"Go'n outside, wanna come?" I invited her quietly.

We slipped out. I rushed ahead in immediate awe of the sight which greeted us. A still calm of night had settled the ocean into a hushed slumber. In the northern sky spanning the small cove was a radiating spectacle of silvers, greys and deep cobalt flecks of light within an all-encompassing dome of aurora borealis. No dialogue was necessary. The young girl was soon as entranced as I and we balanced ourselves on an outcropping of rock, as if the additional elevation of mere inches would carry us that much closer to the atmospheric phenomena.

7.31.97 . . . I've met some great guys again and must return for a longer stay; they'll call when there's a good swell in, maybe get over for a surf during my rest week at home.

Phil's a sweet dude and gave me a Big Audio Dynamite t-shirt, novel by Herman Hesse, and small reflector/signaling kit which is handy. I inquired if he'd ever heard John Frusciante play. We've discovered we're both addicted lovers of music. He's blown away when he hears the name and my convictions of John being the finest guitar player since Hendrix.

"Seen him play lots when he was with Thelonius Monster. Man, *how* did you develop like this growing up *here*!?" he asked me with a quizzical grin. "He's seeing my ex-girlfriend right now." The world keeps on getting smaller everyday.

In leaving, he suits up and paddles with me to the bay's end — my first human companion of the journey. Fitting that it would be someone as unexpected in these environs as a surfer!

I've only made it to the outer point with another strong SW gale blowing. I'll see if it dies out. Meanwhile, I need a break from people. I cooked a fine meal (first in many days) and now have the chance to get my head straight and cleared of all past days' kicks, before I jump into a handful of new ones. This is the first time I've written since Tom's.

With Johnnie's remarks of the past evening re: my likeness to a guy down the shore, it's given me incentive to search a little further. There's a lady just up from here who's been helpful. Haven't spoken to her in many moons, perhaps I'll drop in for a visit. From there I may cross over to Random Sound. It'll be the last substantial crossing before home.

2030 hr — As I write, the sun is setting over the Bonavista Peninsula. I've remained here and it's been grand; pretty warm weather and I've been nude all day. The winds are only now beginning to die out, yet it calls for much of the same tomorrow. Being alone all day was great and definitely needed. Tonight will be the first authentic campout prior to St. John's. I've cooked and eaten better food, napped and taken walks, sang and read, thought of girls, fixed gear, and wrote a couple more cards. My levels of patience and natural connection have reached new heights.

My Odyssey continues . . .

Having retired early, I awoke in the morning refreshed and confident. Only problem with making progress on the water were the conditions: gale southwesterlies continued to blow down the entire length of Trinity Bay.

I decided to hike back to the nearby town to enquire about a spring for water. There were no brooks around, and the prolonged dry spell reminded me that I'd have to be very meticulous in maintaining full amounts of water with me. It was a fine walk and I knocked at the first house I encountered. An elderly lady approached and looked suspiciously through the window of the storm door.

"Hello ma'am," I said. "Sorry t' bother ya, but I been campin' out on d' point and waitin' for d' wind t' drop. Don't s'pose I can fill me bottles wit' water at ya faucet, can I?"

She leaned forward slightly and looked down at the two empty containers that I held up for her to see.

"Well . . . I s'pose, son," she answered slowly as she unlatched the door.

"T'anks, ma'am. I realize it might be a tad spooky t' let a young fella into yer house," I reasoned as I removed my sandals, "but I assure ya, I'm a pleasant soul."

I smiled warmly at her husband who was sitting at the kitchen table as I entered and she motioned to where the sink was.

"Where ya come from now, lad? We don't get many come back 'ere dese days, 'specially none's as fit lookin' as y'self. Sure look at ya arms, I'd swear ya been 'aulin' tackle fer years," he noted.

I did take notice then of my arms, and for the first time realized how much stronger and muscular they'd developed over the many weeks of paddling. "Ha. Can't says I noticed 'till now," I said, quietly marvelling. "I been paddling a boat around d' island, sir. I started in Port aux Basques d' last part o' May an' been at it ever since."

"Well," he declared. Before he spoke another word, he motioned for me to sit at the table with a quick nod. "Fill d' man's bottles for 'e, will ya, Mudder?"

I departed with an incredible high, as two senior citizens waved happily from the open door. The stay had been lengthy and I'd welcomed the conversation with the couple in the cool confines of their simple kitchen. Where only a short time before we'd been complete and questioning strangers, now we left as friends. My pockets were filled with cookies, I had a Coke donated to the cause and as I put on my sandals, the lady gave me a quick kiss on the cheek. I was so gloriously blessed, I felt, as I strolled down the lane.

Within an hour I found myself back in "the hood." Smokin' butts and drinkin' black coffee. I didn't even like coffee. Johnnie and his girl had picked me up along the road. It seems they were inseparable; their relationship, as a result, was doomed to failure I predicted.

"Look who we picked up agin d' road," he called out as we entered.

"Wha'd I tell ya, Johnnie? Told ya he'd be back. Bit o' wind again —
got out to the point, did ya?" inquired Phil as he lazily tossed me the bag
of tobacco.

"Couldn' keep me away from all dis fun sure. Ain't 'ad enough o' ya
bad coffee t' do me," I joked as I tossed him the Coke in return.

It felt good to be surrounded by relaxed souls who were unburdened
by the fraudulent pressures of "the American Dream." Phil had understood
that it was not in his nature and rationally decided to head to a land where
it was less smothering. None of us had swank cars, or new clothes . . . or
stuffy dispositions. What we did possess were fine friends and the time to
appreciate them.

"Before you came along, shit, the crowd figured that I was the wildest thing around since sliced bread. Now ya upped the ante a little, brother, makin' me look like a lazy ol' Yank here sitting on my ass waitin' for
swell. That paddle out yesterday got me inspired I'd have to say. It was sad
to see ya leave so soon," he finished.

"I don't know much 'bout inspirin' no one, but d' gods seen fit t'
keep me aroun' awhile longer, so I found me way back," I grinned
wickedly.

Shortly following, Phil and I walked over to his friend's home. The
lady who'd been part of my welcoming committee the afternoon before
greeted us as we entered. She and her husband had two young daughters
and I got to know them quite well during the remainder of my stay. There
was a mammoth scoff of Jig's Dinner awaiting us. I silently asked forgiveness, understood the benefits I'd receive from adopting the diet of my gracious hosts, joyously foresaw the time when I'd return to a completely
wholesome diet, and dug in!

"Dis is some spread m'dear," I complimented between mouthfuls of
turkey and gravied potatoes. "I don't eat no animals or dairy products by
choice normally. Barely touched d' stuff fer four year, until I came home t'
do dis trip. I figured she'd be best if I weaned m'self a little into it, fer
such occasions as dis."

I looked around to see how it was being received. Most were still occupied with the feast, I surmised, so I continued: "'Tis a bit tough fer

folks aroun' d' shore t' understand ya can live better wit'out meat. Most won't believe I come aroun' d' island wit' little more den pea soup, vegetables and soy milk."

"They must think it's pretty strange for a fellow Newfoundlander to have such a peculiar diet to theirs," offered Phil as he lunged lavishly into the turkey's leg that he held.

"It's a tough t'ing t' bring up, b'y. Dere's few I felt comfortable enough wit' dat could benefit from d' topic," I announced as I battled with the remains of salted beef stuck between my teeth. "If ya could git d' folks off d' salt beef even, or git 'em leavin' d' poison in d' stores and returnin' t' just wil' game, sure, dere'd be an immediate change in d' morale an' psyche of d' folks."

"Ya figure's d' meat d'eir feedin' us idn' very good, eh?"

"B'y, I been t' countries, whole subcontinents, sure, where dey lived fer centuries wit'out d' stuff, an' dey ain't ever heard o' heart disease or cancers. Billions, an' it didn' exist. I don't 'ave t' look any furder den dat t' find a connection. Granted now, we lives in a region where a well-balanced diet 'twould be 'ard t' maintain on just split peas an' d' few root vegetables dat we can grow. But wit' d' fish . . . an' I s'pose dey sees fit t' import d' bloody junk food t' all crannies o' d' island. Wit' some intelligence we could git more sustaining products in dere den dat, surely."

Perhaps it was beneficial. Regardless, it was a start and it felt strengthening for me to voice some of my own personal convictions a little more. I'd sat, observed and complimented during the majority of my journey in an effort to understand. Perhaps it was time to begin voicing some of my own ideals again.

8.2.97 Thankfully my system seems to have adjusted a little better now to the occasional onslaught of flesh. Following the turkey/salt beef scoff only a little discomfort is felt. Plans for the evening were put forth soon afterward: a hike back out to the point for a fire and sunset. Phil packed along his gear and spent the night. An hour of talkin' about it over butts and it's developed into the party spot for the night.

The place began to hop and beer was being purchased. A truck ended up in our possession and our band of merry men (now totaling 6, with another load to come) made our way back to the point, which I'd left *many* hours earlier simply in search of water! I was content to listen to the oft bizarre conversation and hum my little tunes while tending the fire, and lay up next to a girl!

Early in the morning, Phil and I found ourselves walking back to the fire after escorting a number of guests out to the road, well over a mile back along the shore. I spent this time recollecting a lengthy tale of my climbing a peak over on the west coast that nearly killed me one year — much to the appreciation of Phil who was a wonderful one-man audience.

Seems something I rarely do is relate to people any of my experiences. In the past I've always remained very self-absorbed and nearly unwilling to open up to others. Perhaps this trip is teaching me as well many of the benefits that can be attained in expressing my feelings more openly to others . . . Hmm . . .

A breakfast of cod, garlic (my contributions), coffee and cigarettes (Phil's) was the shit, and it was evident that yet another adventurous day on land would be spent. And spend it we did! An entire day of hiking along the shore and then doubling back through moose leads and wood-cutting trails. It also saw the first substantial berry pick of the season: a huge fill of plumboys (a cross between raspberries and blackberries), and my first ever bakeapples picked from the stalk. Simply majestic . . .

8.6.97 Was I conceived thru an act of love? Above all else, this is the question I'd ask of my mother. There's forever been a void, which no physical journeys can fulfill, and no degrees of insight, meditation or reflection can penetrate. Is it possible to continue a spiritual development forward with so many questions from my past left unanswered? Am I even prepared for some of the things I may discover?

I may be caught on a pendulum. At times I feel it doesn't matter, that I've evolved into the person I am due to my environment. But then I listen to my heart further and realize this is rubbish. I've observed other families and have begun to see clearly how their thoughts, actions, deeds are nearly predestined in them through their genetic makeup and their ancestral history. As I grew, I began to see this within my own family as well. They all accept me fully and regard me as an unquestionable equal — yet I continue to feel betrayed. Not by them, or even by my biological parents . . . but by my history.

Through no fault of my own I continue to know nothing of my ancestral background. Did my forefathers feel a kinship with the sea as I do? Is this why I'm drawn to it? Further reasons being unrequired . . . Then, above all else, I feel I must know — was it an act of love which destined my arrival into this world?

I've been away from this homeland for so long. It's now that I've returned that these questions and yearnings have culminated once again. One day it's going to be too late — folks are going to pass on, and the past is going to be buried along with them. I've exhausted all known avenues in search of some truth. It merely ends in frustration and more questions. The bureaucratic red tape of getting access to existing files was so formidable. Inquiring did reassure me of one thing I guess. I'm certainly not alone.

Tonight I feel quite like Thoreau himself for I find myself in a small, abandoned shack. Comforting fire in the stove; hell, even a radio for some evening listens of Liszt and Rachmaninov. The crossing went well — a considerable stretch of open water, 20 miles. The paddle in Random Sound the following morning was beautiful, as I've finally returned to the densely wooded areas of the northeast shore — getting close to home.

The stay with friends was a special treat yesterday and she spoiled me silly. Heck, I was nearly ill from being fed *so* much while there. We fixed up my spare skeg that I'd been meaning to do since the troubles. Seems I've learned to protect the stern with a piece of driftwood all the time now, and I've had no further mishaps. I even got some new threads out of the visit. She begged me to stay longer, yet I could feel the distant yearnings of the oceans beckoning for my return. I've been held up for awhile so I'm content to now be moving again.

The family have expressed interest in meeting me below Terrra Nova Park somewhere for this weekend. This would be wonderful, but to plan it to correspond with the time they get off is difficult — considering my mode of travel and factors of weather. I trust they can understand this.

A small fishing boat with two men aboard approached shortly after I'd rounded the final point of land for the day. They cut the engine and drifted toward me. The day had been long and enjoyable, as I'd met no one else and my thoughts had remained positive.

But I welcomed conversations such as theirs as our voices carried poignantly over the short span of water between us. They tended to be clear and uncluttered and, strangely enough, nearly always uproariously funny. They were soaked with the dry wit and sarcasm I'd learned to tolerate, and even understand, during my trip. For it's apparent that the closer two people are and the stronger their relationship, the more comfortable they are with spraying one another with brash insults and degrading comments as a warped form of admiration and even love. I think it's developed in this culture largely due to the environment and harsh climate surrounding the people. For to survive here, we soon weather ourselves on the exterior, like the granite cliffs and gnarled timber about us, as an instinctive barrier to better absorb the harsh occasions that will inevitably occur. To show open affection toward a friend is rarely seen among the males of this island. It exists of course, as in most cultures. It's just a little more poetic, more subtly administered through a wave of personal jibes and jokes.

"B'y, you'd 'ave trouble 'aulin' any gear in dat t'ing, now wouldn' ya?" remarked the eldest of the two once the engine had quieted. "Where ya come from now in she?"

"Port aux Basques, b'y, not dis marnin' now mind ya," I answered proudly.

"Lord Jesus, you 'ave come a ways den," he said as he stood shaking his head. "Sim 'ere don't talk much. Right queer fer a Newf t' begin wit', I know, but 'e figured ya was DFO when we seen ya out at d' point. But I says t' 'e, 'Sim! Dat feller's rowin' out dere. Das work, b'y. Since when you see d' gove'ment do any o' dat?'"

I looked at the young man. He was my age and very sturdily built after such a short lifetime of harsh physical work. There was a gleam in his eyes as he looked at my boat admiringly. "Any fine spots t' camp, b'y?" I called over.

"B'y, we just goin' out t' check our net. Didn' see 'er when ya come in did ya," he snickered brazenly. "Head fer dat point ya seen us comin' from. Dere's a beach in dere ya can 'aul up on. We'll show ya a toime fer a night I 'llow, wa Sim?"

He grinned wildly and gave the outboard a mighty haul of her cord, and the engine sprang alive. There was no need to await a response and with two swift jerks of their heads in recognition, they quickly left me in their wake. I continued on in the direction he'd prescribed and curiously speculated on the unorthodox occasions that were sure to follow.

There were a few more men loitering about the stage when I came around. The initial looks of bewilderment, for which I'd developed a fondness, welcomed me ashore. They all seemed a little uncomfortable and preoccupied, as I recall. As I changed quickly and grabbed a light snack I gave it some thought, before joining them up on the wharf adjoining the stage. "Gone to haul their net . . . An assorted bunch on the wharf . . . Oh shit, ha — they're waitin' t' pickup!" I soon surmised.

Anxious to verify my Holmesian intuition, I waited along with them for the fishermen's return. A couple of them grew increasingly more anxious with the unexpected arrival of this strange "water dude," which resulted in most unstimulating conversation.

The two gallant warriors soon returned and there was evidently little time for chit-chat until all cargo was covertly unloaded into the inner sanctuary of the stage. It was there that the scene unfolded, one that had been replayed for over five hundred years in every cove and cranny that the island harbours, up until the past half dozen. I contentedly had a "ginnie," as the others did, and marveled at the fine catch.

Codfish. The staple of existence for our humble and stoic race.

The sweet smells of kelp and musty sea water mingled with that of sweat and blood and tears. The slickers were fastened up and the bystanders graciously retreated to a safe and unhindered vantage point. The table was thrown a bucket of sea water, while the sound of knives being sharpened sliced into our eardrums. The masters of their art methodically stood back and hitched up their sleeves in preparation. The ancient, grey wood of the stage was speckled and muddled and stained with the blood and slime of countless other occasions. The seasons of constant additions to the decor had seen the walls' transformation into a near resemblance of the fishes' spotted skin in return.

A tense uncertainty filled the air, which grew tighter and grittier with each passing moment. All who were present seemed to understand what was required in order to relieve the immense pressure that had filled the room. The panel facing the sea had remained open — it was there that I stood, on its threshold, half of me within the sanctuary of the past while the other precariously stumbled along with the future. It was as if the entire structure had been violently cast into the sea, with a weighted cement anchor plummeting us all into the depths.

The pressure increased.

The first fish was reverently removed from the bucket. It was ceremoniously laid on the dampened, dimpled surface of the table. Everyone held their breath. The knife was revealed and all eyes followed its slow arc, as it rested softly on the whiteness of the flesh. The altar had been prepared. The sacrifice ensued.

Fissshh . . .

The knife deftly found its mark and the methodical carnage began. Immediately, enthusiastic conversation filled the air and there was a communal sigh of relief. The boys had returned safely and the mass devastation had once again avoided them. They'd lived to continue their ingrained, unflinching heritage for another day. The ocean was *their* keeper — they'd done nothing wrong.

The heads had been split, the tongues and britches savoured — the flesh nearly worshiped. Once the stage had been cleaned, the entrails were all that remained. Yet even those would be utilized, once the receding tides had distributed them amongst the grateful organisms with which the cod in turn would replenish itself.

The men had all retreated happily to their respective homes each with his small bounty from the sea, which the two men I remained with had provided. They felt no remorse for what they'd done, nor did I after what I'd witnessed. Nothing was wasted. From their reports, they'd gone no further than the point to set out a small net that saw them feed themselves and a great percentage of the community, which they'd dedicated their lives to living in. The fish were large and clearly the thickest, healthiest ones I'd ever seen. They were catching them in an area that even their grandfathers could never recall finding them. In the quietness of the late evening and following the commotion and excitement of being "outlaws," we stood on the wharf and sighed, wondering if our children would ever witness a scene like that which had just transpired.

It was John who'd met me out in the boat with his young friend Sim, and he who spoke then: "D' crowd in SinJohn's, b'y, dey won't be satisfied 'til dey 'aves ev'ry kid on d' islan' stuck wit' 'e's 'ead glued to a computa, sure. Make's no sense, b'y. It ain't what we knows . . . and it ain't right," he said quietly in the stillness. His over-anxious nature had softened to a gingerly calm as subtly as that of the dusky sky before us.

"B'fore we knows, dey'll 'ave de 'ole world turned inta robots," whispered Sim. They were the first words I'd heard him say since we'd met. I had to leave and get something, *anything,* from *Destiny* after he spoke. I was suddenly very scared for the world again.

I returned, having put on my jacket and was met with a request. "Sim, 'e's wonderin' could 'e 'ave a try at ya boat. 'E damn near killed o'er two 'unerd seal 'eself last win'er, and 'e still ain't got d' balls t' ask ya," John frankly informed me.

I immediately brightened with the thought. "Well lord jeez, I been waitin' for d' time when someone was gonna ask. Took me dis far t' find a feller willin' t' give 'er a go! You're damn right ya can try, b'y," I said enthusiastically.

I gave him a couple of simple tips and let him go. Within minutes he was accustomed to the kayak's responsiveness and off he went. I rejoined John on the wharf and we watched as Sim effortlessly paddled away.

"B'y, I swear, ya checks 'e's fingers ya'd find 'em webbed. Take to d' water? My son, you never seen d' like," spoke his friend admiringly. "And 'e's fine 'ead too. Sharp as d' cock in d' marnin' fer gettin' me up an on d' go. And strong . . . oh, my son!"

Listening to him speak so affectionately of his friend and fishing companion, I stood in envy as I became aware of the many years it had

taken to develop such an inseparable bond between the two men. I wondered also, what with my roaming nature, would I ever discover those feelings of deep camaraderie and dedication to another human being?

We ascended the hill to Sim's house once he'd returned and I'd set
myself up in the loft of John's store for my evening's sleeping quarters.
The paddle and extended talks on the waterfront had made him late for
supper. We found his parents shucking bakeapples on the kitchen table and
I was quickly allowed access to the bathroom for a shower. I emerged
shortly thereafter to a plateful of potatoes, peas and bologna, which I graciously devoured before I realized it was the leftover plate that had awaited
Sim's return.

"Ah Sim, b'y," I apologized, "I didn realize dere was only enough fer
one. Sure, ya shouldn'a give me ya meal, brudder, after you been workin'
all day. An' den I come into your home an took ya meal . . . I feels terrible
now, b'y."

"No trouble, I'll grab som'n, b'y. No trouble," he said quietly.

"'E figured 'twas d' least 'e could do, right. See'n ya let 'e try ya
boat. Not many fellers'd be as keen as you was t' let 'e go off wit' ya gear
like dat," added John from the living room.

It didn't help how badly I felt. "Sorry, b'y," I said sincerely, unable to
let it go. "I wish I'd known . . . "

"Ferget it, b'y. Come join us fer a beer out on d' bridge now, luh,"
he invited further.

We stood on the bridge and the beer softened our spirits further. We
delighted ourselves with tales of growing up as youngsters in the small
outports. Darkness fell and it was understood that the proceedings were to
change locales, to a nearby shed.

Within, there were already a number of neighbours gathered around
in a circle, seated on upturned beef-buckets and beer cases. The one bare
bulb in the ceiling seemed to be the nucleus of the proceedings. I'd discover that it was the depot for men of the community to drop by and exchange their meagre currency for the more prized commodity that was
available, the highly revered codfish. There was security in numbers of
course, and others simply gathered to tell a few yarns and socialize. At one

point there may have been as many as ten men seated facing each other. And with nearly half as many conversations criss crossing each other simultaneously, I was lost many times when two or three questions or comments were directed toward me at once.

With one gentleman I'd felt reassured that I, in fact, *had* been invited to his house for breakfast the next morning. This understood, I then relaxed and quit trying to concentrate on the dialogues. I'd been too long removed from such an environment of having to lip-read and quickly spurt out half sentences in an effort to be understood. It was a skill to which I'd grown unaccustomed.

> 8.8.97 Holy Marathon Man . . . I've had some crazy kicks and sweet times. The weather's been magical. I'm exhausted. I left early this morning to the tune of a couple brothers informing me that "the Mafia" would be passing me today. Again they've heard tell it's been towed around the entirety of the island by a Coast Guard vessel. Nothing surprises me anymore. Nice to see the folks finally becoming aware of the farce and decadence which is our governing party. I'd an idea of making a banner to fly off my boat in protest when she went by: YOU'RE SUPPORTING A GENOCIDE. But later reasoned that I must have been napping in the midday heat when the circus passed by. Nearly rode down a swell onto the back of an unsuspecting humpback. He surfaced out of nowhere — It was a trip!

> BIG swell again. A magical time at Cape Bonavista. The spires and rock formations are wild and very reminiscent of the passages I'm currently reading from Homer. Conditions were god-sent again and winds changed as I approached, making another big crossing possible for the evening. Countless times have the winds shifted perfectly for my course. Good karma, baby!

> I need much time to write, yet weather is so alluring and the folks await . . . Must sleep.

185

8.12.97 — Been paddling every day since my last break: 29, 12.5, 19.5, 35, 31, 20, 31, 20 miles. Finally . . . a little time to try and get my head straight. It's been such a mad trip these past nine days; since leaving the surfing scene it's been 200 miles and few breaks later. It still amazes me where I find myself — camped out on the Windmill Brook with my siblings.

Many days ago it seems, I'd paddled into a cove of Bonavista Bay with a strange craving for peanut butter and partridgeberry jam sandwiches. I left with a belly full of salsa and chips, and macaroni salad with massive black olives and crab. Black olives — here!

Entering, I see an old-school skiff set up with a canvas sail and sculling oar, and the man is slowly making his way across the small cove. It was truly beautiful to behold. I'm still disappointed as to the few sailing craft I've encountered. They were a lovely couple and refreshing to speak with, as they've travelled much as well. They were hosting relatives at their home so I kept pretty quiet. They showed much interest in my trip, as I did in theirs, as they've only just returned from southern France. Paul and I speak quite openly of my experiences in India and of his continued disillusionment and disgust for the mindsets of many Canadians. Would've loved to have stayed and spoken with him more; the invitation was there, yet the family would be awaiting my arrival on the other side of the sound early the next day. I pressed on again. . .

I had a fine campsite out in the islands, and the feast of PB & J was divine. The area is very inviting and only one vessel was seen — the supply/passenger boat. Did catch a glimpse of two kayaks pulled up on the beach, yet it was early and there was no sign of life from the tent. Again, I pressed on because I had people waiting.

This past week's sprint has jeopardized a few of my objectives for this trip, all in an effort to join up with the family. I've risked injury and worked myself senseless. I guess kicks will be had regardless.

Shine on Crazy Diamond . . . but bullocks to schedules!

The visit with the family was nice, yet I feel there's so much they don't understand about me. And how will they unless I begin to open up to them more? I struggled the entire time to find the courage to enquire about my reception at home to come — a simple request that no meat be present. I can't understand why I've trouble being honest and open with my own family, as in this case. Am I refraining 'cause I'm hoping they'll discern these things themselves? They've all helped me incredibly during the journey, but I feel I remain selfish and stubborn and unappreciative. I continue to reveal my true nature, my thoughts and feelings to complete strangers, but create a giant mask between the ones I truly love and myself.

Evening now, following a swell day of rest and relax-ation. Brother and I spent majority of it fishing the pond and brought back 9 fine sized trout, which made for a grand supper. I've been eating very well thanks to the efforts of Sis, and hope to have much more energy tomorrow.

Back at it with renewed enthusiasm.

This is the first time the three of us have been together in a setting like this since we were kids. Very nice. It amazes me how similar those two are.

I've had very few thoughts of anything these past days, for I've just been struggling to make a predetermined location. Tomorrow I return to a more spontaneous and uninhibited flow. Oh yeah . . .

PS: This is the first time I've been exposed to campsite environs. What's with the mongolian motorhomes?! I was so exhausted last night that an earthquake could've occurred and I'd have been undisturbed. But the report from the siblings is that some guy next to us had a generator going until 0200hr. To power his fucking television!!?

Michael,

I have always believed that nature is a very powerful force. Beautiful, yet more powerful than any other force imaginable. This power sometimes instills a sense of fear in my mind. A force that makes me anxious, nauseous, and today, scared for your life! As children, camping along this shore was memorable and feelings surfaced that I thought would be fun and reminiscent to experience as adults.

The weather today however, has been synonymous with my feelings since you paddled to shore with the breakers several days ago. I had forgotten how rough and treacherous the ocean can be. The sky being drab and dismal, almost angry, only exemplifies the dread I feel as the cold, grey waves crash upon the sandy beach. I forbid myself to look to the rocky shoreline, as I can hear the waves crashing, exploding with an unimaginable force. It's been a wonderful few days with campfires, fresh trout, roasted garlic, and outhouses, but in my mind when thoughts may drift, I am afraid that nature this time may be a little too powerful for my liking.

You always rely on all things natural to fulfill the necessities of life, to feed you, to clothe you and to provide warmth. In our geographic area we don't experience natural disasters such as earthquakes, tornadoes or hurricanes, and we tend to take for granted our natural existence, sheltered from the storms that may be life threatening. I envision you paddling against the breakers and with all my faith in you and God, I pray your journey will not extend my list of natural disasters.

Now as you sit in your boat, a lot of memories flash through my mind, ensuring me that you would never be careless. Despite the seemingly fatalistic life you lead, I know you are calculating the waves and when they will break. Your calculations prove to be accurate. Your experience, strength and ambition get you through the breakers, and those qualities at this particular moment remind me that you have always had them. Sometimes I tend to forget, yet once again you have gained my respect.

As we stand on the beach, unable to move, unable to speak, we wait until you are out of sight. Then my heart starts beating again and my nausea subsides. I know you'll accomplish this goal and every other goal that you set for yourself.

Please take care!

Love, sis.

Perhaps I'd been a little too anxious for the improvisation of coastal life to return. For in my desire to reinstate the sun and moon as the catalyst for my movements, I found myself in a situation not entirely unfamiliar to me by this time.

I'd left my siblings to return home by land, while I engulfed myself again in the challenges of reuniting with them via a more "advantageous" route. The morning had been damp and a biting chill was to be felt in the air — one which reminded us that summer, after her quaint visit to our shores, had perhaps grown restless as well and was intent on making an imminent adieu. I found myself in a cantankerous forty knot gale of wind. It was in crossing Deadman's Bay that the conditions had developed and the result was a grueling, three-hour physical struggle with the elements, across a mere three and a half mile stretch. The weather had deteriorated so dramatically that I felt an attempt at turning in the sharp seas to return downwind was unwise. I pushed on and slogged my wearied body towards the leeward shore. I was thankful that the test had been conducted immediately following my day of rest. It would've spelt disaster had it come during my nine-day, 200-mile paddling marathon.

I gratefully pulled ashore inside a slip and had little time to gather my thoughts before I was surrounded by inquisitive and stupefied locals. There I stood for an hour, retelling tales of past days and shivering violently from the inactivity.

"Ya don't mind comin' across stretches o' water like dat? Most o' d' crowd sure, yer lucky t' git 'em out o' d' house, days like dis," said a man comfortably from the warm confines of his idling truck.

"Oh, I don't s'pose, b'y. Ya gotta expect times like dis along d' coast, don't matter what time o' d' year," I chattered back. "Makes y' appreciate d' fine stretches all d' more, sure. De natives . . . before we come along an' messed 'em up, sure dey'd go t'irty mile offshore t' d' Funks in d' spring o' d' year. I 'llow I can dabble me way along d' shore wit' dat in mind."

There was little recognition from any of the men present concerning my mention of the native people and their awesome paddling trips offshore to the Funk Islands to hunt. It was as if no amount of time could transpire that would soften the effects of such a terrible period in our history. I searched for a topic that would get the crowd talking again, as difficult as it was in my numbed state.

"Saw a shark a few days back, o'er on d'udder side o' d' cape. First one I e'er come across. Must o' been a Thrasher I 'llow. Dere was talk of a few of 'em up Conception way, a few weeks back . . . I been back at d' park wit' me brudder an' sis . . . yeah, d' shark was makin' some fuss atop d' water, 'ad just grabbed a seal when I come along, I s'pose."

"Son, ya lips is blue, luh," said the man in the blue truck, "git aboard, I brings y'up t' d' 'ouse fer a shower."

That afternoon I visited three separate homes as I walked through the windswept sheeted rain that had developed. I was grateful to the folks who invited me in, as it had become apparent I'd worked myself far too hard the previous week. Only now did my body begin to show telltale signs of how much I'd endured.

I'll forever remember walking the dampened streets and being mildly amused at the hallucinations I experienced. The road itself became a malleable liquid, as that of the surface of the ocean. It rippled and sagged with the effects of the wind. I'd look to the surface of the bay itself, and then return to the road which stretched out at my feet — both were nearly indistinguishable.

There were times when I'd worked on charter boats the previous summer, that I experienced similar visual manipulations. Another fisherman explained later that it was simply the brain's inability to adjust to the solid surface of the land, following extended stretches of being soaked with visions of an ever changing one, coupled with exhaustion.

I spent that evening in the driveway of a house across the road from *Destiny*. As I settled down on hardened dirt, anxious for sleep, I listened for a long time as the angered winds whistled past the telephone wires above my head. They were reminiscent of harsh January storms. I also slept with my winter tuque on that night. In a short time I was planning a return to the southwest coast by vehicle, in an attempt to complete the rounding of the entire island with a late-season paddle down along the Northern Peninsula. How rational an endeavor was this, I wondered.

"'E ain't up yet," I heard the voice of a woman saying when I woke. "We was off t' bingo an' 'e was out dere already asleep when we come 'ome. D'ere's no need fer d' like o' dat, 'e bein' out dere like d' dog all night. I 'llow 'e musta been put t'rough d' ringer yes'day."

I had in fact woken at dawn as usual, long enough to poke my head outside and contentedly enough returned for an extended sleep. The weather had remained devilishly uncivil. A few hours later I was stirred by a pickup truck's arrival in the driveway and quickly got dressed to greet the visitor who'd apparently come calling.

"Hello," I said to the elderly gentleman who'd remained at the porch door talking courteously with the lady. The weather had improved and I arose revived and optimistic. "She's a little better den she was earlier dis mornin', wha'?"

"So, ya *was* up den. I figured if ya come dis far, like d' crowd said ya did, ya didn' do 'er by sleepin' in ev'ry mornin'," he replied with a grin. He quickly informed me I was to join him for breakfast over at his home. Without further ado we hopped into his truck and drove the short distance.

"B'y, I never 'eard you was come 'til an hour ago. If I'd o' knowed, ya wouldn' o' slept out on d' ground las' night. M'name's Bart'olomew," he said as he turned up into the lane.

"I got no trouble wit' sleepin' out, sir. D' folks aroun' helped me enough as it was, an' in d' mornin's it's better if I can git up an' not bodder anyone wit' me risin' early."

"Well said, lad. Ya reminds me of m'self when I was ya'age. Now, I s'pose ya likes bologna," exclaimed Bartholomew as he led me into the house.

His wife and visiting daughter had yet to rise and we had a quiet breakfast together. Once we'd finished I inquired, "I noticed ya fine garden out back. Mind if I go an' take a look?"

His eyes widened and he smiled, "Yes, b'y. Ya likes t' grow a few plants ya self now, do ya? Ain't many yer age got much use fer dat stuff anymore. Dey'd radder 'ave dere chips an' Coke from d' store. 'Tis a shame, b'y."

"I've only done a bit m'self. Been movin' too much. One o' dese years, God willin', I'll find me a place t' grow me own," I said wishfully as we stood overlooking the vegetables.

"Once ya find's yaself a girl, lad, she'll settle ya down and ya can grow all ya likes den," he reassured me.

"Agh!" I said forlornly, "like ya said, all dey cares fer now is dere bloody Coke an' chips. Ain't many aroun', sir, got much interest in livin' d' way I feels is right. I'd radder go it alone sure, den live d' life most is livin' on d' mainland."

"Oh, son," he reprimanded me, "ya don't 'ave t' go as far as dat t' see d' sad way folks is livin' nowadays." He turned to face in the opposite direction and continued. "Take d' crowd next door sure. De gove'ment's made 'em so damn lazy, dey ain't wort' d' air der breathin', really. Dere gettin' new siding put on d' house. Sure dey ain't even got d' energy t' do it derselves. All welfare! While dey sits in dat house and watches der friggin' soaps an' rolls der cigarettes. I don't see no garden bein' kept, no animals. Nudding t' help derselves. If d' crowd in Ottawa or wherever dey says dere from . . . if dey 'ad any sense dey'd let 'em starve for a time —

192

be d' best 'elp dey could give 'em I says. Dey'd come aroun' den, an' realize dey ain't gonna get pampered no more. Den *dat* crowd feels so bloody self-righteous dat dey *loves* keepin' d' folks dependent on 'em; makes 'em feel all powerful and important like. Ah, son, she's in a fierce state, b'y . . . a fierce state. I ain't gonna live t' see wha's gonna come of it all. I fought Hitler o'erseas t' see d' folks come t' dis." He stared blankly at the desecrated lot next to his then, and his eyes became distant and tear-filled.

I left the gentleman shortly afterward and headed for the point to check on the conditions. But more importantly to think over all that he'd said.

In returning to town later in the afternoon, I approached another man as he was picking the few bakeapples that were scattered throughout the bog. "Skipper," I called as I watched him plop one of the divine gifts into his mouth. "I come out figurin' d' bog would be full sure, dere only just ready t' pick now, right."

"Yes, b'y. 'Tis d' best year for 'em dey says since '54! D' bogs' *was* covered wit' 'em. I never saw nudding like it," he answered dreamily, as if it had been a phenomenon he'd never again bear witness to. I began to walk on when he continued, "Dey been out sure, weeks ago snippin' d' 'ard berries from d' plants wit' scissors! In some b'jesus mad rush t' git more den d' rest . . . got d' plants ruined, b'y . . . ruined."

He shook his head in despair while I continued on dejectedly. How was anything going to survive the shortsightedness and lunacy of the human race? They'll wonder why, ten years from now, there's no bakeapples to be found on the bogs. We've only ourselves to blame for the raping of the land. How long before we comprehend that we can't eat rock?

13

Setting my final course for home, I began reflecting on the many experiences I'd encountered: the challenges, the friendships, the glorious splendour of Mother Earth, and the many heartfelt tales that had been told to me.

Had I changed as a result? If so, was it for the better? My conversations with Bartholomew and the man on the bog had lingered with me long after I'd departed their shore. But the exchanges hadn't swelled within me a hurtful bitterness or near neurotic despair that only months earlier I would have struggled to overcome. Did this mean I'd become less sensitive? I'd developed into a happier, contented individual, but was my integrity going to suffer, as I refrained from letting all gross indecencies affect me so personally? Was I being as selfish in my desire for personal contentment, as those folks were who'd been out greedily raping the bogs? Perhaps I'd struck on some questions which would take a lifetime in approaching any satisfactory answers. Maybe there weren't any.

Of all the hospitalities the inhabitants of this rugged coast had given me, it was their uncompromising dedication to their families which had been their greatest gift. This support for one another, to see them through, was the most admirable and life-affirming characteristic I'd ever witnessed.

I know now that no person should walk alone through the formidable troughs and chasms of life. I'd discovered many of the glorious beauties that overcoming these challenges revealed. My convictions hadn't strayed and I'd not begun to question any less. I merely discovered that more could be accomplished through acts of love and patience than could ever hope to be attained through contempt and denial. I'd become less jaded and cynical toward the ever-changing world around me. Confucius said, "There is beauty in all things, but not everyone sees it."

Perhaps there was some relevance within the church, the schools, the government. If I had no clear answers on how to improve the system as a whole, did I have any right to condemn it? I know what I must do for myself to exist with purpose and relevance. Yet these things, quite often, are in fact useless for others. It was unjust for me to dictate to others how they should live their lives. If I was conducting my life honestly, then folks would see this for themselves. There was much to unlearn, I told myself that day, and if destiny felt it was useful I had my entire life in which to ponder, experiment, and discover.

So it was, that my head was full of fragmented theories and philosophies then, as it is now in writing about it. And while I searched for truth, I needed to feel reassured that I wasn't alone, that I had support from those that I'd been neglecting as a result. A sign for me that in some way they understood a little more clearly why it was I'd been struggling with the society by which we were all surrounded. I could remain optimistic and beneficial to the planet, as long as I felt I was being instrumental in my positive actions toward it.

As I drew closer, and closer, my oft unexpressed love and appreciation for my family grew all the more stronger. For along the familiar shore of my childhood came the enthusiastic cheers from mother and father, sister and brother. It *didn't* matter that I wasn't of the same blood. As Mary had said, "So long as dey loves ya, dere was no odds where ya really come from."

I had to slow as my eyes became blurred and I was overcome with the emotion of such a long journey.

There were old school friends and neighbours there who were ecstatically blowing whistles and banging drums. I slowly drifted in among the clatter and bangs of the jubilant reception. There were exuberant bear-hugs of congratulations from buddies and warm, emotional ones from my family.

My great-grandfather had even made the effort to come welcome my arrival. I immediately sprinted up to where he was seated. There sat a man for whom I held so much respect and admiration, for him and his generation who had been subjected to so many incredible changes — as I would, provided I'd the opportunity to witness some more of them. "Well, well, well . . . ya made it aroun' after all," he repeated as he took my hand in his.

The weathered and powerful presence of those hands, an undeniable reminder of the proud and honourable life he'd endured. As he held me in those wonderful clutches, with thankfulness and pride, and I looked around me at all the inspired and optimistic family and friends who had gathered on my behalf, I'd never have to question again whether or not I had their support.

14

"Mom," I began a little reservedly, "I don't s'pose I was breast-fed as an infant, was I?"

"No," she replied simply as we sat alone at the kitchen table. She was diligently repairing some of my clothing.

"How 'bout yer own two . . . were they?"

"No," she repeated as she stopped sewing and turned her full attention toward me. "Back den, no one really did that. It wouldn' really accepted. The general understanding was that d' formulas that were out were better fer your child. 'Twas also seen to be easier and more convenient. When we got you sure, they'd already been feeding you Carnation milk fer weeks."

I was amazed at what I was hearing and became bitter and enraged at the thought of how much the majority of my generation's development had been stunted, by mass acceptances of such profound fallacies. "How could d' folks be so easily persuaded against something you must've realized was *so* essential?" I continued in bewilderment.

"Everyone was so young when dey began 'avin' kids, Michael. Ya didn' really question what d' medical folks told ya. An' it was how everyone else raised dere kids."

"Well, jesus, Mudder. Didn' yer own mudders an' grand-mudders 'ave any say in d' matter?" I barked at her in frustration. "I'm assumin' *dey* was raised a bit more naturally. Didn' yer own bodies, sure, tell ya what was right an' proper? I jus' can't figure how such a fundamental. . . gift, fer a developing child could be so easily disregarded."

I pleaded with her for some insight, some understanding of how, why, the people were so easily misled. In response I received a look of hurt.

I'd been home for a day.

My often insensitive inquiries and remarks, in efforts to comprehend, were once again met with hurt feelings and consciences. I dearly wanted to be open and objective with the members of my family, as I did with everyone. Yet whenever I began voicing my opinions or questions, they were often met with confusion and disappointment toward my unconventional ideals, to which they'd a difficult time relating.

I told myself I'd been fortunate enough to observe the lives and beliefs of so many around the world, while my family, who'd lingered here, had no way of comprehending all that I'd witnessed. My remaining quiet, uncommunicative and reserved created unwelcome results, while voicing my opinions and ideals seemed to dissociate myself further from them. I began feeling trapped and detached in my own home. How could this be — that I ended up hurting the people I loved the most? The faults were clearly my own, yet I had little idea of how to rectify them.

I'd made phenomenal efforts to seek understanding with the people along the shore. Even with those on the other side of the planet. But there I was in my own home, after all I'd felt I had learned, displaying minute levels of patience and understanding with my own family. I was frustrated and disgusted with my own inconsistencies. My only solution was to run away again.

Regardless of the lateness, or the dangers involved, within three days I was headed again for Port aux Basques and the southwest coast. It was obvious that I could be of little benefit to my family until my dream was fulfilled. The problems that were evident took a back seat to my selfish desires.

I'd still a long way to go.

8.21.97 Here I am — at it again.

Most of the time spent confused and uninterested. Uninterested! I'm paddling on the ocean and I was uninterested! The trip home wasn't too beneficial, was it?

The family's gotten me so frustrated and I've not the courage to voice any of my concerns to them — or if I do, it comes out very tactless and hurtful. I'm questioning now, if setting this goal of rounding the island has been a setback to the full potential of this trip.

The seas were the calmest I'd ever witnessed the Atlantic — perhaps I'm being permitted some leniency, in Poseidon's understanding of my preoccupied thoughts.

8.23.97 Yesterday saw my return to a contented and focused state. If I persevere, I'm confident that even the most formidable obstacles shall be overcome.

Spectacular, untouched (even uncharted) coast, many seals and birdlife, including 5 grey herons. Offshore, gusting 35 knot winds have kept me ashore all day, yet I'm content to absorb this rustic, Thoreauian atmosphere I find myself in. A warm fire and oil lamp glow, to relieve all worldly idiosyncrasies.

There've been letters to write when the weather's been uninviting, and out exploring when it has. The sandstone formations here are splendid.

The seals have come to visit periodically. They're still puzzled by my appearance yesterday, I'm sure.

I've thought much of females as well. I wish more could experience life out here — the world would be a better place.

I've given little thought as to what happens following this expedition, but up until this point I've been adamant in venturing to Cuba. Being here in this one-room abode — and with such feelings of peacefulness overcoming me . . . Perhaps it'll be more useful if I were to remain here and winter myself in a like-minded setting in an effort to reflect on all my experiences thus far, before immersing myself into a completely new mindframe and atmosphere. Regardless, I should begin to give it more thought.

This day's been a welcomed rest from everything: the people, the paddling, society and the paranoia. Now I'm much more prepared and apt to deal with those things again. Weather permitting, I'll delve into the lives of coastal liviers again tomorrow.

This guy's cabin is sweet — as he must be a cool dude. He's neat and uncluttered, simple and genuine.

With yet another grueling marathon five hour crossing, I arrived at the Port au Port Peninsula where a difficult decision had to be made.

There's a narrow isthmus which separates it from the mainland. I'd have no trouble finding help in transporting my gear over the short stretch of land, but this meant bypassing an area which was renowned for its French history and rich folk music.

I'd discovered, to my chagrin, that very little music remained along the shores. In nearly every port I'd visited I asked if there were any fiddlers or accordion players left around. The answer was nearly always the same: "Nah, she's all died out, b'y. Eider der's no one int'rested in it no more, or d' youngsters picks up d'electric guitars an' figures dere ain't enough rock stars aroun'. Or d' talent up an' went t' T'rono somewheres."

Considering the lateness of the season and the distance I still had to cover, it was apparent that I'd require every good travelling day available. Confident that I'd made the most practical decision, I slowly set up camp for the night amidst a high-walled enclosure of lobster pots, surrounded by fishing stores and upturned boats which had already been hauled up for the season. It was a bold reminder that the unrelenting gales of fall would soon arrive. I wondered seriously if we'd be blessed with the decent September that was essential for my successful rounding of the Northern Peninsula. I'd developed the confidence, experience and stamina I felt, but it would all prove irrelevant if the season was to change too rapidly. Again, my fate was in the hands of Mother Earth. All was well with my soul as a result.

8.26.97 What times to be had — as I now find myself nearly across the Bay of Islands!

The weather's been excellent apart from a damp afternoon yesterday. In the evening I arrived at a small cove with a few cabins and was welcomed by two men. In no time I was getting my clothes dried over the stove and had a plate of Jig's Dinner in front of me. I was given some fly fishing instruction, while I returned the gesture with some lessons in navigation. Even had a hand of crib before bed.

Before bed!? It was after we'd all retired that it became sheer hell. And following such a lovely evening too. Between the bloody clocks ticking (Clocks!! The nearest community is 12 miles away and they've got to know the time!?), the ceaseless snoring of my fellow cabin dwellers, and the unsettled salt beef and can of soda, I barely slept and was nearly at the point of screaming. I got up at one point and searched for my earplugs. I'm sure they felt I was cracked — up banging into things at some ungodly hour in the morning — some crazy paddler they'd met mere hours before! Dawn finally arrived and I could at least get up. The relief was euphoric as I prepared to move. But not before a scrumptious breakfast of sausages and eggs! I've had it with the vile shit; my body and mind's suffered long enough. Next meal of the crap and I'm turning it down.

Conditions again were Godsent today and I'm relaxed in a lobster fisherman's log cabin for the evening, with finally a belly full of good grub (lentil soup) and I anticipate another fine day tomorrow.

Wrists are a little sore these past days so I've held back a little — a day off is in order at Gros Morne. I needed a fine stretch of weather early, and certainly got it. This last bit of coastline has been spectacular; fine potential for a home.

I was clearly addicted. I'd returned to an environment and mindframe of utmost clarity. Little else was required to maintain my contentment and happiness. I basked in its untroubled peacefulness, fully conscious now that rough and unsettled times would always be forecasted, for such was the framework of life. It was times like these which made it entirely worth-while.

As I paddled silently along the still calmness of the ocean's surface, I marvelled at the subtle interactions of all things: the sun's astronomical effects on our planet, and from such an unfathomable distance away. It was that same dynamo of life-giving energy that I'd witnessed drifting away from the mystically captivating river Ganges; the same which I'd experienced settling graciously into the endless dunes of the Sahara; and those same rays which shone then off the glistening backs of the remarkable antics of the dolphin pod before me.

I arrived in their presence completely unannounced, as with so many other wonders of the ocean. Their displays of playfulness and energy were contagious. The low projection of the sun's early morning rays caught the beautiful streams of water, as they trailed in an arc behind the graceful bodies of the airborne mammals. There were no tanks to contain them, no deceitful capitalists to exploit their splendour and bravado. They were free entities and they evidently rejoiced. They conducted incredibly stunning somersaults and leaps. The only audible sounds were of the numerous individuals breaking and then re-entering the surface. I sat in silent wonder as the pod slowly travelled past me and continued their casual meander up the coastline.

Would I be able to attract their attention to me, I wondered. I pulled a "Flipper" and slapped the blade of my paddle flat onto the surface. Instantly, they all became aware of my presence and the results were astounding.

Within seconds they'd increased their speed to remarkable proportions in a desire to get away from me! No longer did they blissfully leap and play but were only occasionally viewed as they hastily gulped for air in their departure. Within minutes they were far out to sea and nearly beyond the horizon.

I sat disappointedly in the quiet and stillness of my mistake. "So much for my efforts to say hello," I said to myself and lamented "Television . . . television . . . "

I resumed my paddle and continued to enjoy the cooler air of the late season. The flies were no longer much of a threat and the campfires of cool evenings were all the more appreciated.

"I could contentedly do this for the rest of my life," I happily told myself. "Blissfully paddling the coastlines of the planet. How 'bout it, girl?" My silent partner merely slipped peacefully through the sea as she contemplated my proposal.

I met up with a young man out in a boat shortly afterward. He approached me cautiously after retreating from his awkward locale in against the ragged cliffs, where I'd seen him minutes before upon rounding the point. He was in his late twenties, darkly tanned and comfortably at home in his boat out along the shore. It was incredibly rare to meet someone so young these days. The conversation was welcome.

"Jeez, b'y, ya gave me a start when I looked up an' seen d' yellow comin'. I figured you was Fisheries," he said with a sigh of relief.

"No worries dere, b'y, I'm just out paddlin' t' get away from d' buggers," I called over in response.

"Been out checkin' a few pots I got laid. N'er seen nar moose agin d' shore when ya come along, did ya?"

I replied I hadn't and asked him how far it was to town. Then I asked him one more question before we parted ways, "How many fellas yer own age is left home, ya figure?"

"Not many, b'y. D'ere ain't many want's t' get out on a tear once in a while, I tell you dat," he remarked. "Most is too old fer it now - granted now, I gives 'er a good go t' make up fer d' works of 'em!" He smiled proudly. "S'long as I got me boat, b'y, an' can get out fer a few birds an' fish, a coupl'a moose a year t' bring 'ome t' d' missus t' cook up. Das all I needs sure."

"Ah, ain't dat d' trut', b'y. If more o' d' crowd wouldn' so caught up in d' money racket, dere'd be plenty of us 'ome, eh b'y?" I reasoned with him.

"Das deir loss, b'y. Dey're up bein' slaves so dey can collect deir junk. Let 'em 'ave it, I says — we'll 'old our own back 'ere, right b'y?" he concluded before we bid farewell.

We continued on our separate journeys, both happier and wiser from our brief encounter. What more could we do, but "hold our own"?

I arrived at the town, which was shrouded in a beautiful rain squall, and fancied the cratered effect that the droplets produced as they struck the surface. I'd been singing all morning and continued, as I pulled ashore near two young boys who were out, as undaunted by the shower as myself, while they fished from the shore with their makeshift spinrods. "Ya got to go where ya wanna go, Do whatcha, whatcha wanna do, With whomever you choose t' do it wit' . . . ," I sang repeatedly as I drifted in near them. They looked at me shyly and seemed quite amused with the sight of an "adult" so gloriously involved in the damp weather.

"Sir... you win d' Lotto or som'n?" called the eldest of the two.

"Naw, I'm luckier den dat, I 'llow," I answered him with a smile.

"Ya sure likes dat Lotto song den," he said frankly.

"I can't figure what ya means, lad. Whadaya talkin' about?" I questioned, only half interested, as I reached into my gear for some lunch.

"Dat song come's on d' t.v.," he stressed, as if frustrated by my ignorance, "when dey afta winnin' d' jackpot."

"Dat, my young friend, was a tune put out long b'fore you, or I was aroun'. Sound's pretty shifty what you talkin' about, so I ain't gonna ask anymore. D' stuff'll rot ya mind, son, stick t' d' fishin' in d' rain," I happily suggested. "Now, where abouts is ya post office, m' friend?"

"Ya better off paddlin' ya boat over dere, sir. Ya gotta walk up d' riva to d' bridge, den follow d' road back."

"Oh dere's no rush. I'll get dere when I get's dere. 'Twould be nice for a walk t'rough d' town sure."

I left them to their fishing and set out. There were a couple of chats with folks who were out along the road on the less congested side of the river, yet I took immediate notice of a sudden change in people's reactions to me, once I'd crossed into the main area of the small fishing village.

There were questioning looks and even slight feelings of annoyance toward me. This was something I'd grown quite unaccustomed to with the countless other small communities I encountered. I was still pondering the slight difference when I arrived at the post office. I entered and began a conversation with the postal lady.

"Oh my, welcome sir," she ecstatically greeted me. "Have you enjoyed your visit? You been up to d' Pond for a tour I'm sure."

Then it struck me why the mood there didn't seem genuine. Tourists! The locals had been exposed to the near viral-like affects of the visitors with weighted wallets. They'd been subjected to the abuse for a few months by the time I arrived. I quickly adjusted myself accordingly to the probability of encountering many more similar scenes in the days to follow, and took a deep breath.

"You ain't been up on d' tour boat, sir!" she cried out, flabbergasted. "My goodness, ya can't leave wit'out seein' it. It's simply spectacular."

I stood back as a couple of local ladies entered, and observed quietly as she barely gave her own community members recognition in her ceaseless drive to sell me the idea of riding the tour boat up the lake. "I've been in dere, ma'am, years ago, in a canoe. It *is* a lovely spot," I agreed.

"Oh," she stopped sadly, and then snapped back, as determined as ever. "Well, dat ain't d' same as takin' d' tour. 'E takes ya right up agin d' cliffs. We was in dere a few weeks ago. I took me sister in. Sure I lived 'ere me 'ole life and was never up d' pond 'till dey put in d' tour boat."

I mailed my letters and thanked her for the suggestion before retreating comfortably out into the rain again. Before I'd much time to formulate any thought on the matter, I decided it was an opportune time to call home and report in. I quickly ducked into a restaurant, which was bizarre enough in itself, as it stood grossly out of place in the quaint fishing village.

I was met by a young kid, obviously flustered and annoyed in dealing with often discourteous and ill-advised patrons. I asked for the use of a telephone following a botched attempt at a friendly conversation. As I spoke with my brother of happenings at home I casually grabbed the glossy menu and began curiously looking at it.

$13.95 Fisherman's Feast, $12.95 Scallops, $11.95 Caplin Dinner. I was floored! Nearly fifteen bucks for a meal of caplin? Who were they kidding? Oh, I forgot. I concluded my call and happily returned to the street.

"Prepare yourselves brothers and sisters, for the future has arrived." A venerable Disneyland had begun its devolution into the moral fibre of the most unsuspecting and righteously naive of citizens. How many local people had eaten at the establishment, I wondered? How many could afford the "spectacular" guided tour of their own backyard? What kind of an impact was it having psychologically on the town combined? Did it create divisions amongst those who could afford those "luxuries" and those who could not? Divisions that had previously never existed?

Disheartened with these thoughts, I sought refuge in the nearest environment that I felt might harbour the remainder of "unaffected" folk — the general store.

Outside, a bunch of kids were standing about, evidently following a successful crabapple raid. I asked how they were and was thrown one to decide for myself. This instigated friendly relations and the eight boys followed me clumsily into the store. Within minutes there was laughter and joking. The effects of the previous two encounters quickly wore off and I was once again surrounded by the children of the rock.

"Got any pipe tobacco, love?" I said optimistically as I leaned on the counter.

"Now I ain't had a request fer dat in dog's ages sure."

"Try John's," suggested her young daughter who stood beside me to her mother, "'e's d' last I 'eard 'ad any."

The lady called around to the other stores in the community on my behalf, as the boys filled my pockets with the tart fruit and then magically vanished. The confined environs of the store evidently were unable to contain their energetic spirits.

I began a conversation with her daughter. "Whadaya been doin' since ya finished school?"

"Been 'elpin' Mudder 'ere. Goin' t' Scarborough next week, sure. Me brudder's up dere now. Gonna git a job I s'pose. An' dere's no good fellers left aroun' 'ere, right," she said matter of factly.

"Ya ever been dere b'fore?" I asked her.

"Nope. 'E says it ain't wort' shit once ya dere a mont'.

"Hey, ya sees dis gum 'ere in d' blue chummies?" she added quickly thereafter. "Dey says ya can beat d' bret'aliza when ya chews dem. D' cops can't do a t'ing about it eider. Says dey gonna take 'em off d' shelves pretty soon d'ough. I 'llow I'd buy a case of 'em if I 'ad d' money."

"No kidding," I commented as I marvelled at her adaptive ability and frank acceptance of the distasteful course that her life was about to take. *"Oh you'd better start swimmin' or you'll sink like a stone, For the times they are a changin'."*

Happily anticipating a day off, I envisioned the beautiful stretch of coast along the Green Garden Trail that I'd visited a number of times as a young hiker: the group of sheep that I'd encountered lazily grazing along the meadows, the meadows themselves filled brilliantly with seas of violet wildflowers, the pristine waterfall that would welcome my return for an anticipated bath. All these things I silently recalled as I paddled the shore that slowly began to inflict a nostalgic reminiscence.

I thought also of all the influential memories that I was creating from the majority of the island's coastline along my route. Of visions and tales that would remain with me forever, and of the lifetime required to arrive at a clear understanding of all I'd encountered and learned. Many of the things had resulted in bafflement and confusion. Perhaps this was required if I was to comprehend anything of relevance from them in the end.

I paddled on.

From my vantage point I saw a number of young people playing wildly on the beach, as I slowly paddled along offshore. Girls! There were girls there. How I desired a simple, fresh, unencumbered conversation with a girl then. For with every wildly stimulating adventure that I embarked on, there were always some significant sacrifices I had to accept in return for the experience. Once again, it was the unavailability of a female companion and all that this entailed, which seemed to be foremost.

I waved happily at the small group and increased my speed, hopeful to arrive at a suitable landing spot before I planned a jubilant return along the shore. A night of flirtatious silliness with new, young faces was certainly in order. The weather was beautiful. I'd the contented knowledge as well of the following day's objective of mere relaxation to swell my enthusiasm.

I rounded into a small, shallow cove and discovered a boat on the shore where I decided to camp. Upon arrival I found it was the man I'd met in the early hours of the morning, back along the shore. Along with his buddy, they were over collecting a load of driftwood. The boat was dangerously full as I pulled in along side her. He'd removed his jacket which I'd seen him in earlier, and approached me sporting a mustard yellow t-shirt emblazoned with the characteristic lettering of the McDonald's corporation. Instead it read: MaRijuana, over billions and billions stoned.

As a rare treat, "tea" was administered forthwith.

"Brudder, you didn' come by dis stuff aroun' d' shore," he hollered wide-eyed and laughing. "I feels like I been zapped wit' 'lectricity!"

"We figured ya must be smokin' som'n, t' be out paddlin' as far as ya come," giggled his friend.

"Actually, I been at it three mont's. I don't allow I indulged dat many times even. T' be truly appreciated, she requires full respect in moderation I've come t' discover. Like anyt'ing, too much of a great t'ing makes me lazy and unappreciative. An' we can't take anyt'ing fer granted, sir. We're lucky enough t' live 'ere I 'llow, wha'?"

They both nodded in agreement as we all lay on the sand and gazed contentedly out to sea.

"Makes fer a fine gift t' folks aroun' d' shore d'ough," I said in conclusion and tossed him a well-travelled bud. "Use it wisely, sir."

An onshore breeze blew up and quickly the boys had to make a departure. Water was loping in over the transom of the beached boat with her full load. They had little desire to leave the peacefulness of the surroundings, yet fate planned it a little differently.

"So long, my friends, have a safe trip back t' d' wharf. Keep up d' struggle, ya hear?" I called to them as they pushed off.

"You're fine 'ead Michael m'son. Ya needs t' run fer d' Premier, I figures."

"Hold ya tongue, sir . . . I won't 'ave such foolishness spoken on dese sacred shores," I shouted heartily as they turned to leave.

I'd more pressing matters to attend to after all, far more beneficial to our entire existence than committee forming or attending executive luncheons. I had fragrant flowers to inhale, sheep to enjoy the company of and radiant dusks to ensure my optimism . . .

I washed up in the nearby stream and set up camp, before enthusiastically hiking the mile back along the trail to the encounter that I hoped would ensue. Unfortunately, it became apparent that the party I'd seen had moved inland along the trail to camp. But I made the acquaintance of a young couple from Maine and we spent an enjoyable evening at their campsite.

I'd entered the confines of the Gros Morne National Park and was to learn many of the inconsistencies that it had created. It was quite apparent that the government had spent an incredible amount of dollars promoting the area through publicity, only to decide later that they'd have to limit the amount of visitors to certain areas by imposing a fee on hiking trails! A trail I'd many times enjoyed as a youngster was now subject to a schedule, to which the hiker was required to check-in following his or her allotted time in the area. There were now boardwalks and stairs constructed along the path, I was informed. There were bizarre platforms provided for the wilderness hiker to conveniently set their tent upon, all in a brilliant scheme invoked by our "superiors" to preserve the natural splendour of the environment. I quickly changed the subject in an effort to curb our deflated spirits.

I had located the group of sheep which had brought me so much delight years previous. They could be seen far in the distance on a small patch of meadow, just below the steep, precariously angled rock scrub of the overhanging cliffs. It was obvious they'd been driven to such an extreme by the increased presence of humans along their low-lying pastures.

No dice . . . I'd have to try harder.

The young man was an artist and began sketching the brilliant ball of crimson fire that was setting slowly into the sea before us. It had emerged only for a brief, valiant display below a thick bank of cloud. The performance was stunning. I asked his girlfriend if she pursued any arts herself.

"Actually," she began, "I was an avid writer as a kid. Stories and poems were all I cared to do, so it seemed natural enough for me to study creative writing when I attended university. I am the 'proud recipient' of a degree in it now. I don't think I've written a thing since." It wasn't the answer I'd needed to hear.

15

8.28.97 Late evening now following a fine day ashore; couldn't have picked a better one for it; very warm and clear skies, so it would've been uncomfortable paddling all day. Washed clothes and made a killer meal of rice and subjhi, even a naan to top it off.

I was visited while I ate, by a couple from Ottawa, totting camera tripods and mongolian fanny packs. Their understanding of Newfoundland and the sea was heinous. I asked if they'd been here before: "Once, but the weather was so bad we drove maybe 100 miles from the ferry, then turned around and went back." They expressed their disappointment with the Northern Peninsula "with all the trees being clearcut and the barren land."

Had a wonderful bath at the waterfall and visited all campers on my walk back. One was truly bizarre. This kid I'd met briefly last night and he expressed intense interest in coming down to check out my boat. I of course invited him to come and take her out if he wished. He never showed but I meet up with him this evening. After hiking in the previous night (dark by the time he arrived), he hiked out this morning, climbed the Tablelands all day and hiked back in here. A remarkable feat really, yet how silly working himself so hard trying to "do it all." I meet up with him and he's a wreck and cooking himself a box of Kraft Dinner!

"Like, ya see the moose carcass down by the water-fall?" he asked. "A bear must've taken him down not long ago. That's pretty wild, eh?"

"Not unless 'e likes hangin' quarters out in 'e's shed an' digs carryin' a hacksaw wit' 'im," I answered.

His only aspiration is to be a lawyer.

8.29.97 . . . Just prior to breakfast I shat out a nine inch round worm. I figure the super dose of Egyptian chilies and Indian garam masala got him good yesterday. Guess I shouldn't be gender specific; the sex of the thing was quite unclear — bizarre little bastard, if it hadn't have come out of my anus. Nearly a milky white translucence to it, diameter of a pencil perhaps and tapered off at both ends, so I'd no idea where its head was. This was as far as our relationship went. He'd been with me long enough I figured! I must inquire how long would it be in my system to grow to that size? Was that even large? I've heard that tapeworms can be many feet. Could it have been gotten from one of my carnivorous fiascos? Are there any more?

All these things and more, I've had much time to delve over today. I find with the seas as calm as they've been since my venture to the west coast, little thought is required involving the actual paddling.

213

A visit into town today was bizarre again — more stunned and comatose locals, result of a summer-long exposure to tourons. Got shafted when I'd this mad craving for a bakeapple pie. They should be ashamed — the fuckin' thing probably had a handful of berries in it, the rest was dough and it cost me 4 bucks!

8.30.97 As always, the climatic conditions have, and will continue to be, the catalyst for deciding my fate. With gale winds from the NE nearly guaranteed, I decided to pack up and get around the Head and into the next bay, where I'd find better shelter and a vantage point of what's going on outside. It jacked up pretty quickly after I'd rounded the outside and provided a wet, yet almost welcome, challenge following a week of calm seas.

So I'm all set up less than a mile down the shore from town, sheltered from the weather that's expected and I'll now prepare to head in. Looks like I'll see the play by the local theatre troupe that I've been anticipating all summer after all. And being Saturday, it's bound to be an interesting night in town. Even after three months of camping out mostly every night, I'm far from tired of it and feel so content and at peace out here. As I've said many times, in my element . . .

— later — Would you believe it's just come dark and I'm back at the homestead. Very contented after a nice, yet brief visit into town. Brief . . . I was a patron at the pub for the whole afternoon! The folks were the best kind and we all helped two brothers set up their music gear for the night.

There's no chance of seeing the play; they want 20 bucks a ticket! Shit . . . I saw Ravi Shankar play for about one dollar once! How in the hell are the local people gonna be able to afford that? Quite simple I know — they don't! We have to wonder why they're stuck continually with bingo and darts? It's pathetic really to see how much effort is made for the bloody tourists and their cash, then come winter, those that remain are bored silly and seek little stimulation amongst themselves.

Winds have increased steadily since my arrival. Must be +50 knot winds outside, seeing's how much is in here. I took extra time in choosing a spot to set up and am untouched. Had an offer tonight to come up to the house by a fellow bar patron and was a little guilt-ridden, yet amazed at the offense he took after I declined and tried desperately to explain my contentment in sleeping out . . . "No, *really!*"

8.31.97 . . . my tolerance and foray into the drinking world has nearly reached its limit. I also feel that following this packet of tobacco, it'll be the last delve into that "habit of a Newfie". Cultural integration for the sake of one's education can be grossly unhealthy.

. . . I've been experiencing pain in my fingers of late with the arrival of the cold temperatures.

9.1.97 Sometimes I end up amazing myself. Following a long night of socializing — drinking countless donated Indias and obliging well-intentioned splifs of bad oil in the bathroom with the thoughtful bunch — it was well past midnight before I stumbled along the mile stretch of beach and home. A glorious sunset of crimson and pinks filling the entire sky promised for a fine morning.

By 0900 hr I was on the water feeling no ill affects from the previous night, and made a very productive day of it. With the strong, persistent easterlies of the days before, shit, was the water cold! My feet were frozen and I could even feel the muscles in my ass stiffen up with the cold! The air is noticeably crisper and it makes paddling much more comfortable. Extremely clear water up (whoops) down here also. At one point, a large school of herring swam below me; fine sizes as they glistened and reflected the afternoon sunshine.

By 1200h I'd covered nearly 13 miles! With the rising tide of this new moon I was travelling up to 5 knots. A few more days like today and I'll be changing course and heading south in the direction of home. It's amazing how far I've come.

9.2.97 Light winds again from behind, but a little more caution had to be taken — fog all day. It's been awhile since I'd had any major dealings with this obstacle. All this considered, I'm now camped in the rugged tundra setting on the NE side of St. John Island - another long day.

I pulled ashore just long enough to warm the killer spaghetti I'd made yesterday before nightfall. It's getting darker much faster now, especially since I'm pulling away from the sun by about half a degree latitude every day.

More dealings with frozen feet today. Arriving at Port au Choix, parts were frozen *hard* and very white! Worked it out easily enough though. Fingers have held up — it's in the mornings that they're troublesome. I awake now a couple of hours before light with a dull throbbing in them, I must then tuck them tight up under my armpits until I rise so that they function properly.

Calls for 30 knot winds tomorrow — may not move and I'm wondering now if I shouldn't have stayed along the shore instead of cutting across. Was also hoping for a little Thoreauian atmosphere tonight. No dice, for this side at least is pretty uninhabited, period.

9.4.97 early morning — I awoke early, following a fine sleep, to the sounds of howling wind. So they finally have arrived, after all day of dreading them yesterday while I was on the water . . .

I'm staying with a fine family. When I awoke I heard them up, yet following washroom duties I've discovered they've all vanished!

Foreseeing this coming of bad weather, I began looking for decent shelter . . . Interestingly, it seems few people have cabins down this way. Regardless, there was little to be found so I headed for town, with the thoughts of bunking down in someone's store. Following a brief drop-in at the public wharf, where many were busy unloading herring (seven cents a pound), I walked up to the store and bought fruit.

The sky was looking angrier by the hour and I'd still no clue as to where my shelter would be found. The only solution was to move and with faith and perseverance, something would come up. An hour later I was contentedly moving my gear into the loft of a store. I'd pulled up and decided the prospects were good — no sooner was I changed and headed for the nearest house to inquire re: the store, when the young man comes along in a truck. I quickly explain my situation and without a second thought he proceeds to give me the grand tour of his gear shed, my suite for the night.

We were soon joined by other siblings and relatives who'd gathered for an evening's session of cod cleaning in the stage next door. Seeing the extended family in atten-dance and all age groups present for the evening's social was remarkable.

Their mother arrived later to check in on the proceedings following bingo and was appalled at the thought of my staying out in the store. There was an open scolding of her sons for not inviting me up sooner. "No, sir. I won't 'ave it! It's up t' d' 'ouse wit' ya. I got a bed dere; y'ain't gonna sleep out like some dog if I got a bed fer ya," she simply informed me. "Don't matter how scruffy ya looks . . . If one o' me sons was off, an' I knowed no one took 'em in . . . oh, don't even wanna t'ink about it. Come on now, I brings ya up an' fixes ya a lunch."

Little could be said to persuade her that I was quite content with the comforts of the store. It was up to the house I'd go. There were introductions to other family members, as she poured my bath! Followed by a lunch of course, in which Michael's yarn tellin' was included. It was well after midnight before I finally saw sleep, with her glorious and welcome presence.

Now the day awaits . . .

    32.5 nautical miles Table Point to St. John Island
    20.0 nautical miles St. John Island to here
 1,263.0 nautical miles previous
 1,315.5 natuical miles in 58 days of paddling

. . . and keep me waiting it did and wait and wait . . . In retrospect, I'm feeling a little shameful in that I didn't depart. Following the very strong southerlies of the early morning, there's been relatively little wind all day yet heavy rains throughout — and in remaining I've witnessed more of life down here on the Northern Peninsula.

Got my clothes washed as a bonus and was fed *a lot*, 4 meals today! Of mostly the unwholesome variety. Getting my bowels to operate smoothly again will take work. I haven't been able to break this routine of not turning down food — of any kind! The kindness is so incredibly genuine that I can't bear to denounce it in any way. I have been ranting about the benefits of healthier eating, however, with moderate attentiveness shown.

9.5.97 Finally escaped the pampering, yet paid for my sins. It's been many weeks since I've had the misfortune of wetting myself — and I was mightily proud of myself for the accomplishment, yet . . . the record is broken! And of all days . . . Fog, rain and quite cold, and my misfortunes all due in part to the animal/salt intake of course.

Before I was even out of bed this morning, the unmistakable stench of scorching pig could be detected, along with the ghastly sound of all that fat popping and cracking. I immediately explained that another meal of the stuff would not go over well if I was to paddle "safely" and this seemed to work. God love her, she attended to me truly like an honored guest, for which I'm forever grateful. If only for my inability to hold my water, the conditions would've been fine. Yet, soaked in urine, my bottom down was extremely cold.

I've been warmly welcomed here in the cove, but opted to decline the invitation up to a home. I'm set up and need a night alone. It cleared off a couple of hours ago before dusk and the winds picked up; blowing gales now, straight westerlies. Not too bad if the swell stays down. Sounds like this area got off easy over the past couple of days — record rainfall amounts elsewhere. 27 foot swell off Funk Island! It would be nice to get a full urine-free day tomorrow. A day and a bit and I'll be around the most northerly point.

9.7.97 If exhaustion left me too tired to write last night, then it's only through divine intervention that I can pick up a pen and write any thoughts this evening.

Yesterday's travels brought me safely around the most northerly point. Having damp feet since the previous day's "accident", it was most uncomfortable again with the coldness of the water. During the warm summer days, this occurrence was tolerable, now it's 4-5°C and there's no humour left to be found in it.

My only salvation was a spectacular scene of a gannet, less than a boat length directly in front of me, who dove for a fish. They're quite cautious and even flying at 100 feet, they always give me a wide berth, yet this one was *bold*! By the time he'd returned to the surface (and I'd intentionally slackened off), I was so close that I spooked him and all his efforts were wasted: he dropped his herring and "escaped".

Also of note today, a lunch of 4 slices of heavily loaded bakeapple-jammed bread and tea accompanied this conversation with a man in his home: "I don't know wha's wrong wit' d' crowd dese days, b'y. Dey got no fight left in 'em . . . Dey accepts too many 'andouts an jus' goes on bitchin' 'bout it all — like I'm 'ere doin' now, I s'pose. Don't know, b'y, we's all become too selfish I 'llow, wha?"

"Did I tell ya sir, how fine ya bakeapples is?" I responded. Really! I'm trying hard not to instigate negative talk so much, but they seem to search me out. As if I've become some Freudian coach for folks to vent out some frustration...

It was nearly 1800 hr before I departed and I'd be risking much in going out; still large sea left over from the storm on the eastern side and with the winds as high as they were, would I have time before dark to get ashore? I was

220

again and safely made it along — angry, *big* ocean swell at times though.

A brilliant iceberg — so aged it resembled flesh tightly pulled over ragged and bedraggled bones. The setting sun gave an opaque violet glow to it as I explored . . . Beautiful.

I'm exhausted and for supper made tea! I'm making chicken scratches. I think I should quit.

9.8.97 The diversity of weather conditions today was unbelievable; the morning's paddle was lovely — a rugged stretch, so fine weather was essential. I stopped briefly in a small community for lunch and had aspirations of crossing for the afternoon. Skies were clear, hardly a draft. It took me 10 minutes once I'd left the slipway . . . Before I'd reached the outer point of the cove I looked back — the sky was black and within minutes it had turned to white caps and gale winds. Within another 10 minutes there was little decision to be made. I could barely pick out the white houses up on the hills, a third of a mile back in the cove! I headed back.

I figured it had come in so quickly, that it would die out just as fast . . . I'm still here but have had a fabulous day. Bakeapple bread lunches, tying squid-jigging gear and hanging out telling yarns up in the store, getting the 3 brothers out to try my boat (down to visit their grandparents), a fine bath, and molasses bread for lunch before bed — the family's spot on and I'm having a ball.

We figured it out over much discussion and debate. I've less than 300 miles to go!! The next 3 days now and I'll be out of the worst of it . . . I dig being out in the thick ocean swell again. The wind this afternoon was a little sobering though — Take Care of Me . . .

Being surrounded by such a close, warm family has me anxious to get home now and make efforts to improve relations with my own.

As with so many other occasions, leaving those people the following day was shadowed with a tinge of sadness. My thank-yous always seemed grossly inadequate for the generous offerings I've received.

The morning's conditions were bordering on unapproachable, yet I was eager to press on, having an acute understanding that very few days would remain that would be ideally suited to tranquil paddling. To get me home this late, I'd have to rely on the many skills and experiences I'd gained over the previous months. The seas were high as I began the cautious paddle.

I'd experienced a terrible toothache that night and slept very little and the conditions requiring my full attention were a relief from the constant discomfort. I'd wishful hopes of it improving on its own and decided to bypass the larger community with dental services. In stubborn defiance I headed for a vast stretch of coastline, my thoughts exclusively on transporting my one-man craft as far south as possible. I successfully reached the south side of Hare Bay and went ashore in a mid-afternoon downpour on an island, which had once harboured a substantial community.

The sheets of rain whipped wickedly about the many deserted homes that remained standing. Ragged and abandoned, they stood defiantly against the harsh elements. Paneless windows were shrouded with the flutterings of musty curtains as the wind whistled through the skeletal frames. All were too far decayed to provide any comfortable protection so I set up camp in the lee of one of the homes. The remainder of the day was spent exploring the houses, picking bakeapples, hiking over the hills to check on the sea state — anything to keep my mind somewhat preoccupied from the dull throb of my jaw.

I began cursing my stupidity when nightfall arrived. The weather had remained and I'd left the prospect of dental assistance twelve miles directly upwind. A world away considering the sea state. It would be another sleepless night in less than euphoric environs.

I prepared for bed, yet sleep was impossible. I lay awake as the winds howled and my jaw grew increasingly more painful. The second consecutive night of interrupted sleep found me frustrated and irritable. I was alone, completely and unmistakably alone.

In an effort to remain in control, I began focusing on the pain. Unsuccessfully I'd attempted to forget the discomfort by filling my mind with other things. Perhaps the reverse would prove more beneficial. I began to sympathetically relate to those who'd suffered, those who'd accommodated pain in their everyday lives. I'd visited the cemetery earlier in the day. How many had died in tremendous agony as a result of the time in which they'd lived or due to the remoteness of their communities? I lay in the complete darkness and a powerful calm overcame me. I intentionally took no painkillers in an effort to fully understand. I would never take my health for granted again.

Dawn finally arrived and with it, a mild shock as I looked at my image in a small mirror. My jaw had swollen to twice it's normal size. Swallowing and breathing had become difficult.

I lay motionless in my bag — my stiff fingers wedged snugly into my armpits, my groin, anywhere to ease *that* discomfort. It was 3°C and the sheets of harsh drizzle whisked around the house and collided constantly with my shelter. The sea was white with spray and foam-filled. Malignant. Cantankerous.

It was my Nan and Pop's seventieth wedding anniversary.

It was then that I fully understood that I was undoubtedly a truly unconventional character. For I was content. It was an adventure I'd gone in search of, had yearned for, and my wishes had come true. There was nowhere else I'd have preferred to be. Utterly alone and suffering, I accepted it fully. My life now had purpose. My life had substance. *My* life.

I couldn't function properly in the mass ideal of comfort and security. I don't want luxuries. I want to feel alive. I don't want my heat to be adjusted by a dial on the wall, or clothes washed by some energy guzzling machine. My shit is no longer a part of me. It's all too easy, too uniform, and I feel half dead.

That morning on Fischot Island, I woke indisputably alive.

It was evident I'd not be leaving the solitude and discovery of Fischot that day. In not calling for my great-grandparents' anniversary, it would seem obvious to my family that something was wrong. I could barely speak, yet a call to the Coast Guard would be required. They could relay a message to my family in reassurance.

"St. Anthony Coast Guard Radio. This is Charlie Foxtrot Delta Eight Seven Three Six. How do you read, over?" I winced through the pain. I repeated the call twice more before there was a reply.

"You require a message relayed to your contact on shore, sir? Go to channel twenty-four, sir, and we'll patch you through to the radio telephone."

Nooo . . . he didn't understand. He could've telephoned from the station and simply called me back confirming that he'd spoken with the family. Instead, there I was awaiting a direct line to the house. Mother would detect my discomfort and it would only result in their needless worry, and I'd limited power remaining in my radio which needed to be conserved. But I waited.

"Hello?"

Click.

"Hello Mom," I began as I stood atop a rock outcrop, blinding mist slapping my face. "I'm callin' from my radio and it's only a one-way connection, Mom. I'm fine but waiting out a storm down here on Fischot Island. I knew you'd worry if I didn' call t'day, over."

Click.

"Oh my . . . we 'aven't heard from ya. You're alright? We heard you're gettin' bad weather."

Silence. Click.

"Yeah. I'm fine, fine. I've only a bit o' juice left in me radio, so I gotta go . . . Give Nan an' Pop my best will ya? Over."

Click.

"Oh yes. Ya want us t' come git ya at d' next port? It's gettin' late, Michael. Dere's no need fer you t' be doin' dis now. You could go back up in d' spring when d' weader turns fine again, sure . . . Over."

Click.

224

"No, no," I stressed quickly, "I've come dis far, I'll make it. It'll just take time, Mudder. Don't worry now, I'll call again when I gets ashore to a phone, over."

Click.

My jaw was agonizing over the extended stress of speech.

"Ya visa fer Cuba arrived . . . Wha's wrong wit' ya voice? Over."

Click.

"Da's fine, love. I'll deal wit' it when I gets home. Must be d' connection. I, I got a bit of a sore tooth too. It's no problem d'ough. I *gotta* go, Mom, in case I need's d' juice fer an emergency. D'ese calls must be a fortune too. Take care now. I'll be home soon. I love ya."

. . . Silence.

Click.

"We love ya too, son. Call when ya can, over."

Click.

"Bye Mom . . . Out."

Click.

Within seconds I was in conversation with the radio operator. "You are o.k. over der, are ya? Over," he inquired with some concern.

Click.

"No problem here. Bit of a bad tooth, but nudding d' folks 'ere didn' 'ave t' deal wit' years ago, I don't s'pose. I didn' get dis far by bein' impatient. T'anks fer ya help, sir. Over," I said, as a stiff gust of wind nearly toppled me over.

Click.

He relayed that the weather was due to improve by the following morning and then continued, "I can imagine ya had an excitin' summer, son. Don' worry 'bout d' charge fer d' call. Dis one's on us. You stay safe now. Out."

Click. And once again, my contact with all humans was severed.

I was amazed again by the generosity of people towards my efforts. With a little kindness and support from others, it was obvious that I'd be able to overcome any obstacles.

I picked bakeapples, gargled the tears of the earth constantly and thought of the seventy years of marriage and all it must have entailed.

"What can ya remember about your wedding day, pop?" I'd asked him once.

"Wedding day, let me see now," he began reminiscing. "I was workin' on me wedding day — workin' on d' coal boats. And I was gonna be married seven o'clock, ya see. I 'ad it all arranged; evert'ing bought an' so on. And Neve Gill den, 'e was d' box janitor on d' coal boats, well, I come up dinnertime and said, 'Uncle Neve, I want's t' get off afta dinner . . . I'm gonna be married.'

"'What are . . . ya damn young fool!' 'E said it like dat t' me, ya know. 'Gonna be married?'

"'Yes,' I said. 'Gonna be married.'

"'Let me see now, can I get somebody . . . alright,' he said, 'go on.'

"So I come home an' we got ready, an' I went down t' d' store down on d' point, and I bought a ring. O' course, she got'n on 'er finger now. Five dollars 'e was, for a ring, a wedding ring! And she still got'n . . . near seventy year old. And I bought some shoes and udder t'ings, an' so on. De shoes, sure, was only $2.50 I 'llow. And I only spent t'irty dollars t' get married," he proudly exclaimed before continuing. "Anyway, d' toime come, an' seven o'clock we walked down t' d' Quarters. Me and Andrew Dally an' 'e's first wife . . . and d' missus. D' four of us went down, walked into d' Quarters an' got married.

"Well, b'y. It seemed better in d' old days den it do now, ya know," he continued after a contented silence. "Now d' wages an' d' workin' wouldn' a big lot until d' boats started t' come in — but ya know, you enjoyed yaself better, 'cause ya 'ad a pig aroun', goats, and Mudder. She 'ad animals aroun' an' people enjoyed derselves ya know, outa dat. Summer time, Mudder and d' udder women aroun' dey'd go off berry pickin'. Dey'd all do up dere jam den, fer d' winter."

"I figure you were all more active back den," I added.

"Oh yesss," he replied dramatically. "You was always doin' som'n t' make ya life more comf'table. You'd be out fishin' or cuttin' a bit o' wood.

But den everyt'ing got modern, and I figure's we got too comf'table after all."

9.11.97 A day long marathon through excellent conditions has seen me paddle the longest distance for the entire expedition: 36 miles!!

It was very cool, yet no trouble while paddling. My spray skirt is nearly toast and I'm wet through always now (pissing scene or not). Stopping for lunch was very brief, as it was too cold to be held up for too long.

I don't want to pass up a fine morning of paddling, but this tooth has to be looked into first — been 4 nights without much sleep now. The constant salt water has curbed the infection somewhat though.

Two kids showed up shortly after I'd arrived here and it wasn't long before I was up to their home to get my clothes washed and dried. "We seen ya come ashore at d' sewer pipe dere an' knew ya wouldn' from 'ere!"

Following a nice chat with their parents, I returned to *Destiny* and then was quickly invited into the home of the gentleman whose backyard I'd come ashore on. So I've been taken care of once again and with the state I'm in, it's doubly appreciated.

9.12.97 Friday. Today's conditions made having to stay ashore all that much worse — light winds and fog in the morning. By the time I'd gotten some dope it was well after lunch.

Early morning was enjoyed with many tales from my helpful host. The most interesting being stories of people in the community who'd spent time out in the bush, lost in

227

storms, and how he figured many were liable to go "funny in d' 'ead" as a result of their ordeal. He'd no license or registration for his truck, yet insisted that it be the mode of transportation to the clinic. The dentist being on holidays until Monday! I drove and we waited well over an hour before I saw a brother. I felt terrible for the inconvenience . . . and of all days, it was his birthday! He's a fine man and we got along great; I'm forever indebted.

I got a little lazy in navigating this afternoon and ended up giving myself a tour of Little Hooping Harbour before finally getting up into the inlet that I'd intended. There was a fine waterfall and moose down at the shore and a pod of pothead whales to compensate for my mistake though. The inlet has a fine indraft and with the tide falling and stiff breeze blowing out, it gave me a workout I was in no mood for.

Quite a few crab fishermen in here tonight. Some of the brothers had to be towed in, after getting rope tangled around their prop. They've been all day trying to better their predicament. Regardless, they had me aboard for a couple plates of brewis.

9.13.97 That brewis definitely did not cut it! I'd steady headwinds all day and a serious lack of energy.

Hadn't eaten a decent meal since my campout on Fischot until tonight. I dragged my sorry ass into the fiord and spent probably the first hour ashore eating gluttonously from the abundance of raspberries.

If conditions allow tomorrow morning, I'm heading across. I'm not in the mood for two extra days and this coastline keeps me from coming ashore until 4-5 hours later anyway. It's only about 13 miles and certainly less exposed than others I've done. Again, the morning's conditions will decide.

There's a boat moored off the cove - and with 3 cabins upkept here, I'd figured on company for the night. Not exactly . . . It's some gun-totting yankee doodle dandy with a hunting lodge up in the back of the inlet. He just about fired at me with his rifle thinking that I was a bear! He came ashore briefly, we chatted (he kills animals for sport) and he invited me in — then he took a smell of my quite foreign cooking and decided evidently that I wasn't his type! I guess the date was off for he quickly vamoosed and I haven't seen him since . . .

I'm exhausted again. I'm also sure I've written these thoughts more than once!

16

I crossed over to the Baie Verte Peninsula in a mildly contained excitement, for it was the last open-water leg of my odyssey. The sense of accomplishment I felt following one of those fully exposed voyages was remarkably uplifting. With each physical challenge I grew increasingly more mentally encouraged, as if Mother Nature, the earth itself, in permitting my safe passage, was in full support of my ideals and convictions toward a more tranquil and respectful planet. My faith was tested and brought unquestionably to the forefront. It was unnecessary, even ill-omened, for me to complain of anything again. I was clearly convinced that my life was evolving as it should. In maintaining my integrity perhaps *that* was the greatest contribution I could offer to my environment, and towards the fellow human beings with whom I shared it. I was getting ever so close to that seemingly insurmountable goal that I'd set for myself so many moons previous. As a result, anything seemed possible.

I paddled around to the small community indicated on my chart and entered the disguised narrow opening, wedged deep into a cliff. It revealed a sleepy town, impressively unperturbed by the ravages of the twenty-first century. I slowly went ashore amongst the numerous slipways and fishing stages nearly unchanged for decades.

There were children there to greet and welcome me ashore when I arrived. They were inquisitive and refreshing. I was as content as they were to sit for a considerable time and learn of their adventures. All were still deeply tanned and energetic following a summer-long education of freedom.

Shortly afterwards, I returned to the slip following a visit to the general store, where I had purchased two cans of beans and tomato sauce. I was anxiously anticipating a substantial feast of spaghetti. Pleased with the day's accomplishments I decided to search for a peaceful setting and enjoy the evening. Precious little then could prevent me from the prospects of such a splendid evening alone in the wild. As I set down my newly acquired foodstuffs and crouched to study the chart for a suitable camping spot, I was approached by a young man.

"I seen ya come in," he began, "an' figured you could use a night ashore in d' 'ouse. You can git a wash an' relax if ya wants."

We spoke quickly of my trip and of his recent return home from the mainland. "Dere was toimes, even up dere I remembers, when I needed 'elp an' somebody always seemed t' come along. So I seen ya down 'ere an' figured I 'ad t' do d' same."

How could I reject such an honest display of compassion? "Sure, b'y, I'd love to," I replied following a brief pause.

"Dere's one t'ing dough. I works at d' plant 'ere. I'm goin' in now t' work 'til about six. Me sister got a bar up over d' hill, just past where ya come from d' store. Ya can go dere, right, an' I'll meet ya when I'm done."

He gave me his name so I could introduce myself and then left for work. "How lucky am I, wha'?" I wondered aloud as I packed away my ingredients for the long anticipated spaghetti. I began collecting the few things I'd need as a guest instead, then secured *Destiny* on the slip for the night. The beautiful spontaneity of life was truly refreshing.

Without mentioning how I'd come to arrive at the tavern, I comfortably took possession of a stool at the bar where I was warmly received. I was in fine spirits and even with the imposing presence of the television

231

set directly in front of me, I was confident that my optimism could with-stand even its numbing effects. There was a news broadcast on: The Separatists of Quebec were continuing their campaign to seek independence from Canada.

"I can't figure what dey wants," babbled an apparent regular, an old, glassy-eyed patron who sat next to me. "I figures, if English was good enough fer Christ, den b'y d' Lard Jesus, should be good enough fer dem bloody frogs!"

How could I possibly respond to *that*?

"What dey want's, sir, is d' right t' maintain der identity, der culture. 'Cause jus' like 'ere, it's bein' sucked right out of 'em by a government dat got little else but money an' power on deir minds. Dey don't give a tap about t'ings dat sets groups o' people apart an' makes 'em unique, unless it can turn a profit. D' more dey can mutate everyone into a common mould, d' easier it is for dem t' control all of us. No, sir . . . let 'em 'ave deir own country. Might give d' folks aroun' 'ere a kick in d' ass t' start standin' up fer deir own. Instead o' sellin' out like dey been doin'."

I'd noticed while I spoke that the bartender had taken interest in our conversation. When I finished speaking she smiled, quickly opened another bottle and placed it before me. "Dat one's on d' house," she said simply, before returning to the tray of glasses she was drying.

Little else was said on the matter and shortly afterward the man left. All who remained in the establishment were myself and the bartender. As we chatted, I began casually looking at the assorted photographs that she'd placed under a thin piece of plexiglass on the bar. Most were of happy friends and locals who'd visited at various times. Yet amongst all the sinilar photos, there lay a very odd choice that drew my attention.

It depicted simply a scale. On this scale thirteen fish had been cere-moniously laid out. They weighed in at just over a pound. What baffled me and kept my attention was an inability to recognize the species, or its significance for being photographed and placed reverently amongst the pic-tures of friends and family in this lady's pub. They were thick, substantial — vaguely familiar, yet oddly foreign.

"Love, I can't figure out dis picture," I remarked as I finally gave in. "It ain't herring I don't believe."

"Da's caplin sure."

"Nooo," I said breathlessly, as if I'd been violently kicked in the testes. A harsh chill raised the hairs on the back of my neck.

She walked over, leaned on the bar and gazed at the photograph. "'Twouldn' taken yes'day now, mind ya. If we ever really needed a sign dat t'ings is gone sour, I guess dat picture did it for me. Dey figures 'twould take forty of 'em now to reach d' same weight — an' deir out rapin' d' ocean o' dem now!"

"The bottom of d' food chain . . . God help us," I whispered as I continued to study the shot. I was still in a stunned state when I became aware that she'd asked me a question. "Sorry, love. I'm still 'ere gettin' over d' shock value o' dis 'ere. Come again."

"I was sayin' dat someone needs to write som'n to wake d' people up to wha's goin' on. Did ya ever read *Nineteen Eighty-Four*?" she inquired.

I found myself on the approach of the last major headland. All the skills I'd absorbed in reading weather patterns, predicting the sea-state and relying on my judgement and intuition were to be fully tested.

I woke following a long day of paddling and socializing, the latter being the more exhausting of the two.

I'd grown accustomed to the welcome of sleep shortly after dusk had descended on the land, and I woke refreshed with the creeping arrival of dawn. This of course was a drastic contrast to that of the majority of my fellow comrades. Unlike in times previous, when the daylight hours demanded work in the fields or at sea for continued survival, the sun was no longer such an integral factor. It had been replaced by the masses' acceptance of a mechanical gadget on everyone's arm.

I woke to twenty knot southerly winds and rain. I calmly reached for my VHF and listened for the extended forecast, as I snuggled comfortably back into my cocoon. It was expected to switch around to northwesterlies later that day with the high pressure to the south quickly moving off. I was camped on an exposed northwesterly facing beach. Paddling around to

233

the south-facing shore of Cape St. John that day I would find unapproachable conditions. To remain in my current position until the following day would probably result in my beach being totally awash with the newly established northwest swell. This was the dilemma which I contentedly approached from all angles as I lay cocooned in the midst of the blustery weather.

There were no thoughts of government corruption or mass emigration or needless carnivorism. My thoughts were pure; I took delight and contentment in a simple wish to remain mobile and honest to myself. Out there, amongst the jagged cliffs and ever-changing sea, was the only place I felt stimulated or ethically secure.

I lay in the slowly increasing light of morning, the dull ache of arthritic fingers a constant companion now, and decided on my best course of action. There was little need for a committee or any compromise to be taken into consideration. I'd only myself to be responsible for. If my decisions resulted in mistakes, I'd only myself to answer for them.

Perhaps it was time more people began accepting responsibility for their own lives and deeds instead of relying so heavily on a governing body, which I now pitied for accepting such an impossibly mammoth task. It had become so instinctively elementary for humans to push the blame elsewhere, to submit complaints in a constant barrage upon some elite group that felt it had the authority to play God. I'd rather perish with some sense of independence out there than succumb to such an existence of meticulous and subtle slavery.

I pushed on later that morning to the outer edge of the cape. It was the full moon. Somewhere along that exposed stretch of coastline I felt would be a safe haven for me to seek refuge. If fate saw fit and my predictions proved correct, I'd refrain from entering the heavy seas of Notre Dame Bay until the following day, while simultaneously avoiding the risk of dealing with the tumultuous sea conditions expected when the northwest winds arrived.

I bravely ventured forward and within a couple of hours found a small stretch of low-tide exposed beach that would harbour my boldest experiment to date. For *Destiny* would lay on the sand nearly sixty feet away from the high tide mark. The steeply sloping cliffs were home to thick underbrush and only a few trees. High tide would arrive long after dark and at that time the entire beach, well up to the base of the cliff, would be underwater.

I'd been in the lee of the strong winds that were ravaging the southern side of the peninsula. I tucked myself snugly inside the Southern Bill of Cape St. John, but I'd viewed and *felt* the residual effects of the large swell that was wrapping around the cape when I entered. So good, so far.

I came ashore easily on the peaceful sand. The towering cliffs surrounding me continued to offset the violent conditions outside with little wind. The sun broke out of its clouded encasement and graced me briefly with its welcome presence before the steep walls left me in dense shadow again.

I was still many days away from the completion but I'd arrived at a tremendously significant milestone — I'd be entering my own bay in the morning. As remarkably encompassing as Notre Dame Bay was, nearly all major obstacles would then be overcome.

I'd been given many more foodstuffs by a lovely couple the previous evening and contented myself with the chores of cooking that had by now become instinctive, routine and remarkably enjoyable. In finishing the meal I quickly accepted the tremendous chore I'd still remaining, before a relaxing evening around the fire. And so I began the long task.

I emptied *Destiny* of all contents and transferred all the gear to the bush.

I hoisted her empty hull up onto my shoulder and carefully navigated through the field of rarely exposed boulders, my legs buckling at times under the stress.

I reunited her with her innards above the high water line and reassuringly secured her for the evening.

I questioned myself concerning sleeping arrangements. I reasoned that my tent would be useless. I decided on a patch of earth that I leveled adequately below a sloping spruce. I covered the sleeping shelter with my tarp and transported the necessary bedding and articles up to the site.

I returned to the shore and began gathering wood.

I began to cry.

It began and I had little control. I wept and initially had little insight as to why. I sat in the light of the dying season and grew tremendously scared. Not of the ocean. Not of death. But of humans. The efforts to control and conquer had obliterated countless cultures throughout history. Was one more going to make a difference? I told myself it didn't; it was too far gone. My weeping increased.

17

9.17.97 Life is so sweet. My foresight into the approaching conditions saw me execute one of my greatest kayak feats yet. The winds did switch to northerly and after a surprisingly warm night (the full moon reflecting off the cliff face was a spectacular backdrop), the swell-pounded beach was sure to provide another drama-filled entry. Pulled it off without getting too wet and, more importantly, without hull damage or the skeg jamming. Then I'd only a short distance in rough waters before rounding the South Bill and the next step to completion was traversed; the final open-sea cape was successfully rounded — large whoops and cries could be heard from me for many minutes.

Better still, here I am with a beautiful family and fabulous little village. This was a stop I'd envisioned since the beginning stages of this expedition. I'm not disappointed — the people are lovely.

Within minutes I was seated at the table, for I'd arrived just as supper was being taken up. I've made fast and great friends with a young man here. He left once, only to return with gifts of energy bars and gloves. He's an outdoor junkie like me and snorkels the area, is just full of energy and ideas and has no thoughts of leaving or giving up on his home. I was up to meet his wife and newly arrived baby, and of course to have a lunch.

I'd not expected to get over here today, but conditions were excellent. This bay is beautiful — wide, yet with far-reaching capes.

Humpbacks today! It's been so long . . . I thought I'd left those wonderful companions behind for the season. Perhaps they'd come to bid me adieu. Also saw the distant spout of what I believe was a Right whale. Very rare.

Just as life seems to become far too confusing and insane, along comes a fine day such as this to reassure my occasionally doubt-ridden spirit.

9.18.97 It's with very sore wrists that I write these words this evening. A very contented belly and mind persists though.

Didn't quite make it around the head — but am camped out in Webber Bight just before. I figure I'm certainly less than 25 miles to home!

There's been a large sea rolling in from around Cape St. John. They must have gotten hit hard with wind; I rounded just in time. It's calling for southerly winds tomorrow. So entering Exploits should be little problem — may have some stiff winds to put me to work going up though.

My hands and wrists will need the rest upon completion. My legs need some work. At times now, I almost fall over drunken-like, they've been so ill-used.

In the cove out on Cape St. John, I'd been contemplating if travelling to Cuba is the right thing for this winter. There's work of writing to be done; the ideas are coming to me now and I feel a story of truth and integrity must be told. I know it must be written while in Newfoundland — now very much my home — but I feel a potent and crisp, detailed outline is very important and may/should take longer than the actual writing of the tale.

Off the Road, A Plea to our Mothers . . . two titles I'm contemplating. There's so much thought involved that I'll only truly begin it once I've finished the trip. Then the journey really begins . . .

This is my own backyard! There's so much to explore — it would take 10 lifetimes. We don't have to go to the other side of the world for adventure and travel. (And it goes without saying that the folks there would be far better off if we didn't.) How many here have been shuttled off to Ft. Lauderdale or Niagara Falls and have yet to explore their own harbour and bay?

Support Cultural Diversity — Stay Home!

It was tonight that I'd set up my final camp, for the fifty-fourth time.

9.20.97 And finish it . . . I have not! She was quite content in making me work on this last leg, the final step of my odyssey. SSWesterlies all day — coupled with a strong falling tide *and* an inlet that is flowing out constantly anyway. It was a hard, harsh paddle. A couple of mammoth, deep ocean sea swells were quickly avoided, as I rounded Northen Head to bid farewell and give sincere thanks to my dear companion. These were a bold reminder of how accommodating she'd truly been toward me.

So . . . a constant struggle all day saw me drag myself ashore at the cabin. Bewildered and distraught, for I'd have been content if this were to have been the end. My wrists were hurting. There was no one to greet me.

The family did arrive, yet I was too tired, too disappointed, too numb. I was in bed early and now the winds that were approaching have arrived. At least 20 knots. I could be here for days. But I'll get there. If anything, this delay will give those waiting at home some small indication of how much patience was required.

My arms had endured serious strain during the previous day's struggle to finish. Immediately following my crudely scribbled final journal entry, I ventured solemnly down to the shore in the early morning light. Directly upwind lay my destination. I could see it! Only six miles separated me from the greatest accomplishment I'd yet to achieve. It was the fall equinox. The exhaustion and fatigue of the previous day had easily been remedied with a substantial meal and an extended night's rest. The winds were steady gales and unapproachable without risking injury. I sat and reflected on all I'd persevered through.

It was upon completion that I'd fully begin to comprehend many of the things I'd discovered. Would others be able to relate at all to my experiences and come to an understanding of why I held such steadfast views? I'd left on my journey in an effort to escape and forget about a world in which I felt so alienated — only to come around full circle and discover that it wouldn't . . . couldn't . . . shouldn't be avoided. Or I'd simply become part of the problem.

I sat quietly in the cool air.

Nowhere on the entire planet did I feel so intimidated, unstimulated or simply unlike myself than in that small town that lay before me. My family, my acquaintances there, my community — all of whom I'd distanced myself from. It was there that my greatest challenge now lay.

Without examining myself first, I no longer could seek any comfort in voicing my disappointments or frustrations about their lives. If I couldn't accept their lifestyles and beliefs, how could I expect them to display the same courtesy towards my own?

It didn't require increased effort on my part. I'd been struggling against the current, in futile attempts to show them the "right" way, when all along a right way never existed. I'd felt incredible discouragement when others became merely bewildered by my lifestyle, thinking "how could they be so blind?" While it was I who lacked the insight required.

In opposition to a hierarchy that dictated to the people how they should live their lives, I'd been conducting my own set of standards that I fully expected people to conform to. I became introverted and distraught when they never joined me. I'd become a revolutionary all right — without comprehending that what I desired was for everyone to conform and alter their lifestyles to complement my own. I'd neglected my family, my friends, merely for thoughts of my own advancement. Advancement to what? I simply wanted to make it through life now without killing anyone, didn't I?

"There's a family up there that loves you," I told myself, "and continues to support you, regardless of how foreign your endeavours are to them. What more can you ask for? That's unconditional love. Do you realize how rare and precious that is? How many others would've disowned their kid long before now for filling their lives with such radical antics? When are you gonna realize how incredibly fortunate you are and stop taking it for granted?"

I ascended the hill and, joining them for breakfast, attempted to make an effort. A beautifully relaxed and beneficial morning resulted. We picked berries and then returned to our cabin for lunch. Following another substantial meal and with the sun beyond its apex, I felt a yearning overcome me to press on and attempt the final leg homeward.

Bidding a brief bon voyage to my parents, I settled into the hard, intense struggle with the elements once again. Nearly an hour later I pulled ashore on the lee side of a sandspit. I'd only travelled a quarter of the distance to the finish. I was already exhausted.

Time passed slowly and the winds remained high. So close, yet all I could do was wait patiently. I rested and explored the familiar shore before I discovered a sailboat running with the steady wind. I ran for my glasses and confirmed my suspicions. It *was* my friend who'd donated many of his charts to my cause so many months before. I anxiously awaited his arrival, and as he tucked his craft into the shelter of the spit I paddled out to greet him.

"Congratulations, my friend. You've certainly had yourself an adventurous summer, I can imagine. Your mother called when she got home and said you were going to head in this afternoon. We thought we'd come out and give you an escort," he remarked enthusiastically.

His son was with him and we were introduced. Meanwhile, I was overwhelmed with his interest and support and thanked him for coming out on such a wild day.

"We tried to get a few more of the boats out to greet you, but with the weather and such short notice . . . " he added solemnly.

"This is just right," I assured him, "but ya certainly didn' 'ave t' make such an effort fer me, an' I may not get dere yet! She's pretty tough goin' up into dis wind after such a harsh workout yesterday. May 'ave t' turn back down t' d' cabin again if she don't die out b'fore dark. Give 'er a go again in d' mornin' I s'pose."

"We came to welcome you home regardless. Anythin' we can do for ya?" he asked with sincerity.

Many hours had passed since I'd departed and no doubt there were folks waiting for me. He radioed up to get a message to the family that I'd once again been delayed. Following a pleasant conversation, he explained the lateness of the day and reluctantly left me to wait patiently on the beach, while they began the considerable tack back to town. I thanked them again for coming out and watched silently as the small craft filled her sails and began her beautiful voyage upwind.

I was alone again. I watched them pull slowly away. So many along my journey had made incredible efforts on my behalf. Perhaps it made us all feel we belonged. None of us are truly alone, I surmised.

I meditated. "I can no longer doubt that you exist, for I believe now that you're a culmination of good Karma, a remarkable force that's been created with every honourable being that's ever lived on the planet. And you've taken care of me countless times. I thank you — you're helping me to see, to question, and make mistakes, and learn. What more can I ask? But I want to go home today; it's been such a long journey and I need a rest. I just need one hour. One hour," I submitted, "to see me finish. After that you can blow for a month. This is all I ask."

Suddenly I remembered the rock.

How long had it been with me? It seemed like a lifetime ago. That glorious day with the Fin whale when I'd been given a taste of Nirvana — and one of purgatory, as the little girl prepared subconsciously to depart with her family, leaving "the rock" reluctantly, like so many others . . .

Where were they now?

I took the rock out and examined it. It had been such a sweet gift — had seen me through so much, had helped me discover so many valuable lessons. I held it against my cheek; it had retained some warmth from resting against my chest.

"Thank you for keeping me safe. I hope you are too."

I kissed the stone, held it to my forehead and then, with all my strength cast it gloriously out over the sea. It made a hasty plop into the surface and was gone. I'd given up the small gift I'd received, had given it back to the ocean which had shaped it. It was the only thing I'd retained from the remarkable journey, and in an act of spontaneity I threw it away. I sat there thinking that it had been a foolish act, some ridiculously fluffed, Hollywood ending to bring tears to the audiences eyes and pangs to their hearts.

But I wished I could get it back. Yet it was gone . . .

I turned to wander back to my *Destiny* and then stopped short.

The wind. It *had* changed, was less forceful. It was dying out!

I stood motionless and wide-eyed, disbelieving at first.

I *was* remarkably blessed. Remarkably confused most of the time as a result, but blessed none the less. With time, things *would* become understood. I quickly prepared to leave and rounded the spit that only moments before was unapproachable. Yet I *knew* that I would be granted a safe passage; my sufferings had been rewarded; I *was* going to finish my long envisioned dream.

A glorious elation soon overcame me. It didn't matter that this inlet had once been a massively rich pine forest, or that it had been home to a proud and distinguished native tribe, long since eradicated by the forefathers of my fellow citizens. I could no longer live in the past and dwell on the mistakes and ghastly deeds that we were all capable of committing. If only to remain sane, I had to begin reflecting and complementing the good that surrounded me or all would be lost. I could no longer feel shame for travesties that were committed hundreds of years ago, while only an hour ago I may have created barriers and misunderstandings between those who shared my life with me at present.

I continued on, feeling as if I was approaching a new threshold of comprehension. My sailing friends caught up to me and appeared as excited as I. As did another boat that approached with many family members and other friends from the community on board.

A quarter of a mile.

Inside the wharf.

Approaching the beach.

There were whistles and cheers and car horns. A light mist had begun to fall, yet many friends remained out in the foul weather and watched as I slowly drifted ashore. As flares popped overhead, I slowly dipped my finger into the reservoir of the earth's tears and touched her reverently to my forehead. I sat there in unmoving disbelief.

One thousand, six hundred and thirty-five nautical miles later, I stumbled ashore a far different man than when I'd begun.

Then I looked up from my euphoric state and was immediately ravaged with confusion.

There were flags flying — for me! Union Jacks and Canadian Maple Leafs. A wild nausea overcame me. I wanted to burn them. I didn't represent or in any way condone what they stood for. I made a move for them . . . and then paused. I'd only succeed in upsetting those who'd made some efforts to celebrate my return. They fluttered wildly in the heavy wind, taunting me to strike out at them, to destroy all the peaceful values I'd come to question and later established along my journey. Instead, I looked to the people who stood around to greet me and made a sincere gesture to return their welcome positively.

I was pleased to see both my great-grandparents there and quickly went up to them. As those great hands held me again, gnarled with honesty and truth and perseverance and I looked around to all the loving faces that surrounded me, I was deeply grateful. But it was those who weren't there who gave me true purpose, for none of my friends from the community remained. In fact the town was nearly devoid of young people, like so many hundreds of other communities around the coast.

This evident lack of commitment towards our homeland and welfare by my generation had given me another goal, a purpose, a mission. We didn't require some farcical allegiance to a nation. In order to survive we had to retain our sense of community. There were many ways to incite a revolution. Perhaps in writing this, my contribution was being realized.

18

The telephone was for me.

"Hello?"

"Hi, Michael, I assume, this is CBC Radio calling. We've heard about your kayak trip you've just completed. Congratulations. I'm calling to ask you if you'd, like, agree to an interview with us?"

The question didn't appear to require an answer. The man continued: "We could do it now over the phone and I'll record it, or you could come in and we'll conduct the interview live," he aggressively relayed the options to me.

"Well," I began with some indignation, "I guess it couldn't harm. If I'm gonna do it, over d' phone is out o' the question. I'd 'ave t' come in so I can at least see who I'm speakin' with."

"Sure, sure, no problem. Is a couple days too soon? I'll set it up and call you back. It'll be on the Morning Show. Is eight o'clock too early for you?"

Click.

What had I done? Immediately feelings of apprehension and caution swelled within me. But it was unclear exactly why. At least it wasn't television I told myself. I sat there for some time before my silence was broken by my mother.

"Who was it?" she inquired curiously.

"Radio station. Dey want's me t' do an interview. D'ey're like bloody vultures, I been home a day," I said to her as I sat brooding over the usefulness of what I was about to do.

"You can use it t' thank all d' people that 'elped you out along d' way, t' let 'em all know that ya made it 'ome safe," she offered.

"Yeah, I s'pose," I replied in accepting the suggestion. It would have to do. "I can't figure how dey found out about it d'ough."

The days went quickly and I developed an optimism for the interview and its potential. It *was* an opportunity to reach many people and perhaps encourage them to further appreciate where they were living. I wasn't aware of the results beforehand, but it would be live, spontaneous and uninhibited. It was unlikely that they could distort my words to alter my intentions.

I felt up to the challenge.

I arrived at the station stimulated. I was early and walked casually around the inner corridors of the empty station. Radio has such potential, such raw improvised flair. I was soon thereafter invited into the studio and given a chair and cup of coffee. Immediately it was obvious that the man projected himself through life on a much faster pace than myself. Perhaps it was the occupation, the coffee . . . his unsettled conscience? Only then did I fully realize how my lifestyle drastically differed from that man's. Would we be able to relate in a positive manner? I took a great gulp of the lukewarm java and grimaced. It was vile.

"Now," he began breathlessly as he finally settled himself across from me. He'd exited and reentered the room numerous times in the brief moments that I'd been there. "My co-host in the adjoining room there will set us up in a few moments and then we can begin. I've jotted down a couple questions I want to ask you, but perhaps you can, like, tell me a little more before we go on, to help us get started. Now, you did this trip all

247

alone, right? Did you happen to, like, have anybody accompany you at anytime?"

"No, it was an entirely solo endeavour. Did 'ave a surfer escort me out of a bay back in August though, which was a neat trip," I chuckled.

His eyes widened into saucers and he jumped up and reached for a notepad exclaiming, "Surfers? Where was this? You mean *real* surfers? What a story! Would you be able t' get me their phone number?"

Fuck, I felt like I was being raped. He'd gotten me into the chair, his interview was about to begin, so his attentions immediately focused on the next story! I was suddenly old news before I'd even uttered a word. Did he see no problem in treating people this way?

I sat there insulted and resentful. Wanting to leave, to exit the room from this man who seemed oblivious to basic courtesy. I'd tried, I really did, to remain positive and look for the goodness in all people. Only to encounter occasions like this in return. Was it *I* who was being irrational? Only *me* that felt the disregard of human feelings for someone else's advancement was so terribly wrong? . . . so typically Western.

My expedition, which had blessed me with so many joys, challenges and discoveries, was reduced to a seven-minute logistical ramble of my trip. I was allowed seven entire minutes in which to express my thoughts, thoughts which were violently muddled by such a blatant insult.

A number of minutes into the broadcast and I became consciously aware of his sidekick, calling from the other room in panicked dismay, "fifteen seconds, only fifteen seconds!" I kept talking and intentionally got cut off mid-sentence. I sat there and looked across at the man opposite me.

"Judas," I calmly said, "you can't possibly agree that this is the way radio should be conducted."

He was greatly perturbed by my lack of quick and easy answers, dismayed even with my ability and willingness to formulate thoughts requiring more than a couple of syllables. He answered, "No, but what can I do? I'm just doin' my job. Our studies have indicated that our listeners have attention spans of between five and seven minutes. Anything more on one topic, and we're simply gonna lose them."

Who did he think was responsible for molding that general idea?

He continued on, aware that he had me far from convinced. "Unless it's some heartfelt headliner like Lady Diana or something, we're just not gonna keep up in the ratings with extended stories of local people. I'm sorry, that's all we can do."

To treat the public like such simpletons only resulted in maintaining their death-grip on their emotions, their ideals, their thoughts. The media *did* control how the masses now regarded life around them — this was their intention to begin with. Entertain them with predictable fluff, numb their minds with subsidized alcohol, embrace the electronic age and put them out of work — out of purely short-sighted greed and love of self. Get 'em out o' d' bays. Reduce their ability in which to think subjectively. Turn them into slaves.

I drive home in distraught sadness and feel overwhelmingly alone, for few others seem to notice these blatant displays of belittlement. Or most simply accept all the injustices because, after all, it could be worse. And I agree that in many ways this is true — but it still doesn't make it right, or that we should cease to strive for something better.

Out of curiosity I turn on the radio to the station. I cut into a lady talking about her garden. For twenty minutes she's left to inquire about horticultural problems she faces. "These rosebushes I bought from Woolco, now, they've got this wax coating on 'em. Will this hurt them? Do I need to remove it?"

Earth forbid, I should grow old, only to despair that I wasn't completely honest with myself.

> 9.23.97 This country and the way it treats its citizens
> is repulsive. I'd finished this trip with so many ideas of
> involving myself and trying to change people's perspectives
> but getting through to the people with all the control is
> impossible. Speaking with them, they've already transformed
> and mutated into now willing slaves for Big Brother, without
> the actual entity of B.B. even existing . . . For there seems to
> be no "machine" working here at all — Capitalism has taken
> on a mind of its own. The ball's in motion. There's no way to
> stop an object gone so erratically haywire as this . . . Nothing

is important to them — pride, accomplishment, truth, integrity, independent thought — the civil servants, media, police . . . they've all lost those essentials of being healthy, decent human beings. And it's as if it's so commonplace now, so accepted, that they're completely unaware of it.

"As long as I sit here and plinker away at my keyboard, refrain from thinking too hard, no questions which could turn any heads or arouse any suspicion . . . hell, give me a check, let me go home every evening, to sit and stare at my television, eat my chemically altered foods, and I can be content, knowing that I live in the greatest country in the world — blah blah, blah . . . blah, fucking blah!"

So it continues to be a time of frustration and impatience and I wish I was back on the coast, with the folks still holding unto some form of truth.

Epilogue

The following morning, my mother, father and I drove solemnly to the south coast. I was harbouring feelings of bitterness, betrayal and confusion. My unapproachable silence had returned and its crippling effect seemed to influence the mood of everyone present.

Before leaving the radio station in frustration, I'd asked the man how he'd come to find out about my expedition. To which he quickly replied, "Your father."

In a rare display of vented emotions I harshly struck out at my mother. "Jesus, Mudder, I've never been so insulted in my life! Dad knew I didn' want any media attention like dat. Did you hear it? In five minutes d' shmuck reduced it to a fucking vacation!"

"Come on now, Michael," she returned with hurt in her eyes. "You'll 'ave t' bring it up wit' him. I didn' even know he'd gone an' done it . . . But did y'ever stop an' think dat he did it 'cause 'e was proud o' you?"

"An' tellin' me in person would make too much sense?" I asked incredulously. "'Twould be enough fer me . . . I never did this t' receive any special recognition. I did it 'cause I needed d' challenge, and I was losin' my culture . . . and I was searchin' for d' truth. 'Cause d' truth, Mudder, does not lay wit' dose government puppets!"

The rebuke only succeeded in alienating me further and I quickly retreated into my shell again. My father returned from work that evening and nothing was said. I didn't have the courage to voice my frustrations directly to him.

The following morning a bashful, unintentional silence remained between the three of us, as we travelled south through the raped interior of the island. We'd left the north shore and driven for many hours to finally reach the south coast. A journey that would've completely baffled our ancestors. We'd conducted the trip to go fishing.

In a continued drive to destroy the will and independence of the people, the Department of Fisheries and Oceans had decided in all their wisdom that a brief food fishery would open on the south coast, while folks along the other areas of the shore were legally ordered not to fish for a winter's supply of food for yet another year. Many, like my father, had anxiously awaited the opportunity to return to their boats in an honest display of providing for their families, only to be slapped once again into submission by the arrogance of the government.

When the announcement was made, it came as no surprise to me, but to allow it on one side of the island and not on the other was truly puzzling and had, I felt, been a deathly mistake. I was convinced that it would incite a mighty revolt whereupon fishermen would take to the waters everywhere in an act of defiance and communal disobedience. There was much talk of such things.

Our forefathers must have once and for all rolled over in their graves and finally turned their backs on the blinded and misdirectioned offspring. IT training, foreign investment and imported Big Macs had overwhelmingly been welcomed by the people. The crimes of the Premier were just as much our own.

I couldn't change the world — nobody could. Objects in motion were obliged by the intricate system of the universe to remain in such a state. There was no way of stopping "The Machine." As I stood in the boat with my father and friend, with whom we'd established a warm relationship as a result of my summer's paddle, I fully realized that these were the aspects of life which demanded precedence above all else — family and friendships. It was through these that the challenges and despair of life could be overcome. Life was going to evolve whether I felt it was morally viable or not. Races, cultures, species, whole ecosystems, the earth entirely would be eradicated in time by humankind's incessant greed and short-sightedness. What would I do in the mean time I pondered, and reasoned that I could always pull a Black Bart.

As I hoisted another codfish in over the gunwale, I took notice of my hands, throbbing with recently developed arthritis, the jiggers line cutting a deep wedge into the meat of my palms. Thick calluses covering my fingers and the still visible scars of sun damage. They faintly resembled those proud hands of my great-grandfather and supported the cause of "the poet".

"Give 'er a few more decades," I happily told myself.

The remarkable changes they'd witnessed. I'd best prepare myself as well.

There will come a time in the near future when the children of this rock will be sent out into the streets, where they will beg in their ragged clothes to the tourists for "loonies." Those tourists will continue to arrive because the sea will remain. So they'll come.

This prophecy, from many angles, brings a smile to my face for only after a society has reached that stage does it finally discover those things in life which are truly precious. Only then will there be hope for our culture. Where the bonds between family and community and Karma can transcend all else.

These things I discovered while jigging fish with my father. A father who'd willingly taken me in as his own, so many years before, out of love for the wretchedly lost human race of which I was very much a part. I watched silently as the two men comfortably chatted together, as they laughed openly at themselves and the world which surrounded them. While I stood in silent despair . . .

Perhaps they'd discovered it long before I did.

As my mother lovingly prepared a meal back on shore with our friends, I looked up at my father with the newly established pride and respect in his eyes for his son. I then understood the greatest lesson of all.

"I love ya, Dad," I called out, as the wind sucked the words nimbly into the air.

He didn't even hear them, for the jumbled breeze had distributed the sounds downwind. But I smiled. It was a start, for I couldn't recall ever consciously uttering those words to him before . . . and meaning them.

Resist not evil; but overcome evil with good.
  – the Prince of Reformers and Radicals